SOCIAL POVERTY

Social Poverty

*Low-Income Parents and the Struggle
for Family and Community Ties*

Sarah Halpern-Meekin

NEW YORK UNIVERSITY PRESS

New York

NEW YORK UNIVERSITY PRESS
New York
www.nyupress.org

References to Internet websites (URLs) were accurate at the time of writing. Neither the author nor New York University Press is responsible for URLs that may have expired or changed since the manuscript was prepared.

Library of Congress Cataloging-in-Publication Data
Names: Halpern-Meekin, Sarah, author.
Title: Social poverty : low-income parents and the struggle for family
and community ties / Sarah Halpern-Meekin.
Description: New York : New York University Press, [2019] |
Includes bibliographical references and index.
Identifiers: LCCN 2018030572| ISBN 9781479891214 (cl : alk. paper) |
ISBN 9781479816897 (pb : alk. paper)
Subjects: LCSH: Poor—United States—Social conditions. | Low income parents—United
States. | Poor families—United States. | People with social disabilities—United States. |
Social classes—United States. | Social capital (Sociology)—United States.
Classification: LCC HC110.P6 H34 2019 | DDC 305.5/690973—dc23
LC record available at https://lccn.loc.gov/2018030572

New York University Press books are printed on acid-free paper, and their binding materials are chosen for strength and durability. We strive to use environmentally responsible suppliers and materials to the greatest extent possible in publishing our books.

Manufactured in the United States of America

10 9 8 7 6 5 4 3 2 1

Also available as an ebook

CONTENTS

Introduction

Social Poverty in America

Oklahoma couple Ashleigh, twenty, and Mark, twenty-one, arrive hand in hand twenty minutes early for our first meeting.[1] Ashleigh, seven months pregnant, has beautiful blue-green eyes and teeth stained a deep yellow. She is engaged and dramatic while we talk, frequently marking her points by making different faces or acting out moments of her stories. Mark's eyes are noticeably bloodshot—perhaps from working the graveyard shift at KFC last night or from his pot habit. His manner of speaking is at once intense and distracted, leading him to talk emphatically and off topic. They continue to hold hands throughout the hour or so we talk.

The two had been friends before their relationship turned romantic; they moved in together after only a month, and Ashleigh got pregnant—the first child for both—a few months later. Ashleigh feels more emotionally cared for by Mark than she has in previous relationships. She says, "I don't think of him as just a fiancé. I think of him as a best friend, and he is. He's my best friend. If I didn't have him, I'd probably be the loneliest person on the earth right now."

When it comes to social support, Ashleigh and Mark lean heavily on one another. They explain that they've distanced themselves from their former group of friends, with whom they've had a good deal of conflict since getting together (they even say they'd like to move to another state to get away from what Mark describes as the "high school drama"). The couple had lived with Mark's mother but had struggled to get along with her and Mark's siblings. They now live with Ashleigh's mom, which seems to be working out so far, although neither she nor they want the arrangement to last for very long.

With strained relations with family and friends, they're trying not to enter parenthood alone. They've enrolled in a relationship education

1

program called Family Expectations that teaches couple communication and parenting skills. When I ask why, Mark explains, "At least be able to have some type of stability or being nearing stability by the time we're done." I seek to clarify, "Do you mean financial stability?" imagining how a couple that relies on Mark's $1,000 a month in earnings—putting them well below the poverty line—would be laser-focused on dollars and cents. But Mark corrects me: "Not the case of financial, 'cause with the way kids are nowadays, we're not going to be financially stable for years now. And I know that. But just get to the case where we're not trying to rip each other's heads off. . . . Just family stability."[2]

An engaged couple like Ashleigh and Mark, with the man working full-time, isn't usually what we think of when we hear the term "welfare recipient," but due to a little-known twist in the sweeping welfare reform act of 1996, some states now use welfare dollars to fund programs popularly referred to as "marriage promotion"—but known to program developers and staff as "relationship education." Programs like the one Ashleigh and Mark attend, Family Expectations, aim to teach new parents concrete skills for managing conflict in productive ways; the end goal is to have more children raised by both parents in a healthy, committed relationship. In a series of group workshops, couples learn about fighting fair and communicating well. And so, although Ashleigh and Mark do not receive cash assistance from welfare, welfare dollars flow their way nonetheless, paying for the relationship education workshop leaders, the reclining love seats where they relax during their classes, and the dinners they eat during workshop breaks.

Relationship Education: Its Critics, Its Supporters, and a Puzzle

These programs are not new, nor is criticism of them. Journalist Katherine Boo's 2003 assessment of such programs in the *New Yorker* was withering. While the programs funded with welfare reform dollars had yet to be instituted across the country, Oklahoma positioned itself at the vanguard of this effort, offering relationship education programs to its low-income residents. Boo painted a vivid picture of men who were not interested in committed relationships and women too weighed down with the struggles of poverty to attend to much else. Although her portrayal of these men and women was sympathetic, her depiction of the programs was not. She posed the question, "Is wedlock really a way out of poverty?" Her conclusion in the article was so self-evident that she never had to directly articulate the answer—it was a resounding no.

A few months before Boo's article was published, *USA Today* columnist Julianne Malveaux critiqued such relationship education programs by saying the government can't "sprinkle magic dust on poor unmarried parents, hook them up and expect poverty to disappear."[3] *Business Week* columnist Alexandra Starr referred to the Bush administration's proposal to fund such programs as "a little-noticed twist on social engineering by government."[4]

Such criticisms had not gone away by the time Ashleigh and Mark made their way to a relationship education program. Particularly with same-sex marriage now legal, the tendency in the relationship education field to focus efforts on opposite-sex couples was out of date and exclusionary.[5] To some, a focus on any kind of two-parent families was out of sync with the rapid changes in family structure we've seen in recent decades. In a 2016 *New York Times* editorial, Eduardo Porter said, "Marriage is increasingly unpopular. . . . [I]nstead of trying to reconstruct the conventional family of yore, why not devote resources to improving the welfare of families as they are?" National Public Radio's Marketplace hosts *The Uncertain Hour* podcast, which spent an entire show discussing Oklahoma's relationship education efforts, returning to the ground Boo tread years earlier.[6] The reporter's takeaway was that these programs were a waste, with funds misdirected: "In the fifteen years the program has been going, the state's poverty rate has barely budged. Its marriage rate has continued to decline." The headline of Rebecca Rosen's 2016 *Atlantic* article on the topic stated flatly: "Marriage will not fix poverty."

Clearly, media reports have been damning across the board. Meanwhile, in the political arena, liberals love to hate these programs, and few conservatives seem very interested in defending them.[7] This is, perhaps, unsurprising given the limited evidence supporting their efficacy. Randomized controlled trials have shown a modest impact—at best—in terms of keeping couples together. Among the initiatives that were funded under President George W. Bush were the Building Strong Families (BSF) and the Supporting Healthy Marriage (SHM) evaluations; these examined relationship education programs that focused on helping participants to develop skills to facilitate positive interactions and manage conflict in a healthy way. The BSF evaluation focused on unmarried parents and found no significant impacts on participants' relationship quality or stability.[8] SHM, targeting married parents, found small but significant improvements in couples' happiness, distress, and communication, among other relationship qualities. However, couples who enrolled in the program were no more likely to still be together two and a half years after the program than those who did not.[9]

And yet, despite all this evidence, one group staunchly comes to the defense of these programs: the participants themselves, like Ashleigh and Mark. I spent a year diving deeply into one of these programs, perhaps the most famous (or infamous) of them—a program for low-income couples in Oklahoma City, the city that Katherine Boo visited years earlier. Over that year, I talked to thirty-one couples multiple times, both individually and together, for a total of 192 interviews. These parents were about twenty-five years old, on average; more than eight in ten had a high school diploma or less; around a third were white, just under a quarter were black, and more than a third were in interracial relationships; and, on average, they had two children and a family income of about $1,450 a month.[10] Starting from when they first enrolled until their time in the program was coming to an end, I met with these parents, often in their homes, but sometimes in fast-food restaurants or public parks, to learn about their experiences. And what I observed surprised me. Again and again, participants gushed with praise for the program.

Robert, a twenty-one-year-old first-time father, says of the relationship education program he attended, "It was like Family Expectations put a phrase or a word above the problem we had. It was like 'This is your problem here' so now we knew how to take . . . what steps we needed to . . . take care of it, so that was definitely building us up stronger each week." Otis and Denelle, a couple in their thirties, contrast the atmosphere of the housing project where they live with that of Family Expectations. Otis says of their apartment complex, "If we was not here a lot of things would be a lot different. We could get out and laugh and do other things. When you're sitting here, [you're] stuck in this black cloud." Denelle compares this to their relationship education program, saying, "With Family Expectations you get peace of mind. You're around good, positive people. Nothing negative. Nothing."

In short, couples seem to be getting something vital out of the program. Perhaps the value of such programs is not what the program's architects imagined it would be or researchers had been measuring and statistically modeling. After all, "building us up stronger" and "peace of mind" don't sound like the hallmarks of failed social policy, so what do we make of this puzzle? Why do the survey data and commentators conclude these programs have failed at "fixing poverty" and supporting families while participants tout their success? I was perplexed by the enthusiasm parents—including those who dropped out of the program—displayed for its lessons about healthy relationships, its staff, and its influence on their relationships. If programs like Family Expectations were not an answer to material poverty, to which of clients' other needs were they responding?

In this book, I explain how they are speaking to a fundamental need that young, poor Americans who are transitioning to parenthood feel keenly. In doing so, I urge a reconsideration of the conceptualization of poverty as solely a financial experience, which currently dominates our attention to what it means to lack essential resources. The program addressed the sources of what I term "social poverty," which so many parents experience—the "black cloud" Otis describes. Social poverty involves lacking dependable friends or family members who provide emotional support and companionship, and to whom you can safely disclose your vulnerabilities. Recall how Ashleigh says of Mark, "If I didn't have him, I'd probably be the loneliest person on the earth right now." Her young relationship with Mark is all that stands between her and social poverty, and so Ashleigh is on a precipice. Young adults like Ashleigh and Mark often lack the social supports they deeply desire, particularly as they are transitioning to parenthood.

For further proof, we can even listen to the words of the people Katherine Boo interviewed for her article all those years ago. While Boo concluded that relationship programs did not offer "a way out of poverty," like so many other journalists and researchers, she missed that poverty is not just an economic experience; there is a form of poverty that is profoundly social as well.

One of the women Boo profiled in her article, Kim, described being "heart over heels" in love with her new boyfriend, Derrick, whom she hoped to marry. "The first time I slept with Derrick he asked, 'Is this

O.K., does this feel right?' And, after, I just burst out crying. Because when he held me I felt, this is it—this is the something I've been missing my whole life." Kim's mother lived in another state, her dad had never been a stable figure in her life, and her other relatives were less than trustworthy—one found her journal and passed it around for others to laugh at. This made Derrick's caring arms feel like that much more of a safe haven. Another single mother in Boo's story described her divorce as "a living death." Even the pastor delivering the relationship program Boo visited—a man in his second marriage—said,

> I'm not going to lie and say it's easy. So I know some of you will wonder whether it's worth it. But when you know how it feels to go home at night, to have them there every night, to have them trusting you, and to know you trust them back. . . . To find that person and have that feeling—that is worth struggling toward, it's worth crying over. It is the worthiest of personal goals.

Perhaps the profound loneliness—the social poverty—of Kim and others like her is best captured in a detail Boo shares about Kim's work as a telemarketer:

> Some nights while Kim was trying to pitch A.T.&T.'s services to residents of Long Beach or Dayton or Scarsdale, the computers connected her to women who, she suspected, were struggling even harder than she was to get by—women who didn't want to switch phone carriers, who just wanted to keep another voice on the end of the line. Sometimes . . . Kim asked the women about their jobs, the men who disappointed them, the bills they couldn't pay. She learned the callers' names, gave them her own, promised to stay in touch.

Their isolation is starkly on display in this desire to connect with and feel understood by someone, anyone—even a stranger halfway across the country.

This book's premise is that the core need that these relationship education programs address is not marriage or financial poverty but social poverty. It's what gets parents in the door of such programs and what keeps them coming back. This draws our attention to the need for social policies and programs to be crafted and evaluated with an awareness of social, not just economic, needs; our research studies of poverty need to do the same. To productively debate whether or not relationship programs should exist—Is this an area to which government funds should ever be directed? Is this an arena in which interventions can successfully effect change?—we must have an accurate understanding of the motivations and experiences of the people targeted by the policy. A key motivation for many young parents, I argue, is avoiding or escaping social poverty, and their responses to programs and policies flow, in part, from this motivation.

Social Poverty

Research on low-income families has traditionally presented theirs as lives of contrast: a struggle with material poverty set against rich kin ties; these relationships, Carol Stack[11] and others have argued, serve as a protective buffer against financial scarcity. More recently, scholars have begun to call this into question, however, showing that the lives of lower-income families are often marked by mistrust and a lack of durable or reliable relationships.[12] This research does not point to these as flaws in lower-income individuals; rather, relations are shaped, on the one hand, by power hierarchies between low-wage workers and their employers, and public benefit claimants and their case workers and, on the other hand, by an environment of limited resources and opportunities shared among poor people and their kin. Even relatives, romantic partners, and friends may be viewed with distrust,[13] leaving a lack of emotional support and few allies in the fight against economic struggles. That is, social ties may not offset material circumstances—in fact, material poverty can perhaps be exacerbated by social poverty. Social relations are no longer the cozy refuge from financial struggles they were once portrayed to be.

While scholars are increasingly recognizing the multidimensional nature of poverty, as a condition that goes far beyond whether or not one's income falls above or below the government's official poverty line,[14] the research community still has not fully developed an adequate understanding of the social dimensions of poverty. The existing studies on poverty's social component attend to the *economic* consequences of having or lacking relationships. For example, researchers administer survey questions that query whether people have friends or family members who could lend them money in a pinch, or they engage in in-depth explorations of the tenuous nature of the ties forged between those who make ends meet by doubling up in an apartment after an eviction.[15] An extensive set of studies outlines the benefits of what scholars term "social capital," or having social connections with those who can provide essential resources, like a character reference or a job lead, that are key to financial success.[16] However, this conceptualization of poverty's social domain still maintains that poverty is a fundamentally economic experience, with relationships serving as a form of currency that can be used to get by or get ahead—a "rich" social network in this view is one that offers fungible resources, not emotional connections.[17]

I propose an expanded sense of what poverty means by taking more seriously the relational and emotional meaning and consequences of social poverty. Many of the parents I met described purposely separating themselves from their friends because they didn't believe their friends had their best interests at heart; they talked about wanting to be more dependable for their children than they found their own parents to be for them; and they laid out their struggles in trying to trust one another and even trying to trust themselves in their romantic relationships. What they lacked was not just financial; they were coming up short in matters of the heart, not just the wallet.[18]

The consequences of social poverty are far more than hurt feelings. Feeling socially isolated or lacking in the emotional supports to buffer stressful times has been tied to poorer health behaviors and mental and physical health outcomes, including mortality.[19] Better emotional supports during pregnancy are associated with a lower risk of postpartum depression for mothers and better birth outcomes for babies.[20] Greater social support also appears to facilitate better parenting, such as efficacy and feelings of competence, and promotes children's development.[21] In short, just as with economic poverty, the effects of social poverty reverberate throughout families' lives, including impacting the well-being of the next generation.

This social poverty is not unique to those struggling financially, but the circumstances of the parents I met seem particularly ripe for such social disadvantage. These low-income parents, like Ashleigh and Mark, are in the midst of a flurry of transitions that may disrupt other relationships with friends and family and challenge the creation of secure romantic unions. Pregnancies often come relatively early on in relationships, before firm commitments have been made. Therefore, there are multiple transitions taking place, as they work to embrace the roles of *partner* and *parent* and to figure out the responsibilities and daily activities of these new roles. At the same time, most of these parents are quite young—in their early twenties—and, as such, are still engaged in the explorations of this stage of life: developing an identity independent from their parents, completing their educations, pursuing careers, and gaining residential and financial independence. And while our culture expects young adulthood to be an unfettered time, this notion conflicts with the requirements for successful, responsible parenting and partnership; there is a fundamental mismatch between the demands of these parents' new roles and their youth. Their difficulties in progressing down the path to adulthood can stand in the way of their fully occupying the roles of partner and parent in the ways they would like and our society dictates.

These many transitions create a real risk of social poverty. With these parents' selves and lives so in flux, many of their relationships need to be renegotiated, including those with friends and family. For couples, developing trust in one another is challenging; doing so requires believing that your interests and expectations are aligned with those of your partner, which may well not be the case when so much of who you are and what you do is changing rapidly. Further, with little money in their pockets, their romantic relationships and possibilities for success as parents feel constantly under threat, buffeted by the stresses of being unable to afford the lives they want for themselves and their children: having an income adequate to cover needs, and maybe a few wants, and stable enough to do so not just day to day but month to month. But as Mark, whom we met at the start of the chapter, explains, while these financial needs may not go away, he would like to be able to weather them with Ashleigh without "trying to rip each other's heads off." Ashleigh and Mark say they can get by without phone service, but they don't want to get by without one another.

While the parents I met are unique insofar as they've chosen to participate in a relationship education program, their wish to create lasting relationships is a common one. In a study of about 5,000 couples in cities across the United States, researchers found that, at the birth of their child, the vast majority of unmarried parents—73 percent of moms and 88 percent of dads—said they wanted to raise the child together and get married.[22] This embrace of marriage is not unique to unmarried parents either. Monitoring the Future, an annual survey of American adolescents, has consistently found over the last forty years that approximately three-quarters of young people say having a good marriage is "extremely important" in life.[23] Although lower-income men and women may struggle with financial and social poverty, that does not mean that their desires and hopes for trusting, lasting relationships have evaporated. Like their counterparts all along the socioeconomic spectrum, Family Expectations participants don't want to be told to get married—which the program does not do[24]—but most do want to be married one day,[25] and they hope this program can help them secure that future.

I argue that by understanding social poverty, public policy can be recast to better meet the needs of young, poor parents, like the couples profiled here, and help them build stronger social networks that can sustain them as they try to raise their children, in whatever family form they choose. Attending to financial needs alone does not come close to truly addressing poverty in all its forms, as it neglects people's social lives and social needs. To this end, I explore the role social poverty may play in parents' experiences with the Family Expectations program.

Welcome to Family Expectations

When you walk through the front door of the loft-style brick building in downtown Oklahoma City, as hundreds of couples do each year, friendly staff immediately greet you, inviting you in and offering you something to drink.[26] The building is fresh, modern, and well maintained. On the first floor, you walk down a colorful hallway, decorated with black-and-white photos of babies—the decorations are family-friendly but not overly feminine. Here you can visit the nursery, which cares for children under two while their parents are in workshops down the hall or with their family support coordinators in private meeting rooms upstairs. The workshop rooms feature leather loveseat recliners with knitted throws available, appreciated by women in the late stages of their pregnancies. In a nearby kitchen and eating area, couples share a meal during their workshop breaks. Off the dining room is the Crib, the onsite store at which couples can use the "Crib Cash" they earn for participating to obtain a wide array of new items for babies and children, ranging from diapers to cribs, educational toys to baby bathtubs. The overall impression is more of a professional organization than a stereotypical run-down social service program.

What Is Family Expectations?

Family Expectations provides skills-based relationship and parenting education to low-income couples who are new parents. It uses the Becoming Parents Program (BPP) infused with relationship skills materials from the Prevention and Relationship Education Program (PREP).[27] As a site for the federally funded, relationship education demonstration projects Building Strong Families and Supporting Healthy Marriages, Family Expectations has been serving Oklahoma families for more than a decade.[28] Since it began in 2005, the program has served nearly 16,000 individuals.[29] It receives funding through the Oklahoma Department of Human Services and the Office of Family Assistance, including funds allocated from the state's Temporary Assistance for Needy Families block grant—its federal welfare money.[30]

Family Expectations is open to married and unmarried new parents who have just experienced, or will soon experience, the birth of a shared child; the mother must be pregnant or have an infant under three months old. Couples may be having their first child, have had other children together, or have children from previous relationships. Participation is voluntary—not court ordered—with parents recruited via advertisements and information in doctors' offices and baby expos and via word of mouth. It consists of attendance at weekly workshops for two to three months and regular meetings with a family support coordinator for a year.[31] Workshops are intended to help couples create or preserve a positive bond, emphasize communication skills and healthy ways of coping with anger and stress, and offer lessons about understanding and parenting a new baby.[32] Participants may opt to take part in supplementary activities, like movie nights or instruction in infant CPR, once they have completed their workshops. Each December, all couples who took part in Family Expectations that year are invited to a holiday party held at the state fairgrounds; in addition to providing a holiday meal, live entertainment, presents for the children, and a frozen turkey to take home, the party offers an opportunity for couples to catch up with program staff and other participants from their workshops. More than a thousand people—and one bison in a Santa costume, the Oklahoma City Thunder mascot, Rumble—attend each year.

Participants can opt for six- or ten-week workshops, for a total of thirty workshop hours.[33] Couples are eligible to continue meeting with their family support worker until their babies have their first birthdays—this could be a minimum of nine months (if they begin the program when their baby is three months old) to a maximum of eighteen months (if they begin the program as the woman is starting the second trimester of her pregnancy). The frequency of these meetings declines over the course of the program.

Participants are assigned to a workshop cohort when they enroll in the program. This means that they have repeated contact with their three workshop leaders, cohort members (ten to fifteen couples), and family support worker during the program, allowing ongoing relationships to develop. Couples' participation is facilitated by both assistance and incentives. Assistance includes cab rides or gas cards for transportation to and from workshops and meetings, on-site child care for children under two and vouchers to cover babysitters for older children during workshops, and the program is free for participants. Participation incentives include free meals and snacks at workshops and meetings, gift cards, and Crib Cash, which can be spent on new baby items.

During the year I met with couples, more than 1,500 people participated in Family Expectations.[34] Thus, in the evening hours and on weekends, the building is filled with the hustle and bustle of young families who share a common purpose for their visit. People coo over one another's newborns and share parenting advice—which bottles to buy, which diaper brands to avoid. Because multiple sessions run simultaneously, and each session may include as many as fifteen couples, there's a feeling of activity that draws participants in. There is also a sense of hospitality at the program—when workshops are running, staff are at both the front and back doors to greet everyone as they come in. In keeping with this warm hospitality, each workshop has a "host couple" who helps serve the hot meals and chats with participants, sharing their experiences with having recently completed Family Expectations themselves and setting the tone for a friendly atmosphere.

Relationship Education: A Programmatic Attempt to Overcome Instability

All those who walk through the door of Family Expectations have decided not to navigate the challenges of building their personal, couple, and family lives by themselves—they have sought help through a relationship education program. Sociologist Frank Furstenberg notes that young people have "vastly different capacities to make good decisions and . . . very different resources to implement the decisions they do make. Access to the institutions that can provide guidance, support, and resources to better see the road ahead and stay on course is enormously different for those with and without the economic means."[35] For these young parents, a relationship education program could be one such institutional attempt at overcoming the challenges they bring to their transitions to adulthood, parenthood, and partnership.[36]

Through parents' experiences with Family Expectations, we can see how the program tries to create and solidify social supports, in part by minimizing uncertainty and decreasing socioemotional risks. Although not overtly identified as a goal, the Family Expectations program is about establishing expectations; in effect, this means creating an environment of clear norms for how partners are meant to behave in their romantic and parenting relationships—for example, what counts as a healthy way to argue (is yelling off-limits? name-calling?). During workshops and private meetings with their family support coordinators, couples work on setting personal and family goals, making sure they are on the same page about what they are working toward, and laying out the steps necessary to achieve such goals; this makes couples feel they are planning as a team and moving in the right direction. Couples also describe being treated in a consistently positive way by all members of the staff, which itself offers at least a short-term form of social support.

In these ways, Family Expectations provides clear ways of behaving that can potentially reduce volatility in both relationship quality and stability. It offers a set of prescribed ways of interacting that make one another's responses to situations more predictable and more understandable. For example, before the program, when a couple got into an argument and the man stormed off, the woman was left to wonder what this meant—was he avoiding an important discussion, just cooling down, or was their relationship over? After the program, the couple knows about the "time out" technique; the man can leave the room or the house, and the woman knows that this means he's cooling off so the fight doesn't escalate. The couple now has a set of shared behavioral expectations. This brings a greater feeling of security, being able to anticipate how one another will behave and understand what these behaviors mean. This provides a sense of security beyond a relationship's legal status—having a comprehensible, stable way of relating to one another on a day-to-day basis. Valuing a lasting relationship isn't enough—you need to understand and implement the skills necessary to secure such a relationship. As a result, Family Expectations may create an environment for each couple's relationship in which trust is possible and their relationship can be built up as a bulwark against social poverty.

Book Overview

Couples come to Family Expectations because their lives are profoundly unstable and they are negotiating several difficult transitions—to adulthood, partnership, and parenthood—all at once. They feel they need help accomplishing these tasks. The personal, family, and community resources at their disposal don't feel to them like adequate support to secure the family lives they so deeply desire. Family Expectations seems to be a reasonable response to their needs in the relationship realm; the program's lessons align well with the skills and norms couples want to develop in their own unions. As Robert, a young father welcoming his first child, puts it, the program is "building us up stronger." This is enough for some couples to feel their relationship is moving forward on the right path.

But for others Family Expectations is not an adequate response on its own to their many needs, which are inextricably intertwined with how their relationships unfold. Fully addressing mental health issues, felony records, painful family histories, and a lack of transportation, the need for stable housing, or employment that offers some upward mobility are outside the scope of the program. This ultimately limits the program's ability to set some couples firmly on a path toward the more positive, stable family life they desire. As I discuss in the conclusion to this book, some programs, including Family Expectations, are now experimenting with ways to address these other issues; hopefully, my work here can inform those efforts.

The first four chapters of the book share the stories of young parents who are strained by the demands on them, of becoming adults, navigating romantic relationships, and raising young children. Without being able to fully rely on their partners, many feel very alone in managing these strains. And while most couples, nationwide, who are unmarried at their child's birth will break up sooner rather than later,[37] they are nonetheless anxious to avoid such an outcome for their own families.

Most have seen their parents' relationships end. Single parenthood and relationship dissolution are rife today, particularly among those with less education and limited incomes. The parents we meet here hope to carve a different path for themselves, to offer their children a different future; their desires are so fervent that they are willing to go to "relationship school." As we see in the last four chapters, the value they see in this experience and the lessons they draw from their time at Family Expectations tell us a lot about the ongoing dedication to lifelong relationships that remains even in today's individualistic culture, of the need for social connection and support even—or perhaps especially—in a world of brittle relationships. While much of the research on lower-income parents' romantic relationships has focused on their breakups, telling the stories of men and women separately, the present study reminds us that despite high divorce rates and the spread of cohabiting unions, poor and working-class couples still believe in the possibility of a future together, and they are striving to shape that happy family for themselves. But they don't feel they can do it alone. With this backdrop, the last four chapters describe and analyze their experiences in Family Expectations, with a particular eye on the program's ability to address issues of social poverty.

The first four chapters of the book lay out the context in which we need to evaluate the relationship education program, with a particular focus on the role of social poverty as being shaped by and shaping parents' lives. In chapter 1, I introduce the concept of social poverty and detail the multiple challenges faced by the young, low-income parents studied in this book. In chapters 2, 3, and 4, I draw on narratives from the couples to reveal the complex transitions (to adulthood, to partnership, to parenthood)—and the resulting challenges and instability—that young, poor couples can face.

The next three chapters detail couples' experiences in the relationship education program and reflects on how to interpret these experiences in light of the larger context of their lives. Chapters 5, 6, and 7 explain the setup of the Family Expectations program and examine its impact on the participants, as couples and individuals, both in the immediate term and as they reflect back on their year in the program. Throughout, we see how the felt experience of social poverty and the desire to hold on to existing social resources shape these young parents' behavior, objectives, and experiences—from their choice to participate in the program to what they take away from it, regardless of the program's intentions. Despite quantitative evidence that relationship education programs have a relatively limited effect on the likelihood of couples staying together, participants themselves describe a variety of ways in which they see their lives benefiting from their time in the program. In the conclusion, I reflect on how a focus on social poverty might shape our public policy efforts, particularly for lower-income families.

I use this in-depth examination of one relationship education program to explore the nature of social poverty and to consider the potential of this policy approach to combat this often-ignored form of hardship. I urge a more expansive view of poverty and, therefore, of what poverty policy can and should be. More than presenting a story about a particular program in a particular city, the subsequent chapters will tell the tale of lower-income couples who want to raise their kids together, as partners. They want healthy relationships; they want to find forever, together. But the odds feel long.

1

Young, Poor Parents

Lacking Social Support and Social Capital

I meet Jessica and Will for the first time at their house, set back from a busy road. It feels far removed from the city environment. A box that's not yet unpacked from their recent move sits just inside the front door, next to a pair of Will's massive work boots that are covered in a fine layer of red Oklahoma dirt. Jessica has a smattering of freckles across her cheery, youthful face. Her toenails and fingernails show remnants of a bright pink polish. She wears two chunky rings, one on each hand, which she unconsciously plays with while we talk. Will has blond cropped hair and sideburns, and some light blond scruff on his face. He has the bulky build of a former football player. He is wearing a red American Eagle T-shirt, faded jeans, and camouflage pattern flip-flops.

Jessica, nineteen, and Will, twenty-two, have been together since high school, although their path has been rocky, with repeated breakups and one broken engagement. Three of Jessica's closest friends hooked up with Will back when they were in high school; while this ended those friendships, she holds all involved accountable, noting wryly that Will "wasn't the nicest guy" back then. The couple has raised Will's daughter, now two, since she was born. They're expecting their first child together; their new little one was conceived during their most recent breakup, propelling them back together. Will has a relatively well-paying job, especially considering he dropped out after his first year of college to raise a child; this allows Jessica to be a stay-at-home mom. Now that they're having a child together, they're committed to making their relationship work. Will pledged to be far more involved around the house and with the children—the issues behind their most recent breakup—and Jessica is turning to Family Expectations to help with their communication and her trust issues.

Jessica explains:

I think that's why it's hard for me to have relationships, anyways, because with my dad, he has never been there, and my stepdad, he is just not a father figure at all. And losing my grandpa, it was just like, there's nothing left. So I mean, it's just hard for relationships and trust and everything, 'cause my dad cheated on my mom when she was pregnant with me. I know I wasn't there for it, but the stress that she felt, I felt.

She is very aware of how her history with her father and stepfather, and with Will back in high school, affects her today: "I'm always going to have trust issues, but that's just something I'm gonna have to deal with, because it didn't help what [Will] did in the beginning, but the past males in my life, figures that were supposed to be good, weren't." Having her trust violated at every turn—by her father, her stepfather, Will, and her friends—has left Jessica feeling relationally poor. As she notes, when her close relationship with her grandfather ended with his death, she felt she had "nothing left"—an expression of the specter of social poverty in her life. Her otherwise close relationship with her mother is strained by her mother's ailing marriage to Jessica's stepfather. If she can't make things work with Will, she'll lose her mother-daughter relationship with Will's child and her ability to lean on Will in times of stress—in some ways he's been a rock for Jessica, supporting her in her grief after her grandfather's passing and helping take care of her mother and younger siblings when her stepfather has flaked out on them. If her relationship with Will fails, she will feel the full weight of social poverty.

As Jessica and Will's story indicates, there are multiple factors at work simultaneously shaping their union, their parenting, and their satisfaction with their lives. In this chapter, I introduce in more detail what we know about social poverty and how it relates to the lives of young couples like Jessica and Will. I explain how the instability of multiple major life transitions (to adulthood, parenthood, and partnership) coupled with looser norms dictating family life—such as nonmarital cohabitation no longer being stigmatized—make it challenging for young parents to cultivate trust in their relationships; together, this puts them at a great risk for social poverty. Fundamentally, it is this risk of social deprivation that drives them to the door of Family Expectations.

The Contours of Social Poverty in America

Reexamining Social Capital and Social Support

Social capital is the set of ties people have to others through which they accrue resources. A large and growing literature on social capital, examining everything from neighborhood crime rates to morbidity rates for cancer patients, argues for the importance of our social ties to our health, finances, job opportunities, and more. Yet, many have critiqued this area of study for defining "social capital" in so many different ways that its meaning risks getting lost.[1] And so, many scholars have been more deliberate in distinguishing different types of social capital theoretically, boosted by empirical findings that its distinct forms having varying impacts on people's lives.

It is useful to distinguish, first, between social capital as a collective versus an individual characteristic.[2] In the former case, a neighborhood can be characterized by the presence or absence of a dense web of ties that breeds familiarity and trust, promotes collective efficacy, and preserves neighborhood safety. In the latter case, individuals may be part of social networks that provide connections to others who will give gifts, offer introductions to potential employers, or feed the cat while they're on vacation.[3] Whether they are characteristic of the collective or individuals, these ties can arise on their own or through the orchestrated efforts of organizations.[4]

Within the realm of individuals' social capital, we can differentiate between bridging versus bonding ties. Bridging ties are those to others outside one's own immediate context or set of relationships, like the friend of a friend, who can offer new information or opportunities not available in one's close social circle.[5] Bonding ties are more immediate, more intimate relationships, as with friends, romantic partners, and kin; such ties can provide various types of social support, discussed later.[6] An alternative approach to classifying bridging versus bonding ties is to distinguish between those that provide social leverage (help that promotes future upward socioeconomic mobility) versus social support (assistance with "getting by" in the present).[7] Social support itself can be broken down into distinct types, including emotional, informational, and instrumental;[8] some scholars add a fourth category of companionship or shared activities.[9]

Whether studying social capital as a whole or distinct aspects of it, researchers across fields have often treated these social ties as transactional goods, useful insofar as they allow their holders to accumulate other, often financial, resources, such as a better-paying job, child care that facilitates one's pursuit of employment or education, or a needed loan.[10] This means the social capital literature, despite taking human relationships as its object of study, largely neglects a fundamental element of them: these relationships are an intrinsic good.[11] While some scholars do include measures of emotional support in their studies, its intrinsic utility is not theoretically distinguished from the transactional value of informational or instrumental support;[12] an exception occurs among health researchers, who posit emotional support to have unique consequences for health outcomes through its psychological effects and, via the mind-body connection, its physiological impacts.[13] Lacking close, trusting relationships is not problematic just because it blocks access to other resources such ties could offer; it means that basic human needs for companionship, compassion, and understanding are not being met.[14]

Identifying the inherent value of emotionally supportive relationships raises some questions about the definition of social capital itself. Some scholars argue that forms of capital, by definition, can be turned into other resources; sociologist Ivan Light, for example, describes this as "mutual metamorphosis," stating, "Social capital is valuable to individuals and to collectivities because it is potentially convertible into [human, financial, physical, and cultural capital] forms."[15] I emphasize the innate value of high-quality, trusting social ties to human welfare, which belies these transactional notions of social capital. In the end, I suggest, scholars should develop a more encompassing notion of social capital, recognizing its potential for innate, rather than solely "convertible," value.

Feeling safe in revealing one's fears and trusting that the emotional vulnerability of expressing love is wise, for example, are valuable to individuals because they feel good, they affirm one's sense of self, and they help one to feel understood and accepted. Being more financially stable or gainfully employed is not the point of that emotional safety. Likewise, the social integration offered by bonding with others, as through a shared experience such as a group for new parents or a knitting circle, can affirm one's social identities (e.g., as a father or a creative person) and offer fellowship. These, again, contribute to one's well-being even if they never help a person to balance the checkbook or secure an internship. As with food and shelter, these are core human needs.[16]

What Is Social Poverty?

To recognize that the emotional texture of relationships contributes deeply to well-being requires that we account for people's perceptions of their own relationship resources, whether they are adequate to meet their needs or are evidence of "relational poverty."[17] The concept of social poverty I develop here is subjective, a product of the interaction between personality (e.g., introvert versus extrovert); number, type (e.g., friend versus romantic partner), and quality of social ties; and current personal events (e.g., celebrating college graduation versus mourning a family member's death). Social poverty, then, can be marked by a perceived inadequate number of close, trusting relationships or feelings of social disconnection.[18] This isolation does not have to do with being alone but rather with feeling lonely; interacting with others, even family and friends, is not a guarantee of avoiding social poverty. If these relationships are riddled with mistrust, are a site of criticism or hostility, or are undependable, they may create social poverty. Likewise, feeling like an outsider across one's social groups can contribute to a sense of social poverty.

The risk of social poverty, then, will change over the course of an individual's life, as needs change developmentally (with romantic relationships catching up in importance to peer relationships during the transition to adulthood, for instance) and with life circumstances (relational needs may be distinct during times of role transitions, as into parenthood).[19] For example, research has shown that the transition to college can be an especially fraught time, with young people at high risk for feelings of social isolation.[20] Social poverty, therefore, is not simply an individual failure. Rather, it arises due to the complex interplay of personal expectations, opportunities for building social ties, facility with social interactions, and current life events, both in and out of one's control. These, in turn, are shaped by childhood experiences and larger institutional structures,[21] such as educational and employment opportunities or governmental and private organizations' efforts to, among other factors, facilitate financial security, build social ties, and create a manageable balance between work and care obligations.[22] And, as discussed later in the chapter, broader cultural changes can create conditions in which developing trusting relationships is more or less difficult, underlining the role of macro-level factors in shaping an individual's risk for experiencing social poverty.

Sociologist Kristin Seefeldt details the ways in which structural factors—from urban housing policy to practices among low-wage employers—leave families abandoned and isolated from opportunities for economic stability or upward mobility.[23] While she occasionally mentions that there may be social repercussions to this isolation, she focuses on how the lack of social ties may prevent women from accessing financial opportunities (such as job referrals or labor organizing). This focus is undoubtedly important, but it neglects the ways in which this social isolation is meaningful in and of itself. We can see this in the stories Seefeldt details. Shunted into dilapidated and dangerous neighborhoods with many abandoned homes, the low-income women she interviewed found it difficult to make friends and build social connections with neighbors. Jobs on the night shift or with no coworkers, like cleaning an office building or working as a home health aide, and remote or temp work prevented women from developing friendships on the job; this is a real loss, given that research shows that workplace friendships are a key site of socializing for many Americans.[24] By applying the social poverty lens to the insights of Seefeldt's work, we can see a further social cost borne by the women she interviews of the structural abandonment of low-income families.

In elucidating the concept of social poverty, a few distinctions are key. First, receipt of emotional support should not be conflated with having adequate social resources. Having someone offer a hug or an attentive ear in a moment of crisis is not the same as escaping social poverty. As a parallel, consider the difference between a person suffering from hunger being given a meal versus having his or her food insecurity adequately addressed. Exchanging emotional support with a friend or family member, therefore, may be part of one's social resources, but its value is limited unless this exchange is part of an ongoing, high-quality relationship.[25]

Second, the feeling experienced by the individual (loneliness or isolation) is related to but distinguishable from the social problem (social poverty) that government and community groups may choose to target via interventions. By way of analogy, consider the example of the feeling of being hungry and its companion social problem of food insecurity; being hungry becomes food insecurity when it is an ongoing problem that cannot be addressed with current resources. Therefore, I choose to use the term "social poverty" to denote the phenomenon of interest here, rather than "loneliness," due to my focus on drawing out implications for policy and programs.

While social poverty and financial poverty can intersect, as discussed later in the chapter, social poverty is by no means an experience exclusive to those who are struggling financially, as attested to by research describing the prevalence of social isolation among older adults.[26] This point is key for two reasons. First, it underlines that I am not arguing that financial poverty is exclusively a cause or consequence of social poverty; solving social poverty won't solve financial poverty or vice versa. In his foundational work on the welfare state, William Beveridge detailed the multidimensional nature of deprivation. He articulated that while "evils," as he called them, such as a lack of access to health care or education, were related to poverty, they were also distinct experiences that required attention in their own right.[27] Similarly, I argue that social poverty is not a simple by-product of income poverty. While social poverty and income poverty can be related—just as, say, Beveridge's "squalor" or "disease" was related to "want"—recognizing them as separate constructs is essential because it acknowledges the importance of social poverty, apart from income, to the human condition and individual well-being and, therefore, to policy. While it may be more likely for a person struggling financially to also face social poverty, inadequate health care, or lack of access to educational opportunities, it is possible to experience one of these challenges without the others;[28] policy and practice must be developed with these distinct sources of hardship in mind.

Second, the assumption implicit in much of the writing about people in poverty is that they have only one primary source of motivation: money. Social poverty helps us to recognize the core drive to develop or maintain adequate relational resources, which can influence people's decisions and behaviors, aside from any financial incentives. It is only by holding in high regard the importance of relationships to well-being that we can understand why people react as they do to the relationship education program offered to them, for example. The free dinner and the baby gifts the program offers are certainly a motivating factor in getting people in the door, but the opportunities to strengthen their romantic relationships, share fellowship with other parents, and feel the support of program staff also motivate the participants to make the drive halfway across the city after working and caring for children all day. Without this recognition of social poverty, we lack a full accounting of the motivations guiding the people targeted by legislation; therefore, we are unable to fully and accurately evaluate policies and programmatic interventions. And the hardship of such social deprivation has real consequences for physical and psychological well-being.

Social Poverty's Psychological and Physiological Causes and Consequences

Abraham Maslow's hierarchy of needs is a widely researched, popularly known psychological theory that seeks to explain what drives humans to do what they do. Maslow argues that once people meet basic needs, like food, clothing, shelter, and safety, they move on to pursuing other needs, such as having love and, as the pinnacle of human achievement, self-actualization.[29] While Maslow's theory has been debated and his model revised,[30] the area he pioneered makes clear that social relationships are an indispensable part of human motivation, even if they are not critical to physical survival. While in poverty studies the focus predominantly remains on material hardship, Maslow reminds us that "we could never understand fully the need for love no matter how much we might know about the hunger drive."[31] That is, knowing about the nature of people's material needs does not give us authoritative insight into their social needs. As with other unmet needs, going without close social relationships "may lead to a sense of deprivation"[32]—the fundamental idea behind the concept of social poverty I develop here.

And while Maslow and his successors may not consider these needs necessary for physical survival, research in other fields suggests that lacking important social relationships can be fatal, at least indirectly so. Those studying the social determinants of health have found that social support is tied to a host of positive mental and physical health outcomes, whereas loneliness, social isolation, and conflict-ridden social relationships are linked to an increased risk of ill health and mortality.[33] Researchers hypothesize that these effects come about in several ways, including the physiological impact of social interactions and the way relationships may promote or inhibit healthy versus risky behaviors.[34] This is not simply a matter of raising blood pressure by a point or two or having an extra beer; rather, as one study found, loneliness and social isolation raise mortality risk by 26 percent and 29 percent, respectively.[35] It is no wonder that former US surgeon general Vivek Murthy listed emotional well-being—promoted particularly through social connect-edness—as a national priority.[36]

What is particularly key to understand is that the consequences of social poverty can be cascading. That is, lacking social resources can lead to a social spiral, increasing the depths of one's social poverty or the difficulty of escaping its pull. Psychologist John Cacioppo and his colleagues have detailed how feelings of loneliness give rise to an un-conscious "hypervigilance" to social cues and a greater likelihood of negatively interpreting social signals. The result, they argue, is that the lonely person becomes more self-centered and perceives the intentions and actions of others to be socially threatening, making it that much harder to establish trust and ease one's sense of isolation.[37] We can imag-ine how this might play out in the context of a romantic relationship that is already on an unstable footing: ambiguous or seemingly innocuous actions can be seen as slights or insults, further eroding the quality of the bond. The fact that feeling at risk for social isolation is associated with being more aggressive[38] likely increases the chances that a high-conflict relationship dynamic will develop when one or both partners are experiencing social poverty. This means that those who are already disadvantaged in their social resources are more likely to see this disad-vantage magnified, as their ways of perceiving and engaging with others make it more likely that their social fears are realized. The chances of this happening, however, are not equally shared.

Social poverty is not evenly distributed across the population. The economically disadvantaged are often more disadvantaged socially and more likely to experience social isolation, unsteady relationships, and loneliness.[39] The stressful social environments in which today's poor live are associated with cardiovascular problems and death.[40] But social exclusion is more predictive of mortality than is residence in a high-poverty neighborhood, and it is predictive of mortality over and above an individual's poverty status.[41] Social poverty should not be trivialized as a matter of hurt feelings or just wanting to have someone with whom to chat; our social needs as humans are part and parcel of who we are, and whether or not these needs are met plays an essential role in our emotional, psychological, and physical well-being.

Social Poverty in Existing Poverty Research

Carol Stack's famous book *All Our Kin* argued that what poor folks lacked in material goods, they made up for in rich social ties. In her observations of a poor community, Stack described "extensive networks of kin and friends supporting, reinforcing each other."[42] And yet evidence in contemporary America increasingly suggests this no longer holds true, if it ever did.[43] People like Jessica, whom we met at the start of the chapter, face their daily lives with limited support from stable, intimate, trusting relationships; if Jessica's relationship with Will fails once again, she will have few others to whom she feels she can safely turn to consistently meet her emotional needs.

Most research in this area has focused on the economic consequences of lacking social ties.[44] Studies have found that the poor generally derive less financial benefit and support from their personal relationships than do more affluent people, despite their greater need.[45] The reason: their "limited ... friendship networks" make it harder to ask for and to receive assistance.[46] For example, sociologist Sandra Susan Smith's work is part of a broader literature that has detailed the financial benefits of social capital. Smith has found that lower-income job seekers are reluctant to ask for or even accept help in their searches, and currently employed low-wage workers are hesitant to offer it, worrying that someone they refer to their employer might underperform and reflect poorly on them, hurting their own prospects. Smith argues that this mistrust across relationships magnifies existing patterns of socioeconomic inequality, leaving the already disadvantaged struggling to gain a sure foothold in the labor market.

Matthew Desmond's research on eviction also reveals the limited nature of the social support poor individuals sometimes receive. Desmond followed an array of Milwaukee residents through the process of eviction and saw that they often leaned heavily on others to avoid home-lessness. While at first glance this could be seen as supporting Stack's findings from more than forty years ago, in fact, Desmond found that people were more likely to turn to strangers or acquaintances for help than to kin, and these ties were short-lived and shallow. He writes, "Disposable ties facilitated the flow of various resources, but often bonds were brittle and fleeting. The strategy of forming, using, and burning disposable ties allowed families caught in desperate situations to make it from one day to the next, but it also bred instability and fostered misgivings among peers."[47] While these ties can offer temporary relief from hardship, they do not appear to solve the longer-term problem of being financially poor. Nor, we can see, would they address social needs—the longer-term problem of being socially poor.

Shifting attention from the economic exchange benefits of social relationships—like sharing money, information on job opportunities, or a place to live—other work has explored the emotional content of these relationships. This gives us a picture of what social poverty looks like—and, more important, feels like—in its daily manifestations. Social poverty is evident in previous research, once we know to look for and label it.

From interviews Pamela Holcomb and colleagues conducted with low-income fathers, we hear what it felt like for them to grow up lacking dependable relationships and also what a deep desire they have to provide their children with more social resources than they themselves have had. The most common way fathers engaged with their family and friends was in receiving emotional support, rather than any kind of financial assistance (such as food or a place to stay).[48] This is particularly notable in this population, given that most experienced pressing material needs, and it underscores the importance of recognizing the emotional component of relationships; overly focusing on the exchange of material resources can result in missing a predominant role relationships play in people's lives. One father explained, "I didn't have anybody really to support my thoughts or my feelings or my dreams [while growing up]." Another described the sort of father he wanted to be to his children: "Being able to have your kids be like, 'You know what, Daddy? I love you, I miss you.' And being able to say it back and giving them the hugs and the kisses and being able to be their security blanket and somebody that they know that will look out for them, to count on."[49] Among the men they studied, the average number of social ties was five, compared with twenty-three among the general population.[50] Although Holcomb and colleagues don't use the term "social poverty," there clearly are unmet social needs among the men in their study.

Elaine Bell Kaplan's study of teen mothers, interviewed in the mid-1980s, found "a poverty of relationships" for this group as well.[51] These young mothers received little support from friends, family, or their babies' fathers, leaving them desperate for connection; as a response, they often tolerated poor treatment from their mothers and relished their babies' unconditional love. In the foreword to Kaplan's book, Arlie Hochschild wrote, "Living in an inner city today is not simply a matter of cramped living quarters, run-down schools, and absent fathers, but also of severely damaged relationships. . . . It is the injury to these vital bonds, this hidden oppression, that is the secret troublemaker."[52] In developing and deploying the concept of social poverty, I expand on the previous insights of this "secret troublemaker," revealing that its lived experience goes well beyond its financial consequences. To understand why these young parents' social deprivation is so acute and why it matters so much, we must have a clear picture of the factors that shape their lives.

Stressful Transitions

Becoming an Adult

Young adults are particularly vulnerable to social poverty. While most research on loneliness and social isolation focuses on the older adult population, young adults rival the elderly in their incidence of these issues;[53] a recent study found that people report the highest frequency of loneliness during their twenties and again around age sixty.[54] Young adults are at a developmental stage in which ties to peers and romantic partners are especially important. Over the course of adolescence, as young people individuate from their parents, their relationships with peers come to be a primary source of social support. As adolescence rolls into young adulthood, romantic relationships take on an increasingly central role.[55] Therefore, the absence or presence of close, high-quality relationships with friends and romantic partners is more strongly related to feelings of loneliness and psychological distress—such as depressive symptoms—for young adults than for those in other life stages.[56] For developmental reasons, then, we ought to be particularly attentive to social poverty for those young people who are encountering stressful situations, in which social support is crucial to positive coping. The myriad of transitions—in residence, daily activities, and social roles and identities—can be overwhelming as youth navigate their way into adulthood.

Mark and Ashleigh, whom we met at the start of the introduction to this book, have been together for almost a year and are just about to welcome their first child. Ashleigh, twenty, sees herself as college material, despite the fact that she's dropped out of high school. Mark, twenty-one, has no such aspirations. Unlike Ashleigh though, who isn't employed, Mark has worked consistently for several years at KFC, where he spends his time loathing the customers and steaming about not getting a raise. Each of them is traversing the transition to adulthood in a different way.

Mark can't see his way to applying for other jobs when he's exhausted from his overnight shifts and has no phone number to put down on applications. For her part, Ashleigh ricochets between her dreams of being the successful TV reporter she knows she could be if only she could enroll in college as a communications major, versus completing high school online, getting a cosmetology certificate, and working for a while. Were she to follow the latter plan, she says, the next step would then be to "go back to school to be a history teacher or be a nurse or something." Once their daughter is older, Ashleigh says, then she'll abandon what she calls this "logical" path to return to her dreams of television glory. Despite these plans and possible selves that Ashleigh is exploring when we first meet, during the year of the study she never makes it back to high school, but she does enroll in and drop out of a business course at a for-profit college. Like the "office-appropriate" clothing that Ashleigh started wearing while taking the course, she decided this line of work wasn't a good fit for her. Theirs is not just a story of one couple struggling to make it. This weak grasp on the traditional pillars of adulthood is increasingly common across the income spectrum. The transition to adulthood has become an extended affair for all, but a more daunting one for the poor.

Many higher-income young people navigate the time until settling into adulthood by exploring their options in college and waiting to become parents. After college, they can draw on parental resources as a safety net if a career or relationship gamble doesn't work out. Psychologist Jeffrey Arnett points to a culture of "emerging adulthood," wherein people see their late teens and early twenties not as a time to settle down and commit to lifelong partners, careers, or children, as in the past, but rather as a time to indulge in a journey of self-discovery.[57]

Lower-income individuals are not immune to this cultural message. They likewise view the transition to adulthood as an ongoing process and a time of searching, rather than settling, of trying on possible selves.[58] And yet in contrast to their higher-income counterparts, they often take on some of the trappings of adulthood sooner—leaving school, securing paid employment, becoming parents. Despite these early activities, they are less able to gain financial stability, land in a career (not "just a job"), and secure a lifelong relationship commitment.[59]

Unemployment rates are high during the years of the transition to adulthood. With high rates of unemployment, many young adults do not yet fit the bill for "marriage material," so marriage rates are low. But just because young adults are not getting married doesn't mean they put off having children. Across the country, more than a third of young adults have had a child, and the majority of these births are to unmarried parents.[60] Those with less education have their children earlier—starting in their early twenties—and typically have at least one child while unmarried.[61] Because dating and cohabiting unions in the United States tend to be short-lived,[62] romantic commitments are often still in flux while economically disadvantaged young adults tackle the challenges of parenthood.

In short, what looks like an extended period of self-exploration for socioeconomically advantaged young adults is often an extended period of instability for their disadvantaged counterparts.[63] And the task of getting established may not be completed even after they have left their early twenties behind. They have become adults by default but have not transitioned into the adulthood they desire. A sense of searching for a brighter future, of paths still waiting to be explored, remains, alongside the daily struggles they face just to get by. Many of the young people who participate in Family Expectations are taking on the challenges of transitioning to adulthood, partnership, and parenthood without a firm foundation of social support in place to help ease the pressures such changes can bring; as such, the threat of social poverty can loom large. As psychologists Linda Gallo and Karen Matthews explain, individuals with fewer social resources are more reactive to stress because they are less able to buffer its effects.[64] That is, experiencing stressful transitions without adequate social resources makes it more difficult to traverse them successfully.

Becoming Partners and Parents

It may seem perplexing to some readers that, in the midst of such uncertainty regarding their educations, jobs, and relationships, young people would choose to have children. By and large, these pregnancies are not planned. While many couples discuss the possibility of having children, often their happy feelings around this prospect are tinged with ambivalence. Nationally, the vast majority of pregnancies among unmarried women are classified as "unplanned."[65] However, the simple, dichotomous classification—planned or unplanned—ignores the complex feelings and behaviors that often underlie this event. In fact, many women consider their "unintended" pregnancies to be mistimed as opposed to unwanted.[66] Often, such pregnancies occur when couples are not "trying" to get pregnant but instead are lax in using birth control.[67] From the couples portrayed in this book, we similarly hear stories about happy surprises and pregnancies borne of these feelings of ambiguity.

Why would so many young men and women leave pregnancy to chance? Kathryn Edin and her collaborators have interviewed hundreds of parents in an attempt to understand why.[68] Their research reveals that, for many low-income parents, if they were to wait until the time was "right" to have children—when they had a solid marriage, firm finances, and the like—they could end up childless. And because parenthood often stands alone as a source of positive identity and meaning—occupational identities, like cashier, may not be as rewarding—childlessness does not seem like an option. While it might be seen as irresponsible to plan to have a child in less than ideal circumstances, stepping up to the plate in response to an unplanned pregnancy can be interpreted as a young person doing the right thing and can be a huge source of motivation to make his or her life right—avoiding previous bad behavior, like partying, and trying to live up to the role of parent that the pregnancy has provided.

In addition, children often fill an emotional hole. Most of the low-income unmarried mothers Edin interviewed described themselves as having "no close friends."[69] Edin and her co-author Maria Kefalas write that for some young mothers, "pregnancy offers the promise of relational intimacy at a time few other emotional resources are available," adding that children "are the only truly safe emotional harbor" for many poor mothers.[70] One woman explained to them, "I think [I got pregnant] mainly because I wanted to be loved. I went through my childhood without it. . . . It was something that would love me. I would be able to love it unconditionally."[71] In a world in which relationships can feel fleeting, having a child can seem to offer two permanent bonds: one to a child, and another to the child's other parent. While a romantic relationship can end in a breakup or divorce, ties through a shared child are seen as permanent.[72] Though the transitions to partnership and parenthood may not be smooth, they represent a chance to meet core emotional needs that otherwise may be unfulfilled. That is, social poverty may play a role in encouraging many of these pregnancies. And though having a child creates a little companion, researchers have found that it falls short of its promise: parenthood is not associated with a lower likelihood of experiencing loneliness.[73]

Further, the transition to parenthood can place a good deal of stress on romantic relationships. In a study that followed couples for eight years, there was a pattern of a "sudden deterioration . . . in relationship functioning" following the birth of a child, including an increase in conflict and a loss of satisfaction; many couples did not bounce back from this decline in relationship quality.[74] Those who had been together for a shorter period and who had a higher-conflict relationship before the birth saw larger increases in relationship problems afterward, as did women whose families of origin were more conflicted.[75] Thus, while the desires for both partnership and parenthood may originate in a need to escape social poverty, tackling these two transitions simultaneously can also make social poverty more acute; the transition to parenthood can undermine the quality of the romantic relationships, leaving parents struggling to cope with multiple stressors with less support.

Changing Families, Loosening Norms

It is not romanticizing the past to say that relationships today are more fragile and more likely to end than those in the past.[76] Contrary to popular opinion, though, the divorce rate has been basically flat or declining for more than thirty years. This apparent disjuncture is not as mysterious as it may appear at first glance. In part it reflects the fact that couples are much less likely to get married than they once were. None of their breakups, then, show up in the divorce statistics.

Marriage used to serve as the cornerstone of adulthood, with spouses setting out to build a life together, starting at the altar.[77] Today, most couples live together;[78] only some subsequently make it down the aisle.[79] Marriage has become a destination rather than a starting point. Those who can reach these financial and emotional "marriage bars" are more likely to have higher education and income.[80]

Akin to the period of emerging adulthood, creating a family today offers opportunities for exploration and experimentation that did not exist in previous eras. It is far more socially acceptable for couples to live together and have children outside of marriage and for those who are married to divorce. Sociologist Andrew Cherlin refers to the disappearance of the norms that once limited these behaviors as the "deinstitutionalization" of marriage. He explains that what was once governed by community-enforced norms has now become an individual decision; as a result, family patterns are highly variable, both from one person to another and for a specific individual over time.[81]

Despite speculation to the contrary, none of this has meant that marriage is dead in the United States. Marriage is still very much valued, and divorce is still very much feared.[82] But the stigmas associated with not being married and with divorcing have decreased, leading people to feel they can "try out" relationships. This is not the sort of dating that was common in the past, however. Today, while dating, many couples end up living together and having children, raising the stakes in these dating relationships like never before.

Nonmarital childbearing is particularly widespread among those from lower socioeconomic status backgrounds and economically disadvantaged minority groups,[83] and it is more often found among younger women (in their teens and twenties).[84] These are the groups represented by the couples profiled in this book. It's still the case that men and women share households and children, as they did in the past. But while some get married before having children, others wait until afterward, if at all. This isn't merely a difference in timing. Cohabiting relationships, even those in which children are present, are far more likely to end in a breakup than are marriages.[85] Once one relationship ends, another often begins, leading to cohabitation and childbearing with a new partner. The result can be a complex web of nuclear family relationships spread across households, which may place additional demands on parents' financial and emotional resources.[86]

To the extent that romantic relationships are occurring in a deinstitutionalized environment, people are much more likely to experience instability, unpredictability, and a lack of clarity in their family lives. There is a challenge in figuring out how to navigate these new family arrangements. When a mom's boyfriend moves in, for example, there are no institutional structures or norms to suggest whether he counts as a parent, who has a say in child-rearing decisions, or which parenting issues are a part of or separate from the romantic relationship. While for a child's two parents, the romantic and coparenting unions are one and the same, that is typically not the case, at least initially, when a parent introduces a new romantic partner into the family.[87]

Miranda, a twenty-seven-year-old mother of a nine-year-old girl, has been with her boyfriend, Carl, for about two years; she's pregnant with their first child together. Although she never lived with her daughter's father, she and her daughter did live with Miranda's previous boyfriend for a number of years. While her daughter got along well enough with Miranda's ex when they were living together, she has struggled to accept Carl's place in their family. This, in turn, impacts Miranda and Carl's relationship. As Miranda explains, "It gets us in arguments when her and him are not connecting . . . 'cause it's not understood yet what each of their roles is, so it's bumping heads and then it makes me and him argue. So it's not working out very well right at this moment. But it's something that we need to work on." Carl later adds, "That's what we're looking [for from] Family Expectations is understanding everyone's feelings." And Miranda clarifies, adding, "Everyone's part in the family, everyone's role." When I ask what they want their lives to look like in six months, after the baby arrives, they list a "stable" job for Carl, a "better home," and,

Miranda says, "a better relationship with my daughter, happy and, you know, secure in her position in the family." Miranda sums up her vision of their future this way: "And us communicate more. Just being a good, happy family."

Working their way to this "happy family" is challenging because all involved lack clear institutional norms: whether and how Carl should act as a stepfather, how Miranda's daughter should treat him, and how Miranda should mediate their relationship. Such complex family relationships make the transitions to partnership and parenthood all the more difficult to navigate; this, in turn, presents obstacles to the creation of the high-quality, trusting, stable relationships that are needed to avoid social poverty. While bringing important freedoms and easing stigma, broader cultural changes that have deinstitutionalized relationship norms create a risk for social poverty, as partners and parents have fewer social scripts to follow and community-enforced norms to count on as they try to make sense of and construct their families.

Yet characterizing family lives like theirs as deinstitutionalized risks overstating the case on the ground. To folks like Miranda and Carl, not all family choices are equally desirable.[88] Low-income individuals, including parents, express a strong desire to marry and have a "happy family," even if they are less likely than their higher-income counterparts to see this relationship dream realized.[89] Marriage is a relational North Star that creates expectations by outsiders for the couple and between the partners themselves. As we hear from Miranda and Carl, what they want is some guidance in what everyone's roles should be in today's more complex, more confusing family life; clarifying their roles and creating clearer expectations is one way they seek to address their risks of social poverty, as doing so will make it more likely they can develop the close, trusting family ties they so desire.

Social Poverty: A Question of Trust

As a result of the instability associated with financial struggles, navigating the transition to adulthood, and unsettled romantic ties, the foundation that is necessary for a couple to build trust is often weak, if not missing altogether. Without adequate money, an established adult life, or a clear commitment to one another, partners often find it challenging to rely on each other—a necessary precursor to trust. Without trust, in turn, couples remain hesitant to invest further in their relationships or to depend on one another as coparents because the likelihood of being let down feels too high. This is one of the key ways in which these young people find themselves in romantic relationships yet still struggling with social poverty.[90]

Here I focus on trust as a relational element that develops in conditions of familiarity, through self-disclosure in relationships that are protected from overwhelming uncertainty.[91] This is distinct from a focus on generalized gender distrust ("all men are dogs"). As an essential component of close, supportive relationships, trust is intimately intertwined with people's experiences of social poverty. I explore trust and its connection with social poverty because it is central both to understanding how these romances play out and to evaluating the policy responses and programmatic interventions that aim to affect these relationship decisions and behaviors: Can they help couples develop trust?[92]

Given the changes in families and relationship norms over the past few decades, perhaps the struggles couples face regarding mistrust should come as no surprise. Sociologists Ulrich Beck and Elisabeth Beck-Gernsheim write that, when it comes to romantic relationships, "Time-honoured norms are fading and losing their power to determine behavior. What used to be carried out as a matter of course now has to be discussed, justified, negotiated and agreed, and for that very reason it can always be cancelled."[93] It is all the more difficult to know what to expect of a partner in a relatively "norm-free" culture around romantic relationships; in whom and at what point in a relationship trust is well placed may be opaque. The potential for enforceable trust is reduced today by the deinstitutionalization of marriage in our broader culture; because relationships often are without clear social norms, the possibility of community enforcement of "right" behavior is limited.[94] In addition, the myriad forms of instability in their housing, schooling, employment, identities, and finances with which these young parents are coping play a central role in undermining the development of trust.

A foundation of trust is required to feel you can safely commit to living with someone, raising children together, and getting married. Social theorists have explored the bases on which trust develops, finding that a preliminary criterion is familiarity:[95] there's no such thing as "trust at first sight." Trust is based on the belief that the other is acting with one's own perspective in mind.[96] For this to be possible, a mutual understanding born of familiarity is necessary.[97]

This familiarity is cultivated when individuals engage in self-disclosure as their relationship develops. Self-disclosure is risky, as revealing vulnerabilities makes you susceptible to being rejected because of what you have revealed and to having your trust violated in a deeper way. However, the potential payoff is that what is disclosed will be received positively, creating a feeling of acceptance and comfort in the relationship. The familiarity that develops through this iterative process of self-disclosure and greater understanding makes the behavior of each partner in the relationship more knowable and more predictable.[98] Self-disclosure leads to dependability and clearer expectations, which creates greater trust that, in turn, enables further self-disclosure.

As individuals build relationships, the forces of trust and instability are intimately connected. "Trust is a reliance in turbulent conditions on some number of certainties and on other individuals' actions, that affect one's own welfare, that despite conditions largely unknown can be counted on to act in a predictable and presumably benevolent fashion," social theorist Niklas Luhmann wrote.[99] Trust is a way of coping with uncertainty: it is prohibitively difficult to live our lives assuming everyone is out to get us. But trust is also undermined by uncertainty.

The process of disclosure and communication makes partners feel more familiar to one another and makes each better able to predict and understand the behavior of the other, easing uncertainty and further deepening their trust in the relationship. Various external and internal forces that create instability for the couple and erode trust make it that much more difficult for them to engage in those relationship practices that create a secure attachment and strengthen trust. As anthropologist Elliott Liebow concludes, when relationships have not developed over time, through this process of learning and deepening, they are less likely to "stand up well to the stress of crisis or conflict of interest, when demands tend to be heaviest and most insistent."[100] That is, just when that relationship is needed the most, it is the most liable to disintegrate. Without adequate initial investments in the relationship, it may not be a resource that can prevent social poverty. In relationships without deep trust, it is as though you hold a currency that can quickly lose its value, leaving you penniless.

Research finds that lower-income and less-educated individuals tend to be less trusting than their advantaged counterparts, perhaps due to the more limited control they have in some facets of their lives.[101] Sociologist Judith Levine argues that the circumstances for mistrust are endemic in the lives of lower-income women.[102] These women often have been disappointed by so many different people, from family members to bosses to government assistance caseworkers, and thus they approach new people warily, hesitant to trust and be let down once again. Research also shows that those who are currently more socially isolated are less likely to be trusting,[103] possibly because they lack evidence to indicate that relying on others can pay off.[104] Those who report being lonelier are less likely to trust their friends and to believe their friends trust them, and more likely to view these friendships negatively.[105] Social poverty begets social poverty.

People's willingness to trust depends in part on their past and present interpersonal experiences, as well as their current surroundings. Carley, twenty-one, is having her first child with her fiancé, Nick. She says that there are "things we had to work through because we've been lied to by other people. . . . Like if that person can lie to you with a straight face, who else can lie to you with a straight face?" Although she and Nick have been faithful to one another, their past experiences have nonetheless left them shaken, which shapes how their relationship plays out now. They struggle to talk through issues in a productive, nondestructive way. Carley notes, "You can't communicate if you don't trust what the other person is saying." Communication, as Carley rightly notes, is not just about speaking and listening; it is about partners' interpretations of what one another says.

Experiences with parents and caretakers in childhood lay the foundation for trust later in life;[106] without learning that important others can be counted on and seeing trusting relationships modeled, it can be challenging to learn how to properly evaluate others' trustworthiness.[107] When Nick, Carley's fiancé, was only eight years old, the man he had been raised to believe was his father announced to him, "I'm not your dad." The man had also been physically abusive, locking Nick in closets and hitting him. After Nick's mother divorced, she remarried a man who later descended into alcoholism and was violent with her when drunk. Nick feels betrayed by the adults in his life, "Just seeing the hurt and everything else that I had to go through and all that stuff, I vowed on my life to never do the wrong things that my parents did. Like my dad, leaving my child without ever being in my life." Carley, for her part, had various struggles with volatility and abuse in her own family life. It is perhaps no wonder that the two struggle to trust one another today. Like Carley and Nick, many other couples arrive at Family Expectations, as parenthood stares them in the face, with unstable jobs, housing situations, educational trajectories, finances, and relationships—ingredients that make building the solid, supportive relationships they desire quite difficult. What they are looking for, in part, are trusting relationships that provide essential protection against social poverty.

What Does This Mean for Young Unmarried Parents?

There are myriad forms of uncertainty coming from the combination of negotiating the transition to adulthood, tackling the challenges of parenthood at relatively young ages, and figuring out relationships in an environment of deinstitutionalized romantic relationship norms. Trust is a basic foundation of secure romantic relationships, and stability is vital for the development of trust. It is far more difficult for people to behave in consistent and acceptable ways—necessary for the development of trust—when the various norms governing their behavior are profoundly unclear. This emphasizes the role broader social changes have had in shaping the possibilities that individuals will experience social poverty.

Today's young people face a confusing world, in which roles and norms are not entirely clear when it comes to relationships, education, and work. But, while romantic norms have weakened, they've not totally given way; there are rules from the past, but it's unclear to whom and under what circumstances these rules should apply. Monogamy is assumed, but not always practiced; marriage is an ideal, but one that can feel unattainable. There's not a clear pathway down which people must travel as they become adults and start their own family lives. These various sources of uncertainty—broader societal shifts as well as their manifestations on the individual level—make it that much harder for couples to cultivate the trust necessary for stable, happy relationships.[108]

The limitations and obstacles of financial difficulties further complicate coming of age and negotiating romantic relationships. This can range from larger issues like difficulty securing permanent and decent housing to smaller issues like not having money to pay for a babysitter so the couple can have a date night. Money doesn't buy happiness, but it can create an environment in which happiness is more easily pursued and predictability more easily secured. The instability and lack of clarity are particularly marked for those coming from more disadvantaged backgrounds because they are less likely to have the financial capital to easily access higher education, the social capital to secure a stable and satisfying career, and the role modeling to learn how to create a stable, high-quality romantic partnership.[109]

Very few of these young people are set with their educations and on a clear career path before they begin to tackle their roles as parents and as partners. In broader society, young adults are basically seen as preadults, without the responsibilities of caring and providing for a child. But the roles that the young people profiled in this study are taking on, of parent and potential spouse, are constructed as being adult roles and therefore are in conflict with the activities of preadulthood. When relationships, education, and careers aren't settled, even by the marker of having become a parent, it may be harder to know which behavioral norms to follow: Do you have to behave like an adult? All the time, or just sometimes? We see conflict within couples over this issue, with disagreement over what behaviors are appropriate. These complications may be particularly noticeable for the men, especially during the pregnancy with the first child, because there are fewer clear markers for them of the transition they're going through—such as the physical changes mothers experience—prior to the child's birth. This can manifest itself in men behaving in ways that contradict the values they profess—like partying or not settling into a job while at the same time describing what dedicated fathers they plan on being.

That people are trying to achieve a clear end point—a stable, happy family life—without following a sequential set of roles and tasks can create challenges. For example, having children before completing their own education means that parents simultaneously see it as being more difficult to complete their educations (because of the logistics of child care, a need to earn money, etc.), but they also view their children as motivation for continuing their education (to set an example, to provide a better life, etc.). In a way, the stakes feel higher, since it's now more important to complete this task or fulfill this role, yet the chances of success are lower. Further, the lack of stability across so many domains of life makes trust more difficult—if it's unclear whether both partners are in it to play the long game or will quit after a few innings, if when the going gets rough they will decide to take their bats and mitts and go home.

Social Poverty: Focus and Contributions

Identifying the social poverty that permeates the lives of these young, unmarried parents is essential to understanding their responses to a relationship education program. In examining the Family Expectations intervention, we can see what role an outside organization can play in potentially transforming this unstable environment and see couples' responses to it as arising from their wish to avoid or escape social poverty. This serves as a model for how we can include a consideration of social poverty in our policy evaluations beyond the relationship education realm.

Young people do not automatically acquire the complete trappings of adulthood at age eighteen or twenty-one, and so must progress through a series of tasks and transitions while establishing the trajectories they will follow in adulthood. In investigating these tasks, much of the research on "emerging adulthood" has focused on relatively socioeconomically advantaged groups of young people,[110] making studies like mine useful for their emphasis on the complications of transitioning to adulthood for more disadvantaged individuals.[111] This focus is especially significant because this portion of the population is more likely to make early transitions to parenthood and marriage, resulting in their roles and responsibilities being in conflict with the expectations of emerging adulthood's exploration. Emphasizing the role conflicts and the social implications of such conflicts provides an alternative perspective on the challenges of coming of age in America today, including what this all can mean for young adults' ability to create and sustain trusting, lasting relationships; in short, simultaneously transitioning to adulthood, partnership, and parenthood can up the risk of social poverty.

While there are clearly far fewer strict norms dictating acceptable family behaviors than in previous times,[112] people continue to be influenced in their family decisions by a sense of what constitutes the epitome of a good family life.[113] They are at once buffeted by the uncertainty and instability of the lack of norms in creating family lives outside of marriage, yet continue to be oriented in their family decisions toward married family life as the ideal. In the relationships of the couples profiled in the subsequent chapters, and in the reasons that draw couples to a relationship education program in the first place, we see these dynamics playing out on the ground. Without clear roles and rules in relationships, but with ongoing high hopes for relationships, the possibility of social poverty feels that much more likely, with reality falling short of ideals and expectations.

Previous research on the role of trust in the relationships of socioeconomically disadvantaged couples has tended to focus on gender distrust[114] and on distrust arising from concerns of sexual infidelity.[115] I explore trust more broadly here, examining how the intersection of macro-level economic and social changes and micro-level obstacles, such as the experience of role conflicts or weak relational skills, combine to create an environment in which the development of a trusting relationship is extremely challenging. As psychologist Scott Stanley has noted, this can have profound implications for the relationship's future: "Relationships characterized by low trust among partners (whether justified or not) are less likely to move along pathways to deeper commitments, and for some couples, moving toward clearer and deeper commitment is one of the more potent ways to help stabilize an understanding about trustworthiness."[116] The contribution of this book is not to alter our understanding of the nature or function of trust, but rather to see how the confounding factors of life transitions and the deinstitutionalization of relationships create an environment that is, at best, challenging to the development of trusting relationships.

I don't know whether the social poverty I detail here is something new. This wicked combination of diffuse relationship norms, strained romantic and family relationships, challenging and extended life transitions, and limited economic opportunities for less educated folks in part account for its existence today, but its presence in the past could have been created by previous incarnations of our social institutions. For example, at a time in the past when the emotional component of marital relationships was downplayed and when strict gender-dictated roles shaped how partners interacted,[117] many romantic relationships may not have fulfilled needs for socioemotional support. Women were precluded from achieving the autonomy and independence that are likely necessary for true trust—choosing to create a life together, rather than doing so out of necessity. For their part, men were often culturally barred from engaging emotionally and displaying vulnerabilities, even in their friendships and marriages.[118] It will be for future research to determine whether and how the social poverty we observe among the poor and working-class parents profiled here is unique to today, or simply the latest manifestation of an ever-present form of disadvantage.

Lacking key social resources matters. On the simplest of levels, one study found that when facing a stressful experience, simply holding hands with a spouse caused noticeable drops in the brain's neural activity, showing the soothing effect a companion can have as we confront life's difficulties; the effects were even stronger for spouses in high-quality relationships.[119] Failing to cultivate trust can mean finding oneself socially impoverished, without a hand to hold when times get tough.

Becoming an Adult

Getting a Car, a Job, and Paying the Bills

Twenty-year-old Kristina is slender, with beautiful, light blue eyes. She has plucked her eyebrows into just the thinnest line of hair arched high above her brow bone. She tucks the pieces of dyed blonde hair that have fallen out of her ponytail behind her ears. She has a tiny stud in the space between her nose and mouth, off to the left side; this beauty mark of a piercing bobs in and out as she talks. She wears a gold ring with a fleck of a diamond in it on her left ring finger and, in contrast to the rest of her put-together appearance, has dirt caught underneath her fingernails. She's wearing jeans and a crisp, white T-shirt that gets tight over her pregnant belly—she's about six months along. She tells me that she's not a shy person and has no trouble sharing.

The first time we meet, we are at a noisy McDonald's on the edge of the city. When I called her to arrange our meeting, she wasn't sure what was going on with her boyfriend, Lance, and, in the end, he doesn't join us. It's customer appreciation week at McDonald's, making the fast-food restaurant even busier and louder than usual, with toy and balloon giveaways and celebratory announcements over a megaphone. Despite the raucousness around us, Kristina isn't distracted from detailing her tumultuous relationship with Lance.

She and Lance have been together for almost a year and a half. They had talked about having a baby together before she got pregnant, and they'd discussed getting married too, though they haven't made any real wedding plans. They are both employed. Although all this would make it seem like they're relatively prepared to be parents, they're broken up right now—kind of.

Kristina's moving out of their apartment, and she views the next few months as a crucial trial period for Lance to show if he's really going to change his behavior and his attitude; then, she'd be willing to have them live together again, in time for the baby's arrival. Their issues are many and basic.

They check each other's cell phones to see who the other has been talking to. Lance cheated on Kristina a few months into their relationship and then lied about it—even swearing on his father's grave that he had done nothing wrong. Kristina found out the truth several months later and broke up with him, but he cajoled her into getting back together just a few days later. They haven't been able to reestablish trust, though. They struggle to communicate with each other, with neither able to understand where the other is coming from. Whenever tensions arise, they end up yelling, then one of them leaves or else they clam up, hoping their silence will prevent another blowup. Kristina has built up a year and a half of resentments, making each new fight that much worse, fueled by this ready reserve of anger.

They have already talked about how they will parent while broken up, even though their son's not yet born, and it's uncertain whether they'll be together when he is. Lance claims he will be very involved even if they split up, but Kristina's worried. She says that when they've talked about being broken up and parenting, Lance gets mad about the idea of paying child support, saying it would be her fault if the Department of Human Services (DHS) put a child support order in place.[1] He has even claimed he would give up his parental rights if it would get him out of paying child support, but he would still expect Kristina to let him see his son whenever he wanted. It's unclear whether he means this or is just trying to needle her.

Their fundamental problem, as Kristina sees it, is that she has switched her focus to creating a family life and believes Lance should do the same. He tells her that she needs to let him "do him," which apparently involves hanging out with friends—none of whom is a family man—and talking to and texting other women. The precipitating event for the latest breakup was Kristina telling Lance that he couldn't talk to a particular woman. He ignored her and starting texting that woman as well as two others, so Kristina felt like she had to move out to make good on her threat since he didn't seem to be taking her seriously. He says he doesn't understand why he needs to spend all his time with Kristina, since the baby's not even born yet. She maintains that while she has a sense of "we," "ours," and that they're a family, Lance is more focused on

"I" and "his." She sees this in his behavior, especially around his friends. He'll do things without regard for how it might make Kristina feel, and he doesn't take into account how having something negative happen to him also affects her and the baby.

When I meet Lance later, he explains, "I feel like my wheels [are] still turning, just trying to figure out what I want to do [in life]." Kristina, however, has no patience for his need to explore and figure himself out. She tells me:

> He just wants to be doing whatever he wants to do, and he doesn't want to just sit at home with me at this point because he feels like he's missing out. He feels like he's still really young and he hasn't done anything in life yet, but that's, I mean, I told him, "Didn't you think about that before you brought a baby into this world. I don't care what you want now."

The push and pull between them leads to fight after fight, further destabilizing their relationship and their living situation. This young couple is caught, needing to grow up to be parents to their firstborn, but not yet comfortably settled into adulthood.

Kristina sees herself as having become an adult as a result of her pregnancy, a transition she has not seen Lance make. She says:

> It's not about him anymore, it's not about me anymore, it's about the baby and our family. I see that. I'm perfectly fine with that. I'm perfectly fine with not hanging out with anybody. I only have one friend anyways. My best friend, and she's pregnant too, so she doesn't do anything anyways. The only person I go see is my mom. I don't hang out with my friends. . . . People around [Lance's] age . . . have no idea what he's about to go through and . . . they have no cares in the world. . . . [W]henever you're around somebody like that, you tend to be the same as them and think the same as them, and whenever he's around them he doesn't care about how I feel or, if he's about to do something, how that's gonna affect us, our relationship, or the family, or the baby.

Kristina is very socially vulnerable right now. She has separated herself from her friends, leaving her with just her mother and one friend. This makes Lance's role in her life that much more important. His inability or disinterest in being the partner she craves puts her at risk of social poverty—losing not just a boyfriend but the family she very much desires. Deeply embedded in the carefree time of young adulthood, and with his sense of self and his future career up in the air, Lance is hard-pressed to provide Kristina with the secure partnership she is demanding.[2] The volatility of their lives and relationship is far more problematic in Kristina's eyes when what's at risk is the future of their family, not just their dating relationship.

The Transition to Adulthood Today

The transition to adulthood has variably been discussed as the accomplishment of key status passages—such as the completion of one's education, the start of a career, and the commencement of family formation;[3] a change in personal identity;[4] and a distinct developmental period called "emerging adulthood."[5] There is widespread agreement among researchers that the transition to adulthood is now coming later in the life course, with it being increasingly common for people to pursue higher education and to delay marriage and parenthood until at least their late twenties.

Psychologist Jeffrey Arnett argues that this is *supposed to be* an unstable period in life, with an emphasis on freedom and exploration of possible selves and possible roles.[6] That is, there are cultural norms and expectations that have arisen for how young people are *meant* to act during this time in life; these norms include spending time exploring and then establishing oneself before taking on the more permanent commitments of adulthood. In line with these norms, it is now unusual for young people to settle quickly into a career and family life.[7]

Among young adults today, instability in education and work is widespread. Only about one-third of young adults have completed a college degree by their late twenties, with nearly another third dropping out of college along the way; even among those who do complete a college degree, it often takes longer than the designated four years, as people experience setbacks and distractions, and change directions along the way.[8]

Furthermore, young adults face difficulties in finding their way in the world of work. In particular, those without education beyond high school are more likely to go through periods of under- or unemployment and to churn through multiple jobs, rather than settling into a stable job.[9] Young men with less education have been hard-hit in the past forty years by the declining availability of well-paid jobs with stable career paths for those without advanced credentials; the Great Recession only magnified these struggles.[10] Reaching markers of the transition to adulthood—for example, establishing a career and being able to support oneself (and one's family)—has become more difficult over time.

Although achieving these financial markers of adulthood has become more difficult, both marrying and having children at young ages are far more common among the economically disadvantaged.[11] Delaying family formation until the late twenties is most common—nationally, the average age at first marriage in the United States is twenty-six for women and twenty-eight for men;[12] however, approximately one in four women and one in six men marry before age twenty-three.[13] In addition, even though the average age of an American woman when she first gives birth is twenty-six,[14] one in five women has had a baby by age twenty.[15] Therefore, the tension between the expectations of exploration in emerging adulthood on the one hand and the norms around committed relationships and parenthood on the other is not simply theoretical, but rather a reality for a substantial minority of young people, like the young parents in Family Expectations.

It is important to note that such young people are not part of a cultural minority group, such as the Amish, with their own distinct set of values that dictate behavior and attitudes. Rather, these disadvantaged young adults miss out on properly making their transition to adulthood according to the dominant culture of which they are a part. That is, not only do they not experience the freedom and the exploration of emerging adulthood, but they are aware that they are not behaving how people their age *should*.

This is at the root of the conflict we see between Lance and Kristina, whose story began this chapter. Lance describes his "wheels still turning," emphasizing his ongoing need to explore life and its many possibilities. Precisely because the transition to adulthood is a time of eschewing responsibilities and trying out different options, taking on roles that limit such options (such as becoming a parent) is a violation of the norms of this life stage, a reality against which Lance is struggling;

like others, he is influenced by the norms of exploration and freedom in emerging adulthood, whether or not he is able to enact them. The influence of these norms and their inherent contradiction with the roles of spouse and parent are important to understanding the lives of the young parents we meet in this book.

Here we see how these young parents are profoundly unsettled but also highly desirous of stability, as they confront the realities of raising children while trying to transition to adulthood themselves. This is visible in how they deal with education (a work in progress), employment (often short-lived or hard to come by), career plans (optimistic but unfulfilled), living situations (temporary or unsatisfactory), and transportation (unreliable). As parents try to negotiate these various areas of life, we see the impact of their incomplete transition to adulthood on their abilities to pay the bills and to be self-reliant—both essential to their senses of self, but not yet attained. Achieving the markers of adulthood is, at once, more difficult and all the more important because they are parents; when they struggle to hold down jobs, decide to combine work and schooling, or are unable to replace a broken-down car, their children struggle along with them.

An unstable and unpredictable life presents social, as well as financial, risks. It makes it that much harder to trust yourself and your romantic partner when it's unclear what you'll be doing a year—or even just a month—from now. During this period in the life course, young people are transferring their primary focus from their families and peers to their romantic partners.[16] This means that the failure of these relationships presents that much more of a risk for social poverty. This risk is particularly high for those who are transitioning to adulthood and parenthood simultaneously, as their friends often do not serve as supportive figures in their lives; instead, as Kristina does, they jettison ties to these friends altogether, seeing them—and the activities in which they engage—as incompatible with their new role as a parent. If and when the romantic partnership ends, there may not be a ready group of friends on whom to fall back for emotional support. This vulnerability adds weight to these already freighted relationships, a particularly heavy burden to bear for unions that are often new and lacking in permanent commitment.

Building Blocks of an Adult Life

Education

From how they talk about their educational plans, these young adults sound like a pretty ambitious group. Despite having parenting and work obligations, and despite often having had a difficult time with school in the past, most describe plans for continuing their educations. Such plans match the messages communicated by the broader society: that educational attainment is a marker of success and is key to getting ahead and securing the professional careers so many desire.

At the start of the study, eighteen of the parents (29 percent) had dropped out of high school, thirty-three (53 percent) had graduated from high school or earned a GED, eight (13 percent) had some additional education beyond high school, and three (5 percent) had a college degree or more.[17] Across this spectrum of academic accomplishment, the participants consistently described a drive to get more education—a GED for those without a diploma, a vocational certificate or college degree for those who'd completed high school, or a graduate degree for those with a bachelor's. And their dreams of their educational futures often didn't stop with just the next diploma or certificate; many detailed extended plans for additional education, for example, laying out the steps of starting with a certified nursing assistant certificate, then obtaining certification as a licensed practical nurse, and finally completing a bachelor's degree to be a registered nurse.

There are two important features of the study participants' views of their educational plans: (1) this is a central aspect of their lives that is not yet settled—a part of life that's still very much in transition—and (2) although their educational plans are ambitious, they're also often poorly planned or vague, subject to change, and not followed through on consistently.[18] The participants express optimism about and through these educational plans, saying that even if their goals are harder to achieve while juggling parenthood and work, these obstacles won't dissuade them from setting and pursuing high goals. The flip side of this aspect of life being unsettled is that who they are and what they have to offer a romantic partner feel changeable, potentially undermining trust and presenting a risk for breaking up the union and, thus, social poverty.

Nearly all parents in the study described some kind of interruption or break in their educational trajectories. Only one out of the sixty-two parents, twenty-three-year-old Lauren, has taken the traditional middle-class educational path—graduating from high school and going straight through college without any breaks. Others describe a range of events—from parental abandonment to repeated tardies—or a poor relationship with school as getting them off track.

Miranda, twenty-seven, dropped out of ninth grade after getting pregnant with her daughter and has struggled with drug addiction since then. When we first meet, she's clean, pregnant by her new boyfriend, Carl, and enrolled in GED classes. She explains why she's intent on doing this. "I want to get a GED. I want to get a career. I want to have something that's more than working at a drugstore, Taco Bell, or temporary services." Her dream, she says, is to return to school and become an X-ray technician.

When I next see her, three months later, I learn that she never went back to her GED course after the summer break. She tells me, "I was feeling overwhelmed then. [I was] pregnant, with [taking care of my daughter], trying to think about what we were gonna do, where we were gonna move with all the baby stuff. . . . And I . . . just put it off." Miranda's life was thrown into further turmoil when she gave birth only five months into her pregnancy and the baby survived for just twelve hours; their apartment was burglarized while they were in the hospital; and, on unrelated charges, both Miranda's mom and Carl were arrested and went to prison. Not surprisingly, then, Miranda still hadn't made it back on track toward completing her GED by the following spring, nine months later. She says, "That was something that I was thinking I really needed to get in. . . . It seems like ever since the last time [we saw each other] . . . it kind of snowballed. Just big major things going on. [D]oesn't seem like I've really had time for myself. Got to be with my daughter, then this whoops." The "whoops" she refers to is getting pregnant again just months after the baby died, right before Carl went to prison. Although finishing her GED hasn't fallen off Miranda's agenda, the events and difficulties of the past nine months have left it low down on the list of the things she can manage. Pulling off the feat of earning a GED on top of navigating the difficulties of the rest of her life would require more social and psychological resources than Miranda has at her disposal, especially with her two main sources of support—Carl and her mom—incarcerated. Social poverty, therefore, may be both a cause and a consequence of the difficulties young people face as they traverse the transition to adulthood.

Ruby, twenty-nine, who is pregnant with her third child, has seen her education advance in fits and starts. Mental health problems in high school, culminating in panic attacks and a suicide attempt, led her to drop out. After initially misdiagnosing her panic attacks as epilepsy, her doctors began to make progress in treating her depression. "I just got stronger. I went to school. I went to summer school, and I graduated on time. You're supposed to graduate with 40 credits. I graduated with 40.5, but I graduated on time." Her family encouraged her to continue straight on into college, but she resisted. She tells me:

> I didn't go to college because I didn't like high school and I had to go. Why would I go voluntarily to school? But, you know, a few years after that I did try some of those business colleges and then a couple years before I moved [to Oklahoma], I was going to college, community college. I was going for my paralegal degree. I got about a year of it done, but I still got about a year before I'd get my degree.

While trying out the business and community colleges, Ruby had two children by a man who wasn't interested in having a relationship with her or her children—he was simultaneously seeing someone else. She again found herself struggling with depression; her ability to care for her children suffered, and DHS removed them from her custody, placing them with her mother. Estranged from her family, without her children, and without any of the public assistance dollars custodial parents can receive, Ruby fled to Oklahoma to live with a man she'd met online—her current boyfriend, Anthony. In the depths of social and financial poverty, she left behind her children and her half-completed associate's degree. She's been unable to transfer her credits to a new school in Oklahoma because "the schools that I did go to . . . say that I owe them money, which I don't know why because I did it all through student loans, so I can't get my transcripts from them to be able to continue." Ruby's follow-through in resolving this issue is certainly made more difficult by the depression she has continued to battle. During the year we meet for interviews, she makes no progress in getting her education back on track even though she says she wants to finish her degree.

Twenty-one-year-old Nick has also been advancing his educations in fits and starts. Nick transferred to a community college from a four-year college after being put on academic probation for low grades. This setback hasn't deterred him from his goal of working in the "medical field"; he's been in college for several years already and estimates that he has another two to three semesters left before he finishes his "basics" (distribution requirements). Nonetheless, he's determined to finish his education, and his resolve has only been strengthened as he anticipates fatherhood. As he explains at our first meeting:

> I've been busting my butt, trying to get this done. I wouldn't have taken summer classes this summer if [my fiancée] wouldn't have been having a child, but now that all this is happening I have to buckle down. I have to. I feel like I have to do the most I possibly can to make sure this child comes into this world right.

Three months later, when we next meet in the fall, Nick has dropped out. His summer semester hadn't gone well; he failed one course and barely passed the other. Now, he says, "I'm taking this semester off and relaxing for once. This is like the first time since kindergarten [that] I've ever had time off from school." He's also jettisoning his plans to get a four-year degree; he discusses the possibility of starting at the local vo-tech to get a certificate in medical assisting. When I see him the following spring, he has successfully pursued the educational plans he'd outlined in the fall—despite having the new baby, moving, and working through a very rough first year of marriage. Nick says, "I love, just the classes, I love going and I'm doing really great in it. I've gotten nothing but all As. I'm almost halfway through it." He's feeling successful and is excited about the higher wages and career opportunities that finishing his education will bring. It's clear from Nick's description that feeling finished with education and settled onto a career path can contribute to a sense of accomplishment and stability that is missing when educational plans and the life changes they offer remain on the horizon. While Nick's fiancée, Carley, sticks with him through these changes, it also adds turmoil to their relationship, as their daily schedules—juggling work, school, child care, and their relationship—and his career identity bounce around.

Employment

Rather than serving as a counterweight to the hazy nature of their educational plans, parents' current employment situations are also remarkably volatile.[19] When I first met them at the start of the Family Expectations program, many were under- or unemployed. This was, perhaps, not surprising for the women, who were about to give or had just given birth. However, it is important to note that these women were typically out of work, as opposed to on maternity leave.[20] The employment situation was a bit better among their male partners. Eighteen of the men were employed full-time (58 percent) and five part-time (16 percent), while seven women were employed full-time (23 percent) and four part-time (13 percent); two of these employed women were on maternity leave from their jobs. In total, only ten of the thirty-one pairs were dual-earner couples (32 percent). In seven of the couples, both partners were currently out of work (23 percent). Couples' monthly incomes ranged from $0 to $4,300, with an average monthly couple income of $1,452, falling below the poverty line for a family of three.[21]

Tracing the employment patterns of the parents during the focal pregnancy and year of program participation reveals a pattern of strikingly unstable employment. They often report two or three changes in employment, with some describing eight or more transitions, in just over a year's time. Previous research indicates that employment loss is associated with developing a greater sense of distrust in others,[22] which could in turn contribute to feelings of social isolation.

Further, given that the workplace is a site for social connection and forging social ties,[23] employment volatility can sever these ties, creating social poverty,[24] on top of the financial troubles of having a fluctuating income from job turmoil. Plus, job loss puts stress on romantic relationships and can undermine feelings of success as parents.

Twenty-year-old Zach lost his job doing RV repair after a disagreement with his boss escalated into an argument—a burst of hardheadedness that Zach later regretted. After searching for nearly a month, he found a new job on a building and grounds crew at a local school. While he had liked his job doing RV repair, he was dragging himself to this new job and felt compelled to search for something new after spending the summer there. "It was just a miserable job," he tells me. "I mean, mowing the same piece of property week after week after week after week after week after week. . . . Oh my gosh! It just got so old! And it was hot outside, cooking every day. . . . I was miserable, and I was sunburned all the time. I just hated it."

The next job he found was also manual labor, at a landscaping firm and, again, paid less than he had earned doing RV repair; however, he was relieved to escape the tedium of the grounds crew. Instead, he recalls, "You get to the see payout. And it's never the same thing. I don't go back to the same place. So it's all right." Nonetheless, as soon as he was able to find a job doing auto body work—much closer to his old repair job—he left the landscaping company behind.

Unfortunately, the first few auto body repair jobs he had were unreliable. The first company didn't have enough business and, as the last one hired, Zach was the first one to be let go. He'd managed to save a nice little nest egg, however, and with his son about to be born, Zach decided to delay his job search to be home and bond with his girlfriend, Brianna, and their new addition to the family. After nearly three months at home and with the mounting expenses of a new baby, he recalls, "I ran out of money, and then when I ran out of money, I couldn't find a job. . . . I should have started looking for a job way earlier because it took me a month to find a decent job." At this new job, however, he had work, but little income. "In the body work business it's kind of fly-by-night, kinda try to get over on you. I had a guy get over probably $1,500. . . . [W]orked there for a month and I got paid 150 bucks [only] because I asked for it. Yeah, it was stupid. I was pissed," he says with a bitter laugh.[25]

By the last time we met, Zach had finally found a job in auto body repair that provided consistent work and paid him regularly. He'd been with the company for six weeks, and his excitement about this new job was clear. He tells me, "This place has huge opportunity. Brand-new company blowing up fast. Blowing up fast. So hopefully because I got in when they're a small company, by the time they're a large company I'll be making pretty good bucks. . . . Major opportunities!" Zach's enthusiasm about his new situation aside, the array of employment transitions he has passed through in a little more than one year's time is remarkable: (1) RV repair, (2) unemployment, (3) building and grounds crew, (4) landscaping firm, (5) auto repair company number 1, (6) unemployment, (7) auto repair company number 2, and (8) auto repair company number 3.

This sort of transitory employment was common, although not all of the study participants saw as many job changes as Zach during the year of the interviews. Twenty-year-old Lance goes from working at a home improvement store to being unemployed to working at an office supply store; thirty-three-year-old Evan goes through a series of three jobs in the oil industry, punctuated by periods of unemployment; and twenty-one-year-old Carley works in retail, at a fast-food restaurant, and at a home health company, while also having times when she struggles to find work or cannot work (like when she broke her foot). Twenty-three-year-old Leonard has an employment record reminiscent of Zach's. After losing his job as assistant manager in retail, he was unemployed for a time, until he found a job at a butcher. He left for a different job back in retail but soon lost this job and returned to the temp services firm that had found him the position at the butcher; this time, the temp services firm was only able to find him short-term positions. Discouraged, Leonard returned to school and unemployment.

That makes for seven job transitions for Zach, two for Lance, four for Evan, four for Carley, and five for Leonard. These employment trajectories are not exceptional among this group of parents and merely cover just over a year of their lives. Jobs were lost for a variety of reasons, some of which the participants were responsible for (unreliable job performance or quitting due to boredom or distaste for the job) and some of which they were not (downsizing, seasonal or temporary jobs, or a lack of reliable transportation). Among the young adult population nationally, such employment instability is not the norm; on average, people hold about seven different jobs during the decade between age eighteen and twenty-eight.[26] Among those who have not completed high school, however, only half of jobs are held for more than six months.[27]

There was a visible age pattern to these employment experiences, with the older parents more likely to work the same job throughout the year of the interviews.[28] For example, thirty-six-year-old Marvin consistently works in a science lab, forty-two-year-old Otis works for his family's construction business, and thirty-six-year-old Ken works for a cable company.[29] There are, of course, exceptions, like thirty-six-year-old Anthony, who has been without a stable job for more than two years, despite having associate degrees in computer technology and programming; his unemployment is interrupted only by occasional temp jobs.

The story of thirty-three-year-old Hailey captures both the steadier nature of employment among the older parents and the instability that continues to dominate the work lives among the Family Expectations participants. She works a decently paid, steady job for an insurance agency; when she first started her job, years ago, she could see this being her lifelong career, but she'd recently been rethinking those plans. "I was like 'Oh yeah, I can retire from this.' But now I don't. It's just not who I am. . . . [G]etting older, finding myself, I just realized that it's not really what I want to do. I want to do something more productive." Among the parents in the study, a job as steady and career-oriented as Hailey's was rare; however, what she shared with so many other parents was a feeling of not being settled in her job, as well as a broad sense of searching, in which one's employment situation should be a reflection of "who I am" rather than just a way to earn money. Similarly, both Marvin and Ken, two of the older fathers with steady employment, plan to return to school for additional training and then leave their current jobs.

During the Great Recession, when I first met these parents, stories of the unemployed blanketed the media; however, such stories fail to capture the nature of these young adults' labor force experiences. What is striking among these parents is not someone losing a job and being unable to find another; rather, people's résumés tell the story of the transitory, unreliable nature of their employment. This is what is most important to take away from these lists of jobs and changes in employment as we seek to understand their transition to adulthood. Their stories about work are ones of marked instability, not unique to the economic downturn. These changes in employment location and status contribute to social poverty, both disrupting social connections made in the workplace and adding volatility to couples' lives, undermining trust and putting strain on the couple's bond as they grapple with fluctuating and inadequate resources, changing schedules, and shifting conceptions of their future selves.

Career

Despite the fact that many of the young adults had faltered in completing their educations or had struggled to maintain stable employment, it was common to hear of hopes and plans for future careers. Career plans ranged from nurse to doctor, vet tech to hair stylist, and strip club owner to electrician.

In all, thirty-seven of the sixty-two participants (60 percent) described careers they envisioned for themselves in the future; notably, these were spontaneous stories, not responses to any specific question I asked about career plans. Only two (3 percent) said they were already settled in careers, with twenty-two-year-old Will working in construction, and Evan already being in his thirties and earning relatively good wages—more than twenty dollars an hour—in the oil fields, leading him to abandon his earlier dream of being a lawyer. Those who did not describe career goals for themselves either did not see themselves working steadily (like those receiving disability benefits) or else focused on earning a living however they could.

That so many of the parents in this study saw themselves as works in progress—at least careerwise—speaks to the feelings of being unsettled and in transition that so many expressed. Just because they are parents and have responsibilities to provide for their children does not mean most have given up on establishing careers, settling for "just any job," as twenty-two-year-old Necie puts it. She explains, "A good job is a stable job, something that you want for like five years. Not just a job you want for right now. . . . [It should be] worth your feet hurting." However, the level of clarity in peoples' career goals and their progress toward these goals varied widely, with some currently on clear career paths while others had vague destinations.

As one of the older participants in the program, it is perhaps not surprising that thirty-five-year-old Jim has a concrete career goal and is on his way to achieving it. After years working as a baker—a job he disliked—Jim pursued an interest closer to his heart: being an electrician. "I enjoy electric. Wish I would have gotten into it earlier. More my speed," he says. He's currently an apprentice and has been working his way up toward obtaining his journeyman's license for several years. During the year we meet for interviews, Jim faces several setbacks as he works toward this goal. The slowdown in new home construction leads him to decide he can't take his licensing test right away but instead needs to get experience as a commercial electrician. A more comprehensive license, covering both residential and commercial electrical work, will give him more employment security, he feels. After several months of doing this work, he takes the three-hour, multiple-choice, open-book licensing exam and fails. As of our last meeting, he had taken the test for a second time and failed. He's not overly discouraged, though; he says he's been managing to find time to study, despite working full-time and being a father of three (and the only father figure to his wife's three young nephews), and he's considering taking a prep course in the hope that the third time will be the charm when he next sits for the exam.

Lauren, a college student, knew she was going to law school after graduation, until her unexpected pregnancy put a kink in those plans. This hasn't dissuaded her from her dream occupation for the future, but she's willing to settle for an interim career for now. She sighs as she explains, "I guess I'm gonna be a social worker at a hospital . . .'cause I was a CNA for a little bit." Even though this is only a temporary career move in her eyes, Lauren has still clearly thought through her various options, taking into account the jobs her degree in human development and other previous work experience will qualify her for, as well as the pay and work environment of these options. Her time volunteering at a refugee agency made her think that such work would be too depressing. From what she's learned about child protective services, she says she couldn't work in a system that she believes is broken and, besides, "social work in a hospital . . . pays a lot more than just being a social worker at DHS."

Others have far less concrete career goals than Jim and Lauren. Zach, who variously works as in RV repair, on a building and grounds crew, and in car repair, has some ideas for his future career. "I tried at a vo-tech, tried to be an electrician. I stayed for a semester and just couldn't handle it. . . . [I]t seemed neat until you really get the complexity of it. . . . [I]t's just not my thing." He's now discovered his passion, he says. "I've been wanting to go [to school] for either personal training or physical therapy. Those are the two that stuck with me. . . . Wellness. That's my thing. . . . I really want to be a personal trainer. The physical therapist is more a second option. . . . I'm all about 'your body is your temple.'" Zach goes on to explain that he'd be willing to pursue the physical therapy option just because it would be easier to get help paying for school, unlike for a personal training program. None of this takes into account that working as a personal trainer does not require a college degree (that industry is largely unregulated), whereas an entry-level physical therapist is expected to have completed a six-year doctorate in that field. Further, even these fuzzy plans seem to be fleeting; nine months after laying out these possible career options, Zach is doing auto body repair at a used car lot and has decided this is a growth industry in which he'd like to stay—unless, of course, he gets an opportunity to go back to RV repair, which he enjoyed even more.

This process of "occupational identity" formation is among the key tasks of the transition to adulthood.[30] Researchers have found variation among adolescents and young adults in the extent to which their occupational goals are firmly established and tied to achievable plans,[31] ranging from those like Lauren, who have a clear vision of the road they'll travel and have considered their options in an informed way, to Zach, whose goals lack careful consideration or commitment. Further, studies have found that those with well-laid occupational plans have higher self-esteem and better mental health outcomes than those without such direction.[32] Although this may be a product of self-selection, indications are that the focus and sense of self offered by clear plans are beneficial.

When I asked what they pictured their lives looking like in five years' time, parents' visions often started with, or at least included, a career—not just a job. People would often explain that even if they couldn't achieve their dream careers in the next five years, they expected to make good progress along that path by getting additional education or occupational experience. The extent to which people were clear on the steps necessary to achieve their career goals, however, varied widely, as is clear from a comparison of Lauren's and Zach's stories. Most notable, however, was the extent to which this aspect of most parents' lives was still very much a work in progress, which is not uncommon among today's young adults,[33] but may be far more consequential for this group of parents who are trying to settle into permanent romantic relationships. Are you committing to a future plumber or to a partner who will never escape the purgatory of temp work?

Living Situation

Two main features of the parents' living situations stand out: (1) many are or were recently living with other people—typically family members (especially parents), and (2) their living situations change frequently. All the parents in this study are at least eighteen and had moved out of the family homes they grew up in (whether or not they later returned), and they all were having or had just had a baby; nonetheless, members of twenty-three of the couples (74 percent) described living with other people during the focal pregnancy or at some point during the program year.

National studies have called the return to parents' homes by the "boomerang generation" a sort of "new normal," with just under a quarter of twenty-five- to thirty-four-year-olds living in multigenerational households.[34] It is important to understand, however, that this situation—living with others—was not anyone's first choice among the young adults I interviewed. Those who were living with others expressed a desire to live on their own, as "doubling up" was a response to financial needs rather than a preferred arrangement. This desire seems to be born of two main motivations: first, people don't like living as kids in their parents' homes when they no longer see themselves as children;[35] second, people believe that the ideal is for parents to raise their children as a couple in their own home. Their living arrangements, then, were incompatible with how they saw themselves as well as with their dreams for their family lives.

Of the twenty-eight couples whose living situations I was able to track throughout the year of the interviews,[36] only seven couples (23 percent) did not experience a move (and in two of these couples, the men "moved" to prison); more than three-quarters of couples saw a change in living situation during this one-year period. The instability of their living arrangements emphasizes a larger tension explored in these chapters: the transitional nature of the parents' lives undermines their ability to give their children the settled family lives they desire and stresses their relational ties with one another and others.

Mackenzie and Wayan are in their early twenties and have a toddler and a newborn at the start of the Family Expectations program, and they add another "surprise" baby by our last meeting. Their story illustrates the instability of couples' living situations, and their narrative about their living arrangements illustrates just how important it is to people how and where they are living. After a period of time bouncing around Kansas, first living in a motel while they were working at Mackenzie's aunt's business, then living with her father until her stepmother kicked them out, they landed back in Oklahoma several months before we met. Without a place to live or enough money to secure an apartment of their own, they moved in with Wayan's cousin, who has four children of her own. Sometimes Wayan's ten-year-old brother would also stay with them for several nights or even weeks. This shows the social resources Wayan and Mackenzie have at their disposal—family providing places to live. But at the same time we see that these arrangements can be volatile and offer less than ideal circumstances for building a relationship and raising children. The economic resource of housing offered by these social ties undermines the couple's resource of a caring, supportive relationship.[37]

The crowded house—the dirtiest of any I visited—was clearly wearing on them. They consistently expressed three primary goals when I met with them: get jobs, get a reliable car, and move into their own apartment. While at first glance this may sound like wishes purely for adequate financial resources to get by, this interpretation would miss a substantial part of what the couple desires. When I asked them at our second meeting what they wanted their lives to look like six months down the road, Mackenzie explained, "Our place. Just us as a family. Nobody living with us. You know, every time we moved, somebody from his side would stay with us or my brother would come stay with us. . . . I just want it to be us and have our house set up. . . . Just being a family." Wayan underlined her point, adding, "For once." Poverty research focusing on the financial benefits of instrumental support—like shared housing—can miss the emotional costs incurred by such support.[38] Were Mackenzie and Wayan to move into their own apartment, their financial situation might be more strained, but it would ease their social poverty by providing the privacy and space necessary for communication and emotional intimacy, they say.

By our last meeting, they've come a bit closer to achieving their goal; they have left Wayan's cousin's house and moved in with Mackenzie's grandmother. The older woman needs to be cared for, but her alcoholism can make living with her difficult. Nonetheless, their new living arrangement is much less crowded, giving them some breathing room—essential for a young couple with three children under three. In reflecting back, Wayan notes that their relationship was suffering from where they had been living:

> 'Cause when we're at our cousin's, we didn't have no kind of privacy, you know, it's like somebody was always there. . . . Once we were living with her grandma, we got more privacy and I think that's where, you know, the fights stopped happening. . . . So now it's like you go into the other room and chill and then come back in there. . . . Back then we didn't do that. We'd just fight it out about it and stay in the same room. Now, get out of the room for a minute and when we all cooled down then, you know, go back.

Mackenzie and Wayan had learned a communication technique—taking "time outs"—at Family Expectations but had struggled to use it to prevent their fights from escalating when they were living in a house where there was literally nowhere to take a time out. Moving to a less crowded house gave them the opportunity to actually use some of the relationship skills they had learned at the program.

Although this was undoubtedly a positive development for them, they still weren't satisfied with their living situation because they weren't yet living on their own. Wayan explains that what he really wants is

> to have our own house, you know, I mean . . . live comfortably. You know, ain't gotta worry about somebody kick you out. You know, live comfortably, you know, have the car running right and have my kids in the environment, you know what I'm saying, that I ain't gotta worry about them when I'm going to work. I know they safe when I go to work. . . . I just want to live comfortably, finally. . . . Don't want to have no worries. Just live comfortably.

Wayan's definition of having "everything" is heartbreakingly simple: a car that runs so he can get to work, an apartment with his name on the lease so he can't get kicked out because of someone else's whim or short temper, and a neighborhood where he doesn't have to worry about the safety of his three little girls.

Mackenzie and Wayan weren't unique among the couples in their experiences or desires. Packing and moving over and over were quite common, even during the relatively short period during which I met with the couples. Living with family was also quite common and was often a source of stress for couples. For example, arguments commonly arose between Tiana and Stefan as she strained to adjust to living with his parents, brother, and grandmother, who were more raucous and pushy than she was used to. People's living situations, therefore, were an impediment to their feeling like they had established adult lives—the type of lives they wanted to give their children—and to the health of their romantic relationships. There was a tension here between meeting their financial and social needs. Not surprisingly, therefore, plans for newer and better living arrangements were ubiquitous; while these plans offer a sense of optimism about the future—a better house in a more kid-friendly neighborhood beckons—they also add to the general sense of unsettled lives that these young parents carry with them. Both the volatility of their living arrangements and the stresses of sharing a living space with others can increase the risk of social poverty by eroding the quality of relationships and confidence in a romantic union's future.

Transportation

Clichéd visions of American life are rife with cars, with the automobile representing independence, freedom, and the fulfillment of adolescent fantasy, whether purchased on the minimum wage of an after-school job or delivered all shiny-new as a graduation present with a red bow on top. The flip side is that it's hard to feel like you're living a grown-up life when you have to bum rides.[39]

Given this cultural view of cars, as well as the practical realities of living in a country with a relatively limited public transportation system, it is not surprising that a car is more of a necessity than a luxury item. Nationally, even within the lowest-earning fifth of Americans, 65 percent have their own cars.[40] Research demonstrates that issues with transportation impede social mobility, increasing the likelihood of staying in poverty.[41] The Family Expectations couples' stories illustrate how having a car not only is of practical importance but is an essential part of the equation that adds up to feeling like an adult.

Of the thirty-one couples, nineteen (61 percent) brought up car-related issues in the course of describing their lives.[42] In these narratives, the fundamental role a car plays in young people's view of themselves as adults is striking; further, the difficulties with which they must cope without a car (or a reliable car) are severe.

CAR KEY TO ADULTHOOD

Robert, twenty-one, explains that part of the reason he's been putting off marrying his girlfriend, Elyse, twenty, despite the fact that he's fully committed to her and they're expecting their first child, is that they're not financially ready. And the first piece of the financial puzzle that's missing, he says, is having a car of their own; he raises this issue before he brings up their general financial situation or the fact that they're currently living apart, each with their respective parents. As he points out, lacking a car is symbolically important, not just a practical concern. "I can get transportation wherever I need to go, but I just hate having to ask other people. So [buying a car is] one thing that we need to do." This is not just an adolescent-boy car obsession, either; Elyse also says that her primary short-term goal for them is to save up enough so that they can buy a car. The underlying view this young couple expresses is that having your own car means you're self-reliant, and it is only such self-reliant people who are ready for marriage. This indicates how the meaning of resources matters, rather than just their absence or presence; resource poverty, as in lacking a car, is not totally made up for by the availability of instrumental support from friends and family. That is, the social resources that contribute to greater financial well-being are not the flip side of the financial poverty coin: they do not necessarily offer the meaning of the resource, even if they offer the resource itself.

This view is also clear in twenty-two-year-old Abby and twenty-nine-year-old Darren's discussions of why they're not yet married; when I first meet them, they are both recovering addicts in transitional living. Abby contrasts their decision to put off getting married with the impulsiveness of more immature people who would wed without being ready: "When you're younger you fall in love, 'Oh, let's just go and get married. I'll marry you.'... One of you *might* have a job.... We don't even have a vehicle or our driver's licenses right now. We got to get all that taken care of [before marrying]." As for Robert and Elyse, lacking a car is a road-block on Abby and Darren's path to marriage. In fact, Abby argues that it's a sign of their maturity and careful decision making that they put off marrying while lacking a car. Darren reflects this sense—that a car is of primary importance in having their lives settled—as he shares his ideal vision for the couple's future with their newborn daughter: "One or both of us working. Be married, you know. Have our licenses back. Vehicle. You know, just living normal, you know? I just picture having a normal life." Given the plethora of difficulties Abby and Darren are facing in their lives—drug addiction, both having lost custody of their older children, no permanent living situations, no jobs, criminal records, and untreated mental health problems among them—it is telling of the car's fundamental importance to adulthood that having a vehicle even rates on their list of concerns. In fact, as Darren notes, it is a basic requirement of living a "normal" life. Beyond the symbolic importance to people's senses of being independent adults, lacking a (reliable) car creates an array of serious problems in people's lives.

NO CAR, NO JOB?

For city dwellers from New York, Boston, or San Francisco, the idea of getting around without a car might seem to be an inconvenience at worst. However, Oklahoma City doesn't even have sidewalks in many places, so walking to a bus stop can be a death-defying challenge. Although the city council has contemplated ways to strengthen transportation services, its members admit that "effective and efficient public transportation likely will always be an issue in such a sprawling city."[43] As a consequence, people rely tremendously on their cars and are quite literally stuck without them.

Recent studies of the state of public transportation across the nation have ranked Oklahoma City near the bottom among the 100 largest metropolitan areas. Since the late 1990s, Oklahoma City has seen a rapid decentralization of jobs, with employment prospects increasingly found outside of center city areas; by 2006, nearly three-quarters of jobs in the area were at least three miles from downtown.[44] Not surprisingly, then, the share of total jobs that can be reached via public transportation within ninety minutes is relatively low in Oklahoma City—it ranks

80th out of 100 metropolitan areas in the United States on this metric, with less than a quarter of jobs accessible in a reasonable time period without a car.[45]

This is evident among the couples, for whom lacking a car or having an unreliable car is often to blame for their employment problems. Dave, a twenty-nine-year-old father of three, including two children with his girlfriend, Norene, lost his warehouse job after missing work too often, several times because their car had broken down (the other times were when he was sick or had to take pregnant Norene to the doctor). Dave tells me:

> And the last time was Wednesday when my car broke down and I told 'em I couldn't make it and I was on my six and a half write-up. . . . I said, "Hey, I'm trying to make it and there's nothing I can do. My car's down." But they let me work Thursday and Friday. Friday's when they let me go.

The couple continues to be plagued by car trouble throughout the year we meet for interviews. With Dave out of a job, Norene started looking around for work and got a lead on a job, which she decided to turn down because their car was too unreliable. "They was wanting to send me out to [the next town over] and with our car not . . . reliable . . . I don't want to get stuck way out there. Something [could] happen and I'll be way out there."

Thirty-five-year-old Denelle and her boyfriend, Otis, live in a housing project outside the city center. It is located off a main road, not within walking distance of much, and is surrounded on all sides by a tall metal fence. Without a car, they say, they feel like the fence keeps them in rather than keeping others out. Denelle describes feeling "caught" in the projects, where she says the negativity and the gossip floating around among the residents eat away at their relationship. Otis agrees; without a car, he says, "this is what it is. We're here. We don't hardly ever get to go out. That's what it is. We have to listen and sit here and put up with all this crap." If only they had a car, they say, they could, at least occasionally and temporarily, escape. To make matters worse, after their daughter was born prematurely, they couldn't even go visit her at the hospital when they wanted to; to do so, each time they needed to find someone whom they could pay for a ride. In other words, their economic poverty—in this case, lacking a car—contributed to their social poverty by undermining trust and putting strains on their relationship with one another; it also kept them from bonding with and caring for their daughter.

Others also explained how not having a (good) car interferes with being able to parent in the ways they think are important. Twenty-eight-year-old Ann ended up homeschooling her daughter for half a year after their car was stolen and totaled (their liability insurance wouldn't pay to repair the damage, and her income from her disability benefits was too low to cover the cost). With no school bus, no sidewalks on the route to school, icy Oklahoma winters, and concerns about safety, Ann decided homeschooling was the best option for her daughter.

Taleisha, a twenty-year-old mother of one, feels that her car puts her newborn daughter in danger. She starts crying as she explains, "I want a new car. I need a new car. I only have one windshield wiper. I have a baby. It's rainy season." Later, as we talk, she again brings up this issue, which is clearly nagging at her:

> I love [my daughter] so much and I think about her so much, that's really my main thing. If I didn't have her, I wouldn't mind driving it. I'd still be driving with one windshield wiper when it's raining, but it's just like, oh my God, this is my baby and if something was to ever happen, I would feel so guilty, so I need to make sure I'm doing what's right and what's safe for her.

A car isn't just key to Taleisha feeling like an adult or being able to get to work; her unreliable car threatens what she sees as her basic task as a mother, which is protecting her daughter.

The necessity and desirability of having a car to one's sense of being an adult and having one's life together is evident—not only among those who lack a car but also among those who have one. When I ask twenty-two-year-old Necie, a new mother of one, what challenges she's had to deal with recently, she says, "Rent's paid. Car's driving. As long as those two are working, I'm OK." Similarly, Cordell is eager to have his mother come visit him and his girlfriend at their rental home. He tells me, "My mom, . . . she never been up here to see my good part, see me survive in the world. . . . I'm twenty-one and I got a house, I got two cars, two dogs, I got extra cash I can spend on my girl." For Cordell, having a car is among the basic items on the list of an adult life worth showing off.

As explained earlier, Denelle and Otis were stuck in their housing project without a car. By the time of our last interview, a year after I'd first met them, they'd managed to get a car, which Otis proudly brings me out on the balcony to show me, saying, "That's my black car sitting out there. . . . I done come a long ways. . . . I got my license back and everything. . . . I spent a lot of money. It was worth it, though. 'Cause like I say, having [my daughter] changed a lot." For Denelle, having a car has literally been freeing. "We couldn't get a ride to 7-Eleven, you know, nowhere. It's like this [project] was its own city. . . . We got gates, feel like we in prison. Couldn't get out. Now we can leave freely. . . . We just get up and go. But we don't stay gone too long, you know, 'cause somebody can kick in the door." She starts laughing as she relates this newfound freedom—even if they still have a lot of problems, the car provides at least a temporary escape, while also making it easier for Otis to get to work.

A car seems to be a necessary, but not a sufficient, condition for feeling like the basics of life are on track. Parents could certainly feel like they were struggling even when they did have a car, but without one, they felt like they lacked one of the fundamental building blocks of an adult life. This is not, then, just a question of economic poverty but also of social poverty. Having a car is of practical importance—to get to work, to safely transport children to the doctor and to school—and of symbolic importance, as something adults, especially parents, have when their lives are in order. Parents were waiting until this key piece of life was in place before they felt comfortable committing to a future with one another.

Paying the Bills

Because the couples in Family Expectations negotiate lives shaped by limited resources, tales of financial troubles are common. This includes twenty-two-year-old Akira and twenty-four-year-old Ennis, who told me as we walked back from the park after our first interview that they'd suggested going to the playground because they were without furniture or electricity. It also includes Lauren and Cordell, who are able to meet all their immediate needs but explain that they are delaying getting married until they're in a better financial situation, closer to the middle-class lifestyle they plan on living. In all, twenty-six couples (84 percent) say that they face financial limitations. This does not include people saying they can't get the cable package or name-brand clothing they'd like to have; rather, these couples are unable to buy items or pay bills in the ways most middle-class families take for granted—limiting how much they drive to save on gas, living with parents, or relying on meals sneaked home from a fast-food job. Notably, couples would often segue from discussing their financial situations to explaining how their economic struggles impacted their relationships—being a source of arguments and, as for Lauren and Cordell, a reason to put off getting married until things were more stable and settled. While previous research has long recognized the way economic poverty can strain romantic relationships,[46] scholars have yet to conceptualize this as economic poverty contributing to social poverty by eroding the socioemotional resources at one's disposal.

Norene and Dave have two children together, and each has another son with a different partner; they have been together, on and off, for years. They live with Norene's parents in a small, run-down house but aren't close to getting their finances in order to move out on their own. When I first meet them, Dave has lost his driver's license (the reasons why weren't clear), and they don't have the $650 it would cost for him to get it back. The story is the same each time I visit, leaving Dave driving illegally to work—a risky prospect that can result in a large fine should he get caught. Their finances get even tighter after Norene crashes the car when she swerves to avoid a dog that runs across her path. Because they had only liability auto insurance—they couldn't afford more coverage—they can't fix or replace the car. Their car can't be trusted to carry them to employers outside the area of the city where they live, and thus both Norene and Dave can pursue only limited job opportunities. It's easy to see how this vicious cycle will perpetuate itself. Without transportation to reach better job opportunities, it will be harder for the couple to earn the money necessary to buy a better car and get Dave's license back.

Both are appreciative of what they do have, with Dave noting, "We'll make it," and Norene adding, "We always do." However, the couple also says that their plans to get married are basically on hold until their finances improve. Dave says, "She thinks I'm always putting it off, but I'm not trying to put it off, it's just, we're not set yet. And when we do get married, I want us to have a good, decent wedding. Nothing big, but just have the whole family there, you know." When I ask why that's important to him, he explains, "Because it's a big deal. It's marriage. You know . . . you guys are committing." Even though she's ready to get married sooner rather than later, Norene concurs, expanding on Dave's point about the wedding being important. "Something we'll remember too. . . . [Y]ou know, not saying, 'Oh, we just went to the court house.' . . . I would want something big . . . , I mean, not big, but make it a big deal, you know." Dave adds, "And knowing that we're stable. . . . Not owning your own house, but having your own place, you know, just stable, stability, work, job. . . . [T]he kids . . . you know, they know that they have their own place, their own room . . . their toys, clothes . . . anything they need." While Norene and Dave don't face the same struggles as some other Family Expectations couples—they don't see the utilities getting shut off or run short on food, for example—their inability to cover necessary bills in the short term means they're unwilling to take on the long-term commitment of marriage. This is not just about having the "right" kind of wedding, like Norene wants, but also about being "stable" and able to live the adult lives they think they should, the kind of lives they see befitting a married couple.[47]

Unlike Norene and Dave, twenty-eight-year-old Ann and thirty-year-old Trenton do have a stable source of income on which they can depend: Ann's monthly disability check. An on-the-job knee injury led to a knee replacement, but because she's never regained normal function in her leg, she has relied on disability for several years. Neither is a first-time parent, so although they eagerly anticipate their son's arrival, they also know the financial struggles this will bring to their already-stretched budget. Trenton says, "It's all these extras. . . . All these extras are coming up, and it's a strain." They put a positive spin on their tight finances, though. Trenton says with a laugh, "We don't really have any debt. We don't have any credit card offers, so we're not getting foreclosed on!" Although their car barely runs—it was stolen and crashed, which their liability auto insurance doesn't cover—Trenton also casts this situation in a good light, since they had at least paid for the car in full, so they're not stuck paying on a car note for a broken-down wreck.

The fine balancing act they had constructed falls apart, however, when Trenton goes to jail. After assurances from his lawyer that Trenton wouldn't get locked up on some old charges, Ann was surprised when he didn't come home one day, having been sent to the county jail after sentencing. Even though Trenton hadn't been the primary contributor to the household—his income from delivering pizza and under-the-table construction jobs was largely diverted to child support and paying his lawyer—Ann still feels a big economic pinch once he's gone, especially with this coming just weeks after their son's birth. She explains, "It's been hard. A couple of times I had to, thank God for my landlord, I had to pay not the full amount on my rent to pay the electric and the gas. But now I'm glad summer's here 'cause the gas . . . is high. It's the most expensive bill we've had is gas." Ann's lucky her landlord is so flexible because, as she explains,

> even though [Trenton] was paying his lawyer, his little money was help-ing. I had the electric paid, the gas paid, the rent paid. And we had a little extra money for whatever, if an emergency came up and we needed something. [I]f we needed something, we had money to get it. . . . I can't work. I'm on disability. . . . Living off of $800 a month. Thank God for food stamps, though, because without that we'd really be in some trou-ble. . . . And thank God for WIC.[48]

Besides being out the money Trenton contributed to the household, Ann pays to keep Trenton as involved in their family life as is possible from prison—mailing packages with photos and letters several times a week and covering the steep cost of their phone calls, which she can only afford once a month or so.[49] As for Norene and Dave, we see a palpable sense of insecurity brought on by walking a financial tightrope. Ann's spending to maintain Trenton's role in the family emphasizes the finan-cial costs that individuals are willing to pay to secure the family lives they want, paying to avoid social poverty.

Couples also describe finances as lying at the heart of some of their relationship troubles. Akira and Ennis, who have two preschoolers and a newborn, find it nearly impossible to make any space in their lives for being a couple after fulfilling their obligations as parents and Chik-Fil-A employees. Ennis explains the intense stress they're under:

We making the bills, it's just after we get done paying the bills and we look at what we got left, and it's nothing. It's not even change! It's dust! God dang. . . . You know, trying to keep me from crying and [Akira] cry for us. . . . Like we can't take our stress out on our kids. That's one thing we have told ourselves. If we're stressed out we just have to sit down and talk about it or just take ten, fifteen minutes, go walk around the block.

Juggling all their obligations and this stress leaves them with much less time and emotional energy for one another. Akira says that what she'd like is "to have free time to do what we want to do." Ennis adds: "Together." And Akira continues on, "Not just, 'Oh baby, you sleep and I'll take the kids.'"

Financial issues contribute multiple sources of instability to couples' lives. Of course, there is the immediate stress of wondering how to pay the bills while living paycheck to paycheck and raising young children who go through diapers and new shoe sizes like it's their job. But these struggles can also eat away at couples' relationships, as Akira and Ennis can attest. Missed car payments, relying on loans from parents, and the like can all signal to couples that they are not stable or settled enough to tackle the challenges of marriage. If you get married before being financially prepared, as Abby's boyfriend Darren explains, "You just set yourself up for failure." This emphasizes the relationship between financial and social poverty; it's harder to invest in a relationship when money is tight. Couples don't trust that they can create a stable, long-term future together without a solid financial base, and so they wait until their bank account says it's OK to commit.

TAKING CARE OF MYSELF

Implicit in their self-assessments, it was clear that being able to take care of themselves was essential to people's feelings of being established and stable adults. Research on young people feeling they can claim adult status explains that "the preeminent criteria for the transition to adulthood are the individualistic qualities of accepting responsibility for one's self and making independent decisions, along with becoming financially independent."[50] Successfully completing this transition was complicated for many of the couples by the fact that they were struggling economically but were simultaneously responsible for their own children.

The parents want to be independent, although most feel fairly comfortable accepting financial help from their parents and from government programs (like WIC, the Supplemental Nutrition Assistance Program [SNAP; formerly known as food stamps], and SoonerCare, the state's Medicaid program), even if they'd prefer to be able to fully provide for themselves. This tension between preferring independence and accepting assistance is captured in how the people who live with their parents often discuss the situation. When describing this arrangement, they often note (1) that they do contribute to the household (helping with chores, paying rent to their parents, etc.) or (2) that this is just a temporary situation that will set them up to live on their own in the long run by allowing them to save up over the short term. People feel less of a need to explain away smaller forms of assistance from family, like the occasional bag of groceries or help with child care.

As Zach, who has moved back to his mother's house with his girlfriend and their new baby, explains:

> It's stressful on me. I pay the bills. Even though we live with my mom, I pay my mom $250 a month to live here. I pay half the electricity bill. I pay to live here. It's not free. I took that on, the responsibility, when I moved out the first time. That's her deal. You took the responsibility of being an adult when you moved out, so you pay to live.

The extent to which and for how long people feel it is acceptable to rely on help from others is a reflection of their liminal position in traversing the transition to adulthood. The main obstacle to being able to fully take care of themselves, they explain, is their low wages or lack of employment. This is not a matter, in their eyes, of their not being ready or willing to take on this responsibility, but rather of the opportunities available to them.

This complexity of trying to claim the self-respect of independence while still relying on assistance from others can be seen in Joanne and Matt's story. The following exchange occurred during our first meeting, when I asked if twenty-four-year-old Matt had been living on his own when Joanne, also twenty-four, first moved in with him. He replied, "Naw, I'm supporting my mom and dad." Seeking to clarify, I asked, "So you live with them?" Joanne corrected me, saying, "They live with us." Matt repeated her for emphasis, confirming, "They live with us."

Although they claim independence by insisting that Matt's parents live with them, and not the other way around, the weakness of this claim is revealed a year later when they have moved out of the house where Matt's parents are still living and into a trailer. Joanne says:

> We're happier because we have our own place. We have something where we can say, "Hey, we are stepping up in the world. We are making our way." Because about a year ago, we really didn't have something that we had that we could call our own besides our car. And it's still broke down. But . . . other than that . . . it was just our dogs, our car, and we were living with his mom and dad.

Had they truly been feeling independent, as they had initially claimed, moving would not have offered the feelings of accomplishment that Joanne expresses.

It is clearly difficult to feel like an adult, even when you have a child, when you're still living with your own parents. Even twenty-one-year-old Chantelle, whose solidly middle-class parents can easily afford to financially support her and her newborn son, aspires to independence. "I want to be, like, set. I want to have a job. I want to be stable. I want to be able to do for my son myself, instead of depending on my parents as much as I do. It's nice for them to help, but I want to be able to buy him whatever I want to get him." In part, this is about achieving financial self-reliance, but in a larger sense this is about people feeling like they are independent, capable not only of paying their own bills but free to make their own decisions. As discussed earlier with regard to housing, even when these young adults have access to financial resources through their social ties, these forms of support can undermine their feelings of independence and their willingness to commit to their present unions, raising the risk of social poverty.

People want to be independent of relying on their parents and government benefits. The importance of being able to take care of themselves and their families financially often seems to strike even more strongly at the heart of men's identities. Necie captures how essential this sense of independence is as she describes what she'd like for her boyfriend, Leonard. "I know he wants a job that pays a lot. 'Cause that's all he talks about is money. . . . [T]hat's all he wants is a job. All he wants is to take care of his family." When we meet a year later, Leonard has continually fallen short of this goal and, as a consequence, has pulled away from Necie and their son. Their on-again, off-again relationship seems to rise and fall according to Leonard's whims, with his inability to take care of his family the way he'd like driving him to have only limited contact with them, as his family life is the site of his failure.

Settling into Adulthood

As we saw with Lance at the start of the chapter, several parents communicate a sense of needing to explore, of not being ready to settle down in any permanent way, because they still need to see more of the world or figure themselves out. Brianna, an eighteen-year-old first-time mother, moved straight from the home of her grandparents (who raised her) to live with her boyfriend; they now live with her boyfriend's mother. She says, "Been here [in Oklahoma] too long. I want to explore. . . . I want to go to a different state for a couple years. . . . I want to go to Florida. Like Florida or Hawaii or California or something."

Lance shares this sense of still needing to see more of the world. Particularly when he compares himself to his girlfriend, Kristina, he feels like his experiences are too limited for him to feel settled into adulthood. He tells me, "Sometimes I be feeling weird. Everything [Kristina] be bringing up to me. Like she done been on cruises, she done been outside [of the state]. . . . I been in Mississippi and I came to Oklahoma." This is part of his motivation, he explains, for wanting to join the army, since he would see other parts of the world if deployed; it would give him a chance to "explore everything." The other aspect of his interest in the army is that it will help him figure out more about himself and his own interests.

This need to figure themselves out often takes the form of wanting to better themselves in some way. Robert, twenty-one, explains, "I'm trying to increase my mind capacity. . . . I mean, who wouldn't want to be able to know more stuff anyway? . . . I just don't want to be . . . what's the phrase? A deer with his head stuck in the headlights or whatever? . . . I just feel like there's a whole lot more room for improvement."

The need to do this sort of exploration—going to new places, trying out new experiences, and developing a new sense of self—can be limited by the responsibilities that parenthood brings. For precisely this reason, Robert had mixed feelings when he found out his girlfriend, Elyse, was pregnant just as he was dreaming about moving out of state. He tells me, "I was kind of thinking like 'I don't know what I'm gonna do now. I got to start thinking about, well, I can't do this anymore and all my plans are just, man, can't even do anything anymore.'"

Similarly, when I ask Nick about the challenges of being a first-time dad, he says with a sigh:

> Just not being able to do as much as I want to do. I mean, I'm twenty-one, getting ready to turn twenty-two next week, and I haven't been to a single club or bar or anything. I haven't done any of the fun things I want to do. All I've been doing, constantly almost every day, is going to school and work. [M]y friends quit calling, so my social life has ker-plunked completely.

While it's quite clear that both Robert and Nick love their children and want to be with their girlfriends long-term, both struggle with the limitations these responsibilities place on their abilities to explore in the ways they feel are appropriate for this stage in their lives. The simultaneous transitions to adulthood and parenthood can be socially isolating, as their efforts to be "family men" can put them at odds with their peers. Thus, the risks for social poverty come not only through strains on their romantic relationships but also in estrangement from friends.

The Instability of the Transition to Adulthood

We see an optimism among the young parents whose stories are told here. Despite setbacks and obstacles, they have big dreams for themselves and their families—completing their educations, establishing careers, living on their own, driving their own cars, and being able to easily pay the bills each month. In short, they dream of having a "normal life," as Darren puts it.

But the flip side of these dreams is that their lives feel profoundly unsettled for now. For every degree that's unfinished, career path not yet taken, and new apartment not yet occupied, they feel they've not firmly established themselves in their adult lives. Of course, such instability is not unique to this group; the transition to adulthood is conceived of as an extended period of exploration across the population of young adults in America. What is different for couples in Family Expectations is that they are simultaneously trying to figure out how to be successful adults while already having tackled one of life's biggest challenges: parenthood. This makes this period of transition all the more fraught—it's that much more important that they do get established, since their children are depending on them, but it's that much more difficult because their freedom to explore is limited by their parenting obligations.

Robert reflects the optimism of young adulthood, while also expressing the simple concerns of a parent who just wants to do well by his family:

> I want my life just to be . . . , I'd like to say, easy. . . . [G]o to work, come home, you know, take care of the kids and go to sleep. I mean, I don't really want too much more than that right now. . . . I want to take my time to be a father to [my daughter] and just try to make [me and my girlfriend's] relationship a whole lot better. . . . So I just want us to have our own place and our own transportation, and I'll be fine. . . . I really wouldn't want to do too much more than that. . . . I just want it to be easy, you know what I mean? I don't want to have to worry about if I got a job or not. I already got a job. Take care of the kids and just come home, go to sleep. . . . Be fine.

This list of requirements—a stable, predictable life, with a job and car, and caring for his daughter and girlfriend—is, on its face, quite simple. But what should come through from the stories in this chapter is that this simple list can be awfully hard to achieve for many of these young parents. And the process of pursuing these goals can be disruptive, a source of uncertainty itself. This has profound implications for their chances of maintaining healthy romantic relationships and giving their children the family lives the parents so desire for them. Caught between the cultural expectations of their young adult peers and of themselves as parents, they can come up short on both fronts—growing more socially distant from friends while also struggling to fulfill their own and their partner's ideas of what they need to do as parents. The instability of the transition to adulthood, and tackling this transition while simultaneously becoming a parent, raise the risks of social poverty, as these young parents find it difficult to maintain friendships, focus on family, and trust their partners and union in a world veritably defined by volatility.

3

Committing to a Relationship

"You Have to Have Your Trust in Place"

Taleisha calls me about an hour before our last interview to change our meeting from a nearby house to a local playground. Theirs is the only car in the parking lot when I arrive on this windy, chilly spring morning. It's an older car missing its front driver's side window, which is covered with clear tape, and the driver's side front light is smashed and also taped up. While Taleisha, twenty, sits in the car with the baby, who is asleep in her car seat in the back, I sit with her boyfriend, Darrell, thirty-one, at a picnic table in the park.

Darrell's hair is clipped short, and he has a wispy mustache and beard. There's a noticeable buildup of plaque all around his bottom teeth. Underneath the black, long-sleeve waffle shirt he's wearing, which is covered with stains, the necklines of another black shirt and two white shirts are visible; the layers are necessary in this weather. His pants are baggy; he looks thinner than I remember him being at our past visits. He makes a lot of eye contact with me while we talk; it seems important to him that I really understand his intentions in his relationship and with his life. He wants to be seen for more than he is: an unemployed, homeless ex-con.

Darrell tells me that he and Taleisha haven't been staying together for about the past two months, but that they're not broken up. He says the reason for them now living apart is that he needs to be standing on his own two feet and to be able to provide for her and the baby. After his seasonal job on a building and grounds crew ended last fall, he was out of work until he got a temp job in a factory. After about two months at the factory he was fired for being late a couple times. It's been really difficult for him to find another job given his felony record. He's deeply frustrated that a drug-related conviction is still hanging over his head more than a dozen years later.

He loves being a father, but it clearly wears on him that he cannot provide for his daughter like he believes he ought to do. This is apparent in Darrell's description of what he wants from his life as he's making the transition to fatherhood and a committed relationship:

> I can't make nobody hire me. And I love working. . . . I want to get better. Be a better father. I want to, you know what I'm saying, show my girl that I can be depended on. . . . I don't think spending two years with somebody, you're just supposed to walk out on them. I want to make it better. I think it can. Despite what position I'm in, I think it can get better. I do. . . . It's hurtin' but it's good. It's a blessing at the same time. I wouldn't trade it back in.

After Darrell and I finish our conversation, Taleisha and I decide to talk in my car because of how windy it is—unlike Darrell, she's not dressed for the weather. She wears thick, fake nails on each finger that are painted white with colorful swirls and silver glitter on them. She has blond and brown extensions in her hair that are curled and pulled back in a ponytail, although some of her own hair escapes the ponytail's hold. She brings a blue fleece baby blanket out of the car with her to keep her warm in the wind, and she wears it around her shoulders the whole time we're talking even though we're in the car.

Taleisha quickly starts crying during the interview and uses the baby blanket to wipe away her tears. She sits facing forward for the first three-quarters of the interview, when she's particularly emotional. The last quarter of the interview, when we're talking about the Family Expectations program and her tears have slowed, she starts making eye contact more often.

Taleisha tells a different story of their relationship's breakdown than did Darrell. She says the reason they aren't living together is that a neighbor called the landlord on them because they were fighting so often, so loudly, late at night and early in the morning. Because Darrell was not on the lease, he had to move out of the apartment. But Taleisha says there are more reasons for why they're not living together. Like Darrell, she feels like she needs to work on herself before they can be successful in their relationship together. She explains that she needs some time living by herself to grow up (she's a decade younger than Darrell) and to stop being so insecure (she's particularly worried about her weight) so she will have more trust in Darrell and not accuse him of cheating on her all the time.

They have applied for a Section 8 housing voucher for Darrell to live on his own, and they hope to get him, at least temporarily, on her lease because right now he is homeless. Taleisha says he has been living with his mother (he told me he was living with his brother), but his mom's been really mean to him, putting him down and telling him that Taleisha doesn't really want to be with him.[1] Taleisha gets particularly upset when she tells me that last night she called the house looking for Darrell, and his family told her that he was out and they didn't know where he was. She assumed that he was out with another woman, cheating on her, and was furious. When he finally called her back in the middle of the night from his uncle's house, she found out that no one in his family would let him stay with them last night and so he was stuck outdoors. He had sneaked inside to use the phone. She's angry at herself for assuming the worst when he was actually in need; she's felled by her own shortcomings as she remembers seething in anger at Darrell over an assumed transgression when he was actually sleeping outside. They're going to try to get him into the shelter at the Salvation Army on Monday; Taleisha says that she'll pay the thirty-five dollars per week it will cost for him to stay there.[2]

Despite all the fighting and the financial and emotional insecurity, both tell me that they fully intend to get married one day. They say they really love each other and don't want to be with anyone else; they want to raise their daughter together "as a family." Taleisha recalls that their fights weren't so bad when Darrell was working. She thinks it really eats away at him to not be the man he thinks he ought to be, providing for his family. Darrell's old-fashioned sense of gender roles has led him to even greater feelings of failure than his unemployment might otherwise create. Not only does he feel he should be contributing to the household, but ideally, he says, he doesn't even want Taleisha to have to work, viewing it as his responsibility as a man and a father to provide for his family. While Taleisha says she'd be OK staying home, she's also happy to work, particularly when Darrell can't get a job; her income can cover their basic financial needs, but it doesn't solve Darrell's feelings of falling short of what he thinks a father and future husband should do.

Taleisha says things between them got worse after their daughter was born, since her arrival seemed to spur a more intense feeling in Darrell about what he ought to be doing as a father and a man. "I think it's the stress of, he knows he has a daughter and then he's having so much [of a] hard time finding a steady job and having to see her and see me and he knows that he's a man and I think he feels less of a man because he's not able to provide the way he wants to." As Taleisha explains, their feelings of insecurity lead to explosive fights about the tiniest things, since they don't share with one another their feelings of failure and vulnerability. "It was eating away at him inside, and then we were arguing over something about the dishwater or the way he washes the clothes or something like that. And then it would blow up and he would start talking about that and I'd start talking about something else and it would just, we were just eating at each other, arguing at each other, but the argument was over something small. We were just waiting for the opportunity to get out what we had been burying inside."

Although they had wanted to have a child together and say they plan to be together forever, Taleisha's and Darrell's transitions to partnership and parenthood have been anything but smooth. While their financial situation is certainly part of the story, it seems to be more what the lack of money represents in light of their new roles—Darrell's failure in his own eyes—that matters to the future of their relationship and Darrell's involvement as a father. Darrell's family fanning the flames of the couple's mistrust certainly isn't helping the situation either. Lacking the trust to be vulnerable with one another, Taleisha and Darrell are left struggling to right their relationship after months of floundering.

Like Taleisha and Darrell, other couples struggled with their roles as romantic partners—what to expect of one another, how to act, how to feel secure in their connection. Besides the challenges of the transition to adulthood detailed in the last chapter, these young people were trying to figure out how to have a relationship at a time when the social norms dictating them are looser and less restrictive than ever—bringing both freedom and a lack of clarity about how to make a life together. These various sources of instability meant that building a foundation of trust was that much more challenging. And, therefore, the threat of social poverty was that much stronger.

Family Roles and Role Theory

These young adults are making multiple transitions—to adulthood, partnership, and parenthood. The present and subsequent chapters—on partnership and parenthood, respectively—examine what the adoption of these new roles means to them and how these new roles fit together, or don't. Role theory is useful in guiding our attention to aspects of these transitions that may be particularly challenging, highlighting how role conflicts can create or exacerbate social poverty.

Social roles—father, wife, employee, student—come with a set of expected behaviors that are known both to those filling these roles and to those around them. These roles are more than social "costumes" that someone dons to play a part for a moment; rather, the adoption of social roles is related to changes in one's identity. Therefore, taking on social roles shapes how a person sees him- or herself and is seen by others.[3] Darrell evaluates himself far more harshly for not having a job after his baby is born—and he has taken on the role of father—than he did before her birth. Taleisha understands why, since she also knows that the fatherhood role is accompanied by societal expectations of being a financial provider.

Role theory makes clear that the adoption of social roles is not necessarily a seamless process, as someone can experience role malintegration, overload, or ambiguity.[4] Juggling two or more roles that do not fit well together can create role malintegration, when it is difficult to successfully fulfill the expectations of competing roles. As we saw in the previous chapter, when someone tries to simultaneously engage in the carefree role of young adulthood and the responsibility-laden role of parent, role malintegration may result. Likewise, role overload develops when there are simply too many expectations to reasonably satisfy. This could be created when someone is trying to juggle roles like new partner, new parent, student, and employee all at one time, leaving the responsibilities of at least one of these roles relegated to the back burner. In the previous chapter, we heard from Akira and Ennis how the demands of parenting without any help with child care and doing shift work left them without any time or emotional energy to invest in their relationship; their parental and employee roles overwhelmed their romantic partner roles. In contrast, role ambiguity is created when the expectations for a given role are not sufficiently defined, causing whoever fills the role to lack direction. We see this in roles such as cohabiting partner (are you basically married, or just dating and sharing living expenses?) or stepparent (are you a parent or "not my real mom"?), for which a clear set of social norms have not developed.[5]

Figuring out how to navigate a role transition is not a challenge unique to lower-income unmarried couples. Self-help books and mommy blogs are rife with advice for not losing yourself or neglecting your relationship once you become a parent.[6] And laments over the trials and tribulations of finding the ever-elusive work-family balance are a dime a dozen.[7] Lauren, twenty-three, and her boyfriend, Cordell, twenty-one, welcome their first child during the year that we meet. Lauren sounds like many new mothers, across the income spectrum, when she says with a laugh, "Challenges as being a mom? I don't know. Just finding the balance of being a mom, being you, and doing all your different roles that you have to play."

However, the young adults profiled in this book are often attempting to make multiple transitions simultaneously: to adulthood, parenthood, partnership, and career-focused employment. Further, the transitions to the roles of partner and parent are *joint* transitions; that is, they are navigated alongside another person. While this may offer a resource—a companion in sharing the struggles of the transition—it can also be a complicating factor, as the ease of one's own transition is dependent, in many respects, on the facility one's partner or coparent has in his or her new role. What motherhood will mean for Taleisha, for example, depends a great deal on how Darrell does in transitioning to fatherhood. In this way, success at taking on new roles can be threatened by one's social poverty.

Conditions are ripe for these young parents' experiencing difficulties negotiating the expectations that accompany their new roles. The requirements of emerging adulthood, as it is culturally understood, involve searching for a sense of one's true self and passions through a process of exploration, uninhibited by commitments. In contrast, parenthood and partnership both require the opposite, such as dutifully fulfilling the obligations of providing emotional care and financial support, and behaving consistently and with regard for the well-being of others more than yourself. Engaging in these roles simultaneously can result in role malintegration and overload. Avoiding the incompatibility of these various roles may be part of the reason many parents said that the ideal time to have a child is after being settled into adulthood and a committed partnership. We can see how this would minimize the number of role transitions one must accomplish concurrently and also the degree of conflict between the expectations that accompany one's various roles.

Role transitions can be eased by a process researchers call "anticipatory socialization," when those who may later assume a role begin to learn its norms in advance of taking on this role themselves. This can occur by observing those who are currently in the anticipated role—role modeling, receiving advice from others, and engaging in educational efforts, among others.[8] For some, however, opportunities for anticipatory socialization are relatively rare, or the behaviors modeled and advice given are at odds with those most likely to result in an easy role transition and success in the new position.

Arising from the social poverty many experienced in their youth, these young adults often did not have the benefit of positive anticipatory socialization into partner and parent roles. It was rare to hear descriptions of warm relationships between their parents while growing up, with conflicts successfully managed. Instead, seeing physical violence, verbal abuse, and relationship instability in their parents' lives was common. In anticipating their own roles as mothers and fathers, these young adults often used their parents' behavior as a benchmark that they wanted to exceed with their own children. This was particularly true for the fathers, many of whom had grown up without a consistent relationship with their own dads.

In making these major transitions to the roles of partner and parent, then, many were finding their own way in the dark, without the benefit of anticipatory socialization to guide them. As a consequence, they often lacked clear, shared expectations about their own and their partner's or coparent's role, making their own successful fulfillment of their new roles and this jointly negotiated transition quite challenging. The more limited social resources they had as children made it more likely they would experience social poverty in adulthood, by making it more difficult for them to successfully fulfill their chosen relational roles.

Individuals may be less likely to fully accept or prioritize the identities accompanying roles whose requirements they cannot achieve.[9] For example, both Darrell and Taleisha step away from their roles as partners, as they appraise themselves to be falling short of how they believe a future husband or wife should act—Darrell sees himself as not fulfilling the provider role, while Taleisha sees her lack of self-confidence inhibiting her ability to be supportive and trusting of Darrell. We get a view here of the conditions that contribute to their social poverty—falling short in their social roles leads them to pull away from one another. Darrell's family further undermines their identity "verification"—the affirmation of their identities in particular roles[10]—by rejecting Darrell's identity as Taleisha's partner (and even as a father, questioning his paternity and Taleisha's fidelity). Feeling comfortable in these roles, and therefore capable of living up to the accompanying expectations, is complicated by these identity challenges during role transitions. Research suggests that such difficulties in assuming these roles do not bode well for the future of the relationship, since they are associated with lower relationship quality and a higher likelihood of breakup.[11]

As chapter 1 described, trust in a romantic relationship may not emerge or may be eroded when there is ambiguity in expectations or a lack of shared expectations, or when partners are coping with instability. The same forces are behind the issues these young parents face in their role transitions. Difficulties with trust and role transitions likely reinforce one another. For example, a lack of shared meaning or expectations about what a role entails can erode trust within a couple.[12] Likewise, having personal difficulty accomplishing a role transition could make someone behave in less trustworthy ways or have less trust in him- or herself. Similarly, a lack of trust may contribute to struggles in taking on a new role. For example, a troubled relationship, riddled with mistrust, could make it more difficult to have the salience of this partner identity win out when it is in conflict with one's other roles (like that of a friend, whose buddies want to go out drinking). Ambiguity and discordance in partners' expectations of one another are more likely today, as the cultural environment around romantic relationships provides less guidance than in previous eras about how those in family roles—boyfriend, girlfriend, husband, wife—should act.

Deinstitutionalization and Roles

Today's young adults are trying to navigate a world of romantic relationships that is lacking in institutionalized guidance.[13] Old norms around gender and marriage have weakened but not fully given way, leaving a lack of clarity about what partners can expect from one another. This is particularly apparent among those who are not married but whose relationships are more than casual dating. Roles like "boyfriend"—a term that can be used to describe the person you started dating a month ago or the father of your child with whom you've lived for the past three years—carry a fuzziness about how one should act and what a "girlfriend" can expect that creates role ambiguity, making it difficult for partners to be on the same page about their relationship. Without the guiding hand of social norms, the expectations around monogamy, finances, commitment to a shared future, and a focus on family can be unclear, opening up space for relationship conflict as partners' expectations for one another's behavior may not match.

In the past, role transitions typically occurred in a particular order, with marriage preceding parenthood. The rituals surrounding marriage offer a social process for easing this transition, demarcating a change in roles and expectations.[14] The flexibility of today's social norms around marriage and parenthood gives people the wonderful freedom to construct their family lives according to their own interests. At the same time, however, it raises the likelihood of partners having differing expectations of themselves and one another—when a couple moves in together, for instance, one may see this as akin to being "roommates with benefits" while the other sees this as only one step away from marriage.[15] Further, with unstable romantic relationships and multiple-partner fertility creating increasingly complex family arrangements, role transitions may occur multiple times, and role expectations then need to be negotiated across a dizzying array of relationship ties.[16]

Among the couples in Family Expectations, I had purposely chosen to interview those participants who were unmarried when they initially enrolled in the program. All those I talked to either currently lived together or had done so in the recent past. Despite their relative youth, in all but two couples at least one partner had lived with, been engaged or married to, or had a child with another partner in a previous relationship.[17] That is, their current relationships were rarely their first experiences of union or family formation. This means that, for many, role transitions were that much more complex. Becoming a boyfriend could mean taking on the role of pseudo-stepfather to a new girlfriend's child; becoming a wife could mean navigating the potential pitfalls of a new husband's ex, the mother of his children.

Deinstitutionalization in the world of romantic relationships also means opportunities are rife for role overload and misalignment. The easing of social norms around family formation has meant that romantic and parenting relationships may be disconnected; whereas previously parenting almost exclusively took place in the context of a romantic relationship (and a marital one at that), today coparents often have to establish a relationship that is separate from a romantic union as the requirements of parenthood outlast their partnership.[18] Despite the rising prevalence and declining stigma of nonmarital parenthood, the separation of romantic and parenting status remains incomplete; the fulfillment of parenting roles often continues to depend on the nature of one's role in the romantic sphere, and vice versa. For example, research shows that a father's involvement with his children is affected by the end of his relationship with their mother, as well as by his and their mother's subsequent repartnering.[19] Likewise, cohabiting parents who break up report being drawn back together by their shared children, creating an on-again, off-again relationship;[20] that is, their roles as parents may encourage their ongoing engagement in their partnership roles.

This means that people's abilities to enact roles in the ways they would like depend on others' actions. A woman who sees her role as a mother as protecting her kids can't do so if her enactment of the wife role involves a high-conflict relationship with her husband. Likewise, a man who sees his role as a father as spending lots of time with his kids can't feel he's fulfilling his role if his ex makes it difficult for him to see his children.

On its face, the transition to a new role may seem like a social fact: you are a parent or you aren't, for example. However, particularly in an environment with weaker social rules for what is expected in roles, there can be a good deal of ambiguity, and therefore variation, in partners' expectations around when these transitions truly occur. For example, do you become a parent—and take on the expectations associated with this role—when your girlfriend gets pregnant? Not until you see the ul-trasound and find out you're having a little boy? When that little boy is born?

The differing expectations partners and parents have around role transitions are captured in Kristina and Lance's story, profiled at the start of the previous chapter. Both twenty, they are about to have their first child after being together for a little over a year. Theirs has always been a volatile union, with cheating and frequent, though never long-lasting, breakups. When we first meet, Kristina says that she is in the process of moving out of their apartment. Though she wants to be with Lance and raise their child together, she feels she has to make good on her threat not to be with him if he continued to text other women. After snoop-ing through his phone and discovering that, despite her warnings, he had even initiated some of these exchanges, Kristina decided she had to make him see that she was really serious; she hadn't followed through on previous threats to leave if his behavior didn't change, but this time she decided things would be different.

She says of Lance, not without some anger:

> He's like really immature and he's kind of selfish. Like, he doesn't think about what would be best for the baby or what would be best for our family. He just does what he wants and doesn't think twice about it, you know. So that has taken a big toll on [our relationship] because I feel like now is the perfect time to where he should change and grow up and ma-ture a little bit because our relationship needs to be very intact when the baby gets here because I don't want to wait until the baby gets here and be like, well, what's going to happen then.

Beyond the texting, a major sticking point is Lance's continued in-volvement with his friends, most of whom are single, and therefore not the sort of people with whom Kristina thinks a family man should be spending his time. The root of the problem, Kristina believes, is that while she has already taken on the roles of committed partner and mother, Lance is still trying to avoid the expectations of father and fu-ture husband. In fact, he doesn't yet see himself as being a father, a major point of contention between the two. "If he doesn't show me what I want to see, then it'll just be me and the baby," Kristina says. This is a threat, though, that she doesn't want to carry out. She explains:

> I think he needs to just care less about just going and hanging out with his friends and doing his own thing because he's always telling me "Just let me do me." . . . I think whenever the baby's here, he'll probably change that up a little bit, but now is like when it needs to happen. Now, the time before the baby gets here, is when is most important to me in our relationship. . . . He just says the baby isn't here yet. That's what he says a lot.

As Kristina had expected, Lance does step up more in his role as a father after their son is born, although they continue to struggle as a couple, with fights frequent and the status of the relationship unclear. Indeed, the baby's arrival is a time of transformation for Lance. As he explains, "[Kristina being pregnant] didn't really have an effect [on me] all the way through the whole pregnancy. It didn't seem real. I could feel him in there, but it never hit me. But when he came out, you know . . . ," he struggles to put into words how he felt in that moment. "When I first held [him], it was weird. My whole body got hot." This overwhelming rush of emotion seemed to propel Lance into fatherhood. He had planned to join the military as a way of seeing the world, but he abandons this because "I got a kid back here and if I do that, I'm gonna be gone at least a year and a half. I don't want to be gone that long." Initially reluctant to take on the father role during Kristina's pregnancy, Lance now says of being a parent, "Love it. Love every minute of it. . . . [J]ust being there, being able to provide for him, just keeping a smile on his face is good enough for me." He acknowledges how this has changed him: "Like before [he was born] I was being real childish, calling [off work], all this other stuff. From the minute he got here, from then on, it's all about working, all about trying to take care of him." Unfortunately, Lance arrived at fatherhood about nine months after Kristina wanted him to, leaving a well of hurt feelings that wasn't filled by the baby's arrival.

By the end of our year of interviews, Kristina and Lance have been on and off more times than we can count. Nonetheless, they still want to be together in the long run. Kristina explains:

You know, whenever [our relationship is] good, it's really good. It's just whenever it's bad, it's just *bad*. And, you know, I want us to be together for our son anyways, but I know that that's not what has to make us stay together, but I want it like that because I know that [our son] likes having us both around. And I like seeing him with [Lance] . . . because it makes me love [Lance] more, and seeing him be a good dad makes me happy. They have a totally different relationship than [I] do [with our son]. And he makes him laugh like I can't even make him laugh like that, and they just have so much fun together, so that, I don't ever want to take that from [my son].

It is a combination of her bond with Lance and her enjoyment of and appreciation for Lance in his role as a father that makes her want to see their romantic relationship continue; we see how interrelated these roles remain. Similarly, Lance describes Kristina as being a good mom— "[She's] everything I wanted [in my son's mother]"—and says he wants to stay together.

But the difficulties they've confronted in transitioning to parenthood and partnership have undermined the relationship and their trust in one another's intentions. A clash between roles for Lance—of being a young adult hanging out with his friends versus a father and partner—and a disagreement between him and Kristina over when the transition to parenthood takes place and how he should prioritize his various roles have left their relationship with seemingly permanent scars. In their words, we can hear how when their relationship is working, their family life is a prized resource, a source of joy. But their difficulties with transitioning into their roles as parents and partners have sapped their relationship, leaving them struggling with social poverty.

Role Transitions: Partnership

As we see for Kristina and Lance, the diffuse social norms around romantic relationships have left many of these young parents treading murky waters. Strikingly, however, nearly all are enthusiastic about the positive power of romantic relationships, with marriage as their ideal end point. They see romantic relationships as offering the possibilities of lifelong love, a partner, an advocate, a best friend, and someone who

knows and understands you better than anyone else. These emotionally rich connections are deeply desired, if not always achieved. Because
social poverty is, by its nature, subjective, having our relationships fall
short of hopes or expectations can leave us feeling a lack of adequate
social resources.

What this group of young adults wants from their relationships is
shaped by several factors. First, there are the dual cultural narratives
of expressive individualism and a high symbolic value placed on marriage.[21] Second, there are economic conditions that necessitate a dual-
earner household for financial survival. Third, they are deeply influenced
by what they observed growing up. Nearly all offer the relationship examples their parents provided as typifying what not to do. Such negative
role models create a mystery around how to navigate the nuts and bolts
of daily life in a committed, long-term relationship, such as dealing with
peccadillos, arguments, and misunderstandings. They wonder, does
fighting mean the relationship is doomed? Is it OK to curse, call names,
and yell? They didn't like being around their own parents' explosive arguments, but, as parents themselves now, it's hard not to cuss and shout
when that's all you know, especially when self-control goes out the door
in the heat of the moment.[22] Emotionally investing in these relationships
can feel all the more fraught when an explosive ending seems so likely.

Therefore, relationship ideals, prevailing cultural norms, economic
conditions, and family backgrounds create a confusing jumble of direc-
tives and expectations. These couples deeply desire forever relationships,
marked by meaningful communication, the revealing of their most
vulnerable selves, and true partnership. Yet they aren't sure how to do
these things and whether they trust their partners, themselves, and the
relationship enough to take such emotional risks. Their current social
poverty makes their long-term pursuit of these social resources all the
more difficult.

Previous studies of romantic relationships among lower-income couples often emphasize their instability and a pervasive lack of trust. The
stresses of poverty, gender mistrust, and a sense of uncertainty erode relationships, researchers point out, making men and women reluctant to
even get involved with someone, and they play a strong hand in doom-
ing the relationships of those who take this gamble.[23] However, while
scholars' discussions of women's uncertainty about romance can make it

seem like a relationship is something women simply don't have the time or energy to pursue, the reality is that they do get invested in romantic unions, and they do want these relationships to last.[24] Here I focus specifically on describing what it is these young parents want from their romantic partnerships. While they may be wary, they also have romantic visions they hope will one day be fulfilled, and these views play an important role in driving their decisions around their relationships with their children's other parent. That is, they want to gain social resources and escape or avoid social poverty; they want a partner to lean on and to parent alongside. Their assessment of their success or failure in doing so depends on the standards against which they judge their relationships.

Relationship Ideals

Darren, twenty-nine, is having his fourth child. It's his first with his girlfriend, Abby, and Darren's previous relationships with his children's mothers have ended acrimoniously. Nonetheless, Darren has a vision—shared by many of the other men and women in this study—of what it takes to have a good relationship. He explains:

> You have to have your trust in place. You have to be committed and loyal to one another. I believe you've got to compliment each other all the time. I don't see any problem in criticizing as long as it's constructive. And just being there for each other. That's one of the main things. Being able to be open, that's why the trust thing is a major issue. I just think that it takes a hundred percent. You just have to give everything you have, and I think it works both ways.

This narrative of support and emotional openness, aiding one another's personal growth through compliments and constructive criticism, captures many of the tenets sociologist Andrew Cherlin argues undergird our culture's ideology of expressive individualism, in which relationships serve as a location for self-expression and actualization.[25] However, Darren goes further than this, also emphasizing the importance of commitment and trust. The ideal, as he explains it, is not the "pure" relationship of sociologist Anthony Giddens' imagining, driven by a relentlessly individualistic orientation and subject to ending once it no longer serves the interests of one partner.[26] The relationships Darren and others want are not ephemeral but rather lasting resources that can sustain them throughout their lives, a secure social asset.

Similarly, we hear this emphasis on the overriding importance of a union that lasts from Hailey, thirty-three, who is having a baby with new boyfriend, Evan. A good relationship, as Hailey sees it, requires "of course the communication and the trust. And supporting one another. Believing in each other. Loving one another unconditionally. You know, loyalty." But there's more, she says. "I think the big thing is just developing that strong foundation so when high winds come through it's not gonna blow your house down. You know, you're still gonna stand tall . . . because you have mastered, to a point, the art of all those other things."

Even though Tiana, twenty, can feel tired and frustrated by her relationship with Stefan, there are moments that are small but powerful that let her know this is the right place for her. As she describes, "We have our arguments and we have our moments and stuff like that, but at the end of the day when we're sitting down and relaxing and watching TV . . . and you're in that moment where you're comfortable with each other and everything's just right at the time, that's worth it. There's no way you can explain it." This feeling of quiet comfort in one another's presence, born of the understanding and acceptance of each other's quirks that Tiana and Stefan so highly prize in their relationship, is key to balancing out the more difficult times. It is this social resource that couples treasure.

Likewise, Zach, twenty, who is having his first child with Brianna, eighteen, explains how their strengths as a couple make their struggles tolerable:

We haven't really figured out how to speak with each other about our problems the correct way. . . . But the love that we do have for each other and the fact that she's gonna stick up for me no matter what, and she's proven that. And it's vice versa. . . . I know she's got my back on anything. Anything. Even if I was to be wrong, she would stick up for me in the wrong.

Zach knows Brianna is in his corner. He tells me, "If I've got an issue with life I can go and talk to her about it and she doesn't necessarily have to have an opinion back, but I know she's there to listen. Same way, I don't always know what to say to her to make her feel better, but I'm there to listen." As for Tiana and Stefan, the power of acceptance and support fulfills Zach's most important needs in the relationship, rendering their issues problems to solve rather than reasons to break up. What Tiana and Zach describe is that feeling of having an essential social resource—of not being socially poor.

Much of the previous research on romantic relationships among low-income couples has emphasized the destructive force of life's stresses on these unions.[27] In the present study we see that these young parents value, desire, and fight to keep a partner by their side with whom to weather life's difficulties. It may be precisely because so little else—jobs, finances, friends, and even kin—can be relied on that having someone in your corner feels all the more essential. Ann, twenty-eight, and Trenton, thirty, are having their first son together; both have daughters from previous relationships. Ann says:

> My feelings for him has grown. Even though we went through some things . . . , I guess that's why [my feelings grew]. . . . Just trying to make him happy. Try to tell him not to stress so much, 'cause he wants to take it all on his shoulders by himself. But what he don't realize is that it ain't just him. I'm here for a reason.

As she sees Trenton's reaction to what she's saying, she interrupts herself and exclaims, "Don't cry! You're gonna make [me cry too]. Don't do that! Why on earth would you do that?" Trenton explains his tears, "Just realizing somebody's there, whole-heartedly. . . . Thank you." In this moment, my presence in the room disappears, as the two focus on one another. "Love you, guy," she answers. They share a kiss, and then she turns back to me and adds, "He's my soul mate." Their roof may literally be caving in, and they may struggle to pay the bills, but they do have a key asset: their relationship.

These parents have a strong, and commonly shared, set of ideals for what they want from their romantic relationships. They want to have a safe haven and steadfast support in their partner, someone who knows and accepts their innermost selves. Although these young adults and their relationships are buffeted by problems—financial struggles, imprisonment, unstable employment, unrealized educational dreams, and difficult living situations—this has not meant they've abandoned their hopes for a true and lasting relationship. Experiencing financial poverty does not mean acquiescing to social poverty as well.

Relationship Roles

The world of relationship options for young adults today is vastly different than those contemplated by their grandparents fifty years ago. If the relationships of the past were a fixed-priced meal, today's are a smorgasbord. Freed from the confines of externally enforced social norms and laws, there are far more decisions to make about what you're going to "eat" and in what order.[28] Nonetheless, we see mixed emotions about embracing the buffet-style freedom of today's romantic unions.[29]

Every parent in this book has been pregnant (or gotten a partner pregnant) outside of marriage. While a few chose to marry before the baby's arrival or soon thereafter, most did not. It was not uncommon, when I asked about possibilities for marriage in the future, that reactions were dismissive. Marriage is "just a piece of paper," some would say. "We're already basically married," said others. Cohabiting, raising a child together, and struggling side by side to make ends meet—what would getting married really mean? they wondered. This response could lead one to conclude that marriage is a dying institution.

And yet its power would shine through time and again. Those same men and women who dismissed marriage's importance also said they did want to get married someday. Even if it would change nothing about their daily lives, they explained, it held deep symbolic value to them. Marriage represented something ineffably better. Ruby, twenty-nine, initially dismissed marriage during our conversation but then explained that it does still appeal to her. "It's just . . . [an] old-fashion type of thing, husband and wife type of thing. When you're a little girl you always dream of having a husband and a house and everything being perfect kind of thing." While there may be far more options today, the more limited family possibilities of the past still evoke nostalgia for the good old days. Marriage represents "everything being perfect."

As Taleisha, twenty, describes it, marriage is the ultimate end point of relationships. Even if cohabiting is fine, it's still a relationship that has fallen short of the finish line. "I would like to get married at some point to show my daughter that, you know, this is real, this isn't just mommy and daddy being boyfriend and girlfriend and having kids. You know, this is a relationship." But it's not only for her daughter, she explains. "I think we both deserve it. I want those memories. I want those photos. I want to be able to look back with him, so we can look at them, and I feel like we deserve a big, nice wedding. Not big like Kim Kardashian's wedding or nothing like that." She laughs at the thought. "I just want it to be right. I don't want to just get married on the splurge of the moment *just because*. I just want it to be right and to where everybody can be comfortable and I can be comfortable without worrying about other stuff."

The roles of husband and wife remain desirable to nearly all the men and women profiled here. Marriage may now be one choice among many, but its symbolism still exerts a powerful pull, leading most to measure their relationships against this bar: Are the relationship, their finances, and their achievement of life goals marriage-worthy yet? As other researchers have also found, low-income couples often do not marry not because they reject marriage but because they judge themselves as having fallen short of its requirements—decent jobs, stable incomes, a solid financial base, and a loving relationship, marked by open communication and trust.[30] They want to marry, but only under the right circumstances.

Gender roles are a core aspect of the traditional social norms around relationships that have relaxed.[31] This is reflected in the work and family behaviors of many of the young men and women in this study. For a time, Mackenzie, twenty-one, was the only one working while Wayan, twenty-four, stayed home with their two daughters. As we talked during our first interview, each simply did what was necessary to take care of the kids. While Mackenzie fixed their older daughter's hair, Wayan pushed the baby's swing, lulling the little one to sleep. Likewise, Tiana, twenty, and Stefan, twenty-one, each worked full-time jobs—she in a day care center and he at a grocery store—to help their family make ends meet; Tiana owned the couple's only car.

Despite these realities, however, it was often a couple's preferred option for the woman to not work or to work a "little job" if financially possible. As for marriage, while the traditional gendered division of labor is no longer a dominant social norm, it remains the ideal state of affairs for many. This was a measure against which men saw themselves either achieving or falling short.[32] Zach, twenty-one, was happy that his girlfriend did not need to work during or after her pregnancy, since they were squeaking by on his earnings (while living with his mother). Similarly, Will, twenty-two, earned enough that Jessica, nineteen, could stay home with their baby and his daughter from a previous relationship. In contrast, Wayan and Darrell were unable to work enough to keep their girlfriends from having to work, leaving the men feeling frustrated and inadequate, despite their girlfriends' willingness and ability to find jobs. While a wider array of roles offers more legitimate family options than were available in the past, the "classics"—husband, wife, breadwinning dad, stay-at-home mom—still hold sway. At the same time, achieving these roles has become all the more difficult.

Obstacles to Ideals

The challenges standing between these young parents and their ideal family lives are many. First, they lack the financial resources they associate with being "marriage ready." Low-income couples, like others across the socioeconomic spectrum, have a marriage bar they feel must be met before walking down the aisle. Unlike their more affluent counterparts, however, couples like those profiled in this book find it much more challenging to get established financially.[33]

As Robert, twenty-one, explains, "You can't just get married on a whim. To me, you have to have everything in order . . . as far as finances are concerned. The transportation, you and your family as a whole, they have to be ready to be in that married position." His girlfriend, Elyse, twenty, adds, "I want to be stable. . . . [W]hen I come back from getting married, I don't want to have to come back to stress. I want to have everything already together and, you know, organized, so we can enjoy our time. . . . You know, we're married now, just have fun and live life." Elyse describes a financial position these two—who are still living with their respective parents and have to go in with a friend to afford a used car between the three of them—are far from achieving; interestingly, however, she has still brought up marriage repeatedly to Robert, showing the power of the ideal. He follows up on Elyse's thought by saying, "I'd love to go with my wife and pick out our first house. . . . I want to live in a nice home. I don't want to just stay cooped up in an apartment for the rest of my life, so definitely I need both of our finances to be right so that we'll be able to do that." It's not just that Robert and Elyse want to live a more middle-class lifestyle. Rather, they feel that these financial preparations are part of the way you make sure your marriage will succeed. As Robert puts it, "Stuff doesn't come and blindside you as much [if] you've taken steps to prepare yourselves to be ready for that."

Dave, twenty-nine, has two children with his girlfriend, Norene, and a son from a previous relationship. He feels like he needs to be a stronger contributor to the household, getting himself on a career path and doing more around the house. As he sees it, what stands between him and a good relationship, and between him and the type of partner he wants to be, are his own limitations. As he explains, "I wasn't raised relationship-wise. . . . Like helping around the house, and there's times that I do want to cook but I don't know how. My grandfather didn't really show me." It's also hard for him to follow through on his own best intentions. "I do get [depressed] and I just don't want to do anything," he says. On top of never having seen a good relationship while being raised by his grandfather, he feels incompetent when it comes to taking care of daily tasks. Overcoming this limitation is made all the more difficult by his mental health struggles.

This illustrates how, although finances are important, they aren't everything when couples are judging whether they and their relationships are marriage-ready. Like Dave, some young adults feel clueless when it comes to knowing how to have—or even how to recognize—a good relationship. What it takes to enact the roles they want to embody can be unclear, creating a sort of role ambiguity. They sense they're lacking another resource that goes beyond money. Evan, thirty-three, felt like he ruined his relationship with the mother of his twelve-year-old son, though the pair spent fifteen years together. He is desperate to do things right this time around with new girlfriend, Hailey. But he doesn't feel much better equipped to succeed at making the relationship healthy and lasting than he was before. When I ask him what makes a good relationship, he mentions a few characteristics like communication and loyalty, before trailing off and concluding, "I don't know. . . . I've never had a healthy relationship. I've never been around people with healthy relationships." While Evan wants the riches of a positive, supportive relationship, this feels nearly impossible to him as his history of social poverty has stood in the way of his anticipatory socialization into the role of a successful romantic partner.

Similarly, when I ask Ciara, twenty-one, what makes a good relationship, she says, "I don't know. 'Cause I haven't had a good relationship. The only good relationship is me and my kids. That's the only thing that makes me happy. Until I know real love with a man, then I don't know." After hoping she had found a good companion in her younger son's father, only to see that relationship end during the year of our interviews, she's back to square one in trying to figure out this romantic relationship business.

Carley, twenty-one, has found herself feeling as confused as Evan and Ciara. She elaborates:

> I didn't really understand how a relationship was supposed to go. I just assumed that however a relationship was going was how it was supposed to be. No one ever actually said this is how it needs to be and how it's supposed to be. I dated a lot of abusive people. I did a lot of things that were hurtful and awful, that I wasn't aware that other people didn't do.

She explains how it is that relationships have remained so mysterious to her: "My parents never fought in front of us. My mom and my stepdad, never. They always fought behind closed doors, so I thought for the longest time that when you fought that there was something horribly wrong in your relationship." The effect on her, as she explains, is that "I had no idea it's OK to fight, just got to get it out at some point. . . . I want [our son] to know that we will fight, but we will make up. It's all right. I wish I'd seen that." As Carley explains, she lacked an understanding of the everyday mechanics of how to make a relationship work. What does having a fight mean? Is it the end of the relationship? How do partners fight fairly and without undermining the foundation of their relationship? In this and so many other ways, these young adults described themselves as lacking in the role models and experiences—the anticipatory socialization—necessary to learn what it takes to fulfill the roles they desire. These roles, therefore, remain more ambiguous and potentially challenging to successfully fill.

More broadly, transitions into partnership are made more difficult for these lower-income, unmarried couples because they are trying to take on these new roles amid profound instability. This is created and compounded by their liminal financial position, their unsteady progress toward adulthood, and the deinstitutionalization of romantic relationship norms. Lacking a clear and cohesive vision of what a relationship should involve and what roles partners can reasonably expect one another to play, these couples are left plunging into a great unknown when they try to create a healthy, lasting relationship. Feeling insecure in these relationships that are so central to their lives can create feelings of social poverty. As sociologist Jennifer Silva writes, "The unpredictability, insecurity, and risks of everyday life come to haunt young people *within* their most intimate relationships, not only by shrinking their already limited pool of available social resources but also by disrupting their sense of security, destabilizing their life trajectories, and transforming commitment into yet another risky venture."[34] Even though the risks are high, we see in these young parents a deep desire to have the gamble they've taken on their romantic relationship pay off. This desire is made all the stronger by their shared bond as parents, a role transition I explore in the next chapter.

4

Becoming a Parent

Doing Better and Settling Down

Throughout the year we meet, Zach, twenty-one, and Brianna, eighteen, live in Zach's mom's house, a simple, ranch-style house with lots of cars in the driveway and lots of dogs jockeying for a scratch behind the ears. Though he's moved back in with his mom, Zach clearly feels like an adult, particularly once his son, Kayden, is born. The last time we meet, while Brianna and I talk, Zach, with his straggly facial hair and a bit of gray paint on the side of his right temple, is in the back bedroom with the baby. Later, they soar down the hall with Zach flying a giggling Kayden like an airplane. Yet Zach still vividly remembers his deeply mixed feelings at learning Brianna was pregnant. From him we hear hints of the ambiguous feelings so many parents expressed about an unplanned pregnancy at a young age, in a struggling relationship, in a bad economic position. Upon receiving Brianna's phone call after she took a pregnancy test, he says, "I was excited, scared, emotional. It made my head explode really. You know, scared, didn't know what was gonna happen, but happy. I was really happy. You know, start my life. I wish it was further along in life, of course, really, but I mean it was a happy moment, it really was."

Knowing he was going to become a father made Zach feel he was going to "start my life." He describes how this entailed a dramatic change in his daily routines:

> Financially, had to really get my head together. . . . It really, yeah, it made me stop partying as much and going out and drinking all the time as much and it just, it really made me lay off the social side of life a little bit to be with [Brianna]. . . . Which was, I mean, it wasn't a problem, not at all, but it was, I mean, kind of like "Uhhh." But it wasn't a problem.

With a quiet pride, he says, "Grew up a little bit, I guess." Notably, Zach experienced these changes in how he saw himself before his son's arrival.

After Kayden was born, Zach fell in love with his new role even more, reveling in the minutiae of his responsibilities. As he describes it:

> I love every minute of it. It's a lot of work. They always tell you in high school, "Don't do it 'cause you can't afford it." They never talk about the responsibilities. Oh God. Oh God. Cutting a baby's fingernails once a week, twice a week? Never even thought about it. . . . Giving a baby a bath. You got to take thirty minutes out of your day to give that baby a bath. . . . That's every day, and it's a priority. And things, I mean, having to keep the vacuum going every day 'cause we have this many [pets] and he's on the floor a lot. . . . You got to buy baby soap. You got to buy baby shampoo. Laundry detergent. Bottled water. Just stuff that you don't even fathom. It's a whole lot more than anyone could ever think of as a teenager. It's amazing, though. I love it. I love it. It's a challenge. Always up for a good challenge.

We see Zach defining himself as an adult—capable of taking on the demanding role of father in a way a teenager could not—and constructing his own sense of fatherhood as including both financial responsibilities ("buying baby shampoo") and caretaking ("cutting the baby's fingernails"). While Zach's other roles as boyfriend and son are sometimes frustrating—he feels Brianna's not pulling her weight in the family, and he butts heads with his mother—his role as Kayden's father simply leaves him elated.

Especially in a world in which so little else is going as you'd like—education, career, finances, living situation, and, sometimes, a romantic relationship—a child can represent enormous hope for the future. Hope to make things better for your kid than what you had. Hope for an amazing relationship with this child. Hope for finally doing something right. Hope for at least one "forever" in your life.[1] And so, the transition to parenthood is freighted with immense weight for these young adults. It feels essential to get it right, and that much harder to do so when so many other parts of life are unsettled. Wanting to do right by their kids—warding off social poverty for themselves and their children—is part of the motivation that leads parents to Family Expectations.

Role Transitions: Parenthood

For these parents, having children was transformative. They feel it helped make them into adults, and their children are a tremendous source of motivation to remake their own lives for the better. They seek to change themselves to be the sort of parents they want to be, but also to give their kids the kind of childhood they often lacked—Zach wants to do far more for Kayden than his father, an abusive alcoholic, did for him. Parenthood changes how they view themselves and experience their daily realities. It plays an essential role in pushing young people into adulthood, ending the exploration and self-centered ways of emerging adulthood, while also transforming what they feel they need to achieve personally and in their relationships.[2] Parenthood raises the expectations partners have of one another, and its demands can challenge their romantic relationships, increasing the risks of social poverty.

Like many of the parents, Stefan, twenty-one, feels that his infant daughter is the one unambiguously good thing in his life. "My little girl, she's the only thing I have in this world to actually be completely proud of," he says. Stefan is more successful than some other fathers profiled here: he has earned his GED, he's consistently employed, his relationship with girlfriend Tiana is fairly solid, and, by living with his family, they're able to cover most of their bills. Unlike his daughter, however, all these other facts of life have a dark side: he dropped out of school, works a job he dislikes, has some difficulties with Tiana, and isn't fond of living with his family while still scrambling to make ends meet. His daughter really is the light of his life.

Nick, twenty-one, says that it was his girlfriend's pregnancy that drove him to want to marry her more quickly than he otherwise would have. He explains:

> We have really strong beliefs that the child needs to come into this world right and nothing should be wrong. . . . I think now [marriage is] kind of more than necessary because now the child's on the way and the child needs to know that Daddy and Mommy was married. Like I said, the best it possibly could be when the child comes into this world. I just want everything to be perfect. I know everything can't be perfect, but I would like it to be.

Knowing a baby is on the way pushes Nick, like so many other parents, to work hard to create the life—and the relationship with his now wife—he wants for his son.

Being a Parent Means Growing Up

These young people often described the transition to parenthood as a simultaneous transition to adulthood. The carefree, irresponsible behavior—partying, hanging out with wild friends, not being serious about a job or finances—that they associated with being young was often brought to an abrupt end by the news of a pregnancy or a baby's arrival. Zach's girlfriend, Brianna, gives birth to their first child when she's eighteen. Although Brianna hasn't achieved nearly any of the traditional markers of adulthood—completing her education, supporting herself with a job, or living on her own—knowing she was going to have a baby still changed the way she thought and acted, making her see herself as more of an adult. She tells me, "It made me more responsible with everything. It made me grow up real quick. Real quick. Since I have a baby I have to grow up. . . . I clean more than I used to. . . . I used to just sit around the house and do nothing. . . . And now I clean and . . . take care of myself better and everything." While she's out of the room, Zach quietly shares with me that Brianna does less around the house and with the baby than he thinks she should; nonetheless, Brianna's view of herself has changed—she's become more of an adult in her own eyes.

Ken is the opposite of Brianna in many ways. Thirty-six, Ken has a college degree and is taking course work toward a master's degree. Yet in Ken's words, we hear a transformation tale similar to Brianna's:

> The feeling you have once you have babies, it's a feeling you can never describe to other people. But you feel good. At the same time, it can also come with responsibilities. You feel like, before I could do whatever I want to. Even before when you were in a relationship, sometimes a relationship don't work and you can go your separate ways, but once you have a kid, that's a different ballgame, you know. So you're more responsible and you're more [thoughtful] about that baby. You're more [thinking] about how to protect her and how to make sure she's safe all the time. That's something that worries me. But it's a good feeling.

While the arrival of parenthood brings emotions and challenges we don't typically think of as positive—more cleaning, more responsibility, more worry—both Brianna and Ken are, on balance, happy about the changes the new role of parenthood has brought to their lives.

Being a Parent Means Doing Better

For many, parenthood means stepping it up and changing who you are and how you act for the better. This is a fundamental transition in roles. Ciara, twenty-one, has her second child during the year of our interviews. Of her first son, now two, she says that if she hadn't gotten pregnant with him, she and his dad would "probably both be dead. . . . [H]e saved us." The partying and substance use that previously had played a part in Ciara's life were brought to an end by the pregnancy. She and her boyfriend, under some pressure, "did the right thing" and got married before the baby was born. The union lasted only a year. Still, they've managed to negotiate a decent relationship with one another, centered around raising their son, and haven't returned to their old ways. Ciara credits her son, rather than her own willpower or strength, for her transformation.

Taleisha's life has fallen short of what she'd wanted for herself, with a shaky relationship with boyfriend, Darrell, and her having dropped out of college, but she completely lights up when talking about what it's like to be a mother:

> I've grown so much since I've had her. [It] just transform[ed] my whole life. . . . I just love her. I love it. I love being a mom. I want to have some more [children] someday, just not now. . . . She motivates me to do a lot of stuff and, you know, continue toward my goals and my dreams.

Taleisha sees the parenthood role as fueling her drive to achieve. While the role of parent makes those of student, employee, and romantic partner feel more important to Taleisha, trying to do all four at once risks role overload.

The transition to parenthood offers an enormous challenge to these young adults' romantic relationships, discussed in previous chapters. However, as with their personal transformations, some do describe the difficulties of parenthood as offering a way to witness a partner's growth. Carley says, of seeing Nick be a father to their son:

> I never thought he was gonna turn into a dad. He used to make me crazy [when I was pregnant]. I'd be like "Love on my tummy. Rub my tummy." He's like "OK." I was like, "OK? Is that it?" I didn't think "dad" was gonna kick in, and then as soon as [our son] was born, it kicked in. It was very strange. He would sit with the Boppy pillow and feed him. He woke me to pump. He has pictures of me holding up bottles of breast milk like a trophy. Just, he was supportive in every way and I never, I didn't see that until he was born. . . . And that was a big blessing. . . . It just like kicked in. He's been amazing. Absolutely amazing.

Both Nick and Carley witnessed his transformation into a father. Taking on that role changed how Nick saw himself as an adult and his drive to make his son's life "perfect," but it also changed how Carley saw Nick, putting him in a more positive light in her eyes as he stepped up to be the partner she wanted and felt she needed. Because, for Carley, the roles of husband and father were intertwined, seeing Nick successfully take on the role of dad has boosted her estimation of his success as a spouse.

Elyse's pregnancy had a similar effect for her and her boyfriend, Robert. She explains that even though—or perhaps because—the pregnancy came at a difficult time in their relationship, it made them work to create a stronger union, since they were bringing a baby into this world together: "It helped our relationship a whole lot. We were kind of going through a lot, so when I found out I was pregnant, he opened up a whole lot more. . . . He was more supportive, and he was more into our relationship than he had been for a little bit." For many of the parents, when they thrive in transitioning to parenthood together, having that partner by their side and seeing a partner blossom as a parent bolster their social resources—that is, when the transitions to parenthood and partnership successfully coincide, they can move parents farther from the ranks of the socially poor. When the multitude of transitions these young people are experiencing do not successfully combine, however, it raises the specter of social poverty that much further.

Although he no longer has custody of his three oldest children, Darren, twenty-nine, says without a hint of irony, "I'm the best dad."

Though he's basically never lived with these three older children—his fourth child is with current girlfriend, Abby, with whom he occasionally stays—he sees them as having transformed his life. "I always put them first, and that's probably the reason I quit hanging out with a lot of the people I did. I didn't make the best choices in life for a while, but they helped me change what I was doing. They keep me focused. I think I'm a really good dad. I love my kids a lot." Over the year we meet, he struggles to hold on to this changed self as the difficulties in his life with Abby mount. After their daughter is born, Darren loses his part-time jobs, and the two flirt with homelessness, drifting between their parents' houses and motels. He looks to his infant daughter time and again for the strength to do the right thing. Even though he's dejected after weeks of looking for work without any luck, he says he has to press on: "What choice do I have? You know, be like, 'Screw it?' . . . If I didn't have children, I probably would have. [My baby] means the world to me. Any time I feel like it, I just . . . I don't let myself." Continuing on this path is made all the more difficult by the fact that he knows that he could return to dealing drugs, making their financial problems disappear and giving Abby the material goods she wants—an apartment, a car, enough food. But to do so, he knows from experience, means a good likelihood of eventually going back to prison and leaving Abby to be a single parent, while he misses out on his baby's life, just as he did with his older children.

He bangs his cup on the table in frustration as he grinds out his words:

I could go make a thousand dollars a day. I sit here all day and hear [from Abby] about how we don't have money, and I choose to sit there and take it. I don't think she understands . . . how easy it would be for me to just step away and be OK if I chose to go do those things, you know, and how hard it would be on her. . . . I kind of like knowing, I mean, it makes me feel better about myself, you know, being able to do what I do.

The kudos he can give himself are cold comfort, though, when he knows he's letting down Abby. His failure as a father to fulfill the provider role strains his bond with Abby, leaving him feeling misunderstood, especially by the one person who is supposed to have his back. It's his children, he says, that make all the difference. "[My baby] makes it easy. And [my older kids], they make it easy. 'Cause I lost them. . . . I don't want that to happen with [my baby]. It's not gonna happen. I don't care if I have to sleep in the street. She would have a place to be. And have me there every day. That's what's important." The intense joy his children offer is his only source of happiness now. "[My baby] makes it worth it. And seeing my son at [my] mom's and seeing them play together, that's awesome. And I forget everything! I wouldn't think that that'd be possible, but I just forget everything." As he and Abby struggle to get by and be supportive of one another, the emotional fulfillment his children offer him stands between him and deep social poverty.

A central problem for Darren and Abby, as he sees it, is remembering how vastly important it is to make their relationship work for their daughter's sake. Part of being good parents, as Darren says, is being good partners. He tells me, "[My dad] wasn't really there when I needed him to be because him and my mom were too wrapped up in their own bullshit. That's the way it is. So I try to explain to Abby that no matter what we're going through, we need to be parents. . . . [S]he is a great mom, but she hasn't got that figured out." Neither of them saw their parents together in a healthy relationship, but Darren doesn't want their daughter to see what they did. He explains, "I think that raising her in a loving family [is important] . . . and also setting good examples relationship-wise with us, 'cause kids look at that. . . . So that'll be something we need to work on, so we can change that. Break that cycle there." Just as they don't want the baby to lack food, clothing, and shelter, they want her to grow up free from the social poverty they experienced as children and continue to struggle with as adults.

Being a Parent Means Giving Your Kids a Better Life

For many parents, the arrival of a child creates the urgency to become an adult and a better person as they contrast their experiences growing up with the life they want to give their own kids, as we hear in Darren's story. While this narrative emerges in both men's and women's descriptions of taking on the parenthood role, it was more frequently mentioned by fathers. This is, perhaps, driven by the fact that so many grew up without fathers themselves, leaving them feeling that they were floundering without role models and more intent on sparing their children the scars they gained in their youth.

This motivation of providing children with a better life was at the center of these parents working to transform themselves. Aaron, twenty-three, is about to have his second child with Illisha, whom he marries during the year of our interviews. He describes how life-changing he found the birth of their first daughter. Before, he says, he was surrounded by friends who were bad news; he no longer spends time with them, even though this means he doesn't have many friends anymore. As he describes it:

> We'd go chill, or have fight night, or talk stuff, or get our drink on here and there. They would always have women coming in and out. So at the time, all of a sudden, we have [our daughter], I was like, there needs to be a change . . . because I don't want [her] to be in my shoes where I don't have a father around.

Wayan, twenty-four, describes how his family and friends have seen a change in him since he became a father:

> I got a bad temper, and they see now that I'm more calmer now. I don't yell. . . . [B]ack then I didn't have kids. Just me and [my girlfriend] would go at it. But now I seen, you know, [if my children] see me like that, they may grow up like that, and I don't want them to have something like that. So I just learn how to control it. . . . I seen my parents and how they was and how they'd yell at each other and fight and stuff, and I told myself if I have kids I'll never want them to see me like that.

For Wayan, as for Aaron and many others, part of being a good father, and providing for his children's social and emotional needs, is raising them in the context of a good relationship with their mother.

Ann, twenty-eight, describes being similarly motivated to change how she behaved in her relationship once she became a parent:

> I wish that I was taught to be able to trust . . . [and that] it's OK to let some people you love in on your feelings and it's OK to show your feelings, because I used to bottle it up. I felt it was more convenient to just be quiet

and shut up, don't ever let nobody know my feelings. . . . The kids help me. Having kids and then it dawns on you, "I do not want them to grow up like I grew up." . . . And that's exactly what I do with these ones. I don't want them to think I don't love 'em. I try to show 'em, I tell 'em.

It was not just the birth of the first child that necessarily spurred these changes in parents. Ann hadn't been in a relationship with her older daughter's father, or any man since, so it's her more recent relationship with Trenton and the birth of their son, in addition to her role parenting her elementary school–aged daughter, that has prompted her to push herself to open up emotionally. Likewise, Evan, thirty-three, saw himself repeating some of the destructive behavior with the mother of his now preteen son that he had seen growing up. This motivated him all the more to do better in his more recent relationship with Hailey as they anticipated their baby's arrival:

> I learned how to drink and how to fight from my parents. . . . And it defi-
> nitely showed in my last relationship. I wasn't abusive, but I drank. And
> that's what breaks my heart with [my son], is that he's a really good kid,
> and I know that he's forgiven me 'cause I've changed so much, but he's
> seen things that he don't need to. That's why I want him to know that you
> can be with a girl, and it can be OK.

While Evan still is clearly in pain over the hurt he knows his past behavior inflicted on his son, he sees his new baby and new relationship as a second chance to get things right this time around.

Akira, twenty-two, and Ennis, twenty-four, share a bond in the wounds their upbringings caused, and the experiences of their youth also serve as a major motivator in their parenting. Akira's rape by a relative led to her being in foster care, including a variety of abusive homes. Ennis's mother, who was also abusive, raised him. Despite their current extreme material hardship—no utilities or furniture at times—and their occasional inattentiveness to their children, a by-product of their combining shift work with parenting three young children without any child care, Akira says, "We're the best parents that we can be." Ennis adds, "Not trying to live like our parents was living."

Their struggles to parent, to give their children a life better than they had, are apparent as Ennis quickly segues from describing his upbringing to how those experiences shape how he is as a father:

> [My mom] always put that in [my brothers' and my] faces, like "Oh, I wish I had flushed you all down the toilet." . . . So that really made me rebel. . . . I mean, it took me to have my kids to be a man now. Sometimes I still ask myself, "What is a man supposed to do? If you ain't got no money and your lights go off, what I am supposed to do?" It's tempting to go back out there and make a quick buck, but at the same time if I make a quick buck, get popped off, then [Akira]'s by herself with three kids. So I just step back and bust my butt at work and at home. But it's just . . . you know, what you learn from your parents is how you do not want to live. How you do not want your kids to be raised up.

Just learning from one's parents that being abusive is bad still leaves an awful lot unclear about what it means to successfully fill the roles of boyfriend, father, and, as Ennis says, man. Like so many others, Ennis wants to give his children a better life than he had growing up, but he doesn't have a clear picture in his mind of what he's working toward—an ideal he never experienced—let alone how to get there. His lack of anticipatory socialization into these roles has left them ambiguous, making him feel it's that much harder to fulfill them successfully. But it is crystal clear that he wants more—especially more love and security—for his kids than he and Akira had growing up.

Just as parents like Evan, Ann, Wayan, and Darren struggle to provide for their children financially, so too do they prize providing for their children emotionally—not just in the short term, with a hug or a loving word, but over the long term, with a set of social resources that can help them to create healthy relationships in adulthood. They see part of their role as parents as providing a context for their children's anticipatory socialization into healthy romantic partnerships. Evan's girlfriend, Hailey, explains, "I still want my son now to see that it's us, and we've got a strong bond, and we can communicate . . . so that they have some kind of grasp of, you know what, people can make relationships work. That not every relationship fails." Evan agrees. "I want [my son] to be able to know, to have the skills to be able to get married and stay married and teach his kids." As for financial poverty, parents want to avoid the intergenerational transmission of social poverty, hoping to give their children the social resources they lacked growing up. While parenthood leaves much less time for a couple to focus on their bond and adds a whole new element of stress to the relationship—that is, the parenthood role can make the achievement of the partner role more difficult—for many, a hotly pursued part of parenthood is parenting alongside a committed romantic partner. This underlines the presence and importance of social poverty in these young parents' lives. The desire for a stronger romantic relationship for themselves is at once a wish to address their own social poverty and prevent their children from experiencing the hardship that can come when their parents' union falters and fails.

Interactions between Role Transitions

Having children changes daily routines and self-concepts, as young adults stretch their emotional and relational capacities and behaviors to match the demands of the parenting role as they perceive them. Children are a motivator like no other, and each new baby offers the chance for redemption.[3] Parenthood brings feelings of adulthood, even if the other pieces of a responsible adult life aren't in place—a baby's demands don't stop just because you have no job or your car breaks down.[4] As the previous descriptions of the transitions to adulthood, partnership, and parenthood indicate, the processes of taking on these new roles interact with one another, facilitating and exacerbating the challenges of role transitions. We can see how the roles of emerging adult—marked by exploration and self-discovery—come into conflict with parenthood and partnership roles. For nearly all these young adults, the unsettled nature of emerging adulthood, with incomplete educations, unfulfilled career goals, and unstable employment, housing, and finances, contrasts with the expectations they carry for how parents and partners will act.

Becoming an Adult and a Partner

Many young adults find themselves in insecure economic positions. Previous research has extensively detailed the close relationship between finances and couples' willingness to marry, with even substantively small improvements in finances tied to a greater likelihood of walking down the aisle, as the symbolic value of finances is what seems to be of predominant importance.[5] Erica, twenty-two, describes how she talked her boyfriend, Joe, out of wanting to marry her when she got pregnant with their first child, in part for financial reasons. She constructs it as the responsible thing to do to *not* get married, given their difficult financial circumstances and with her only in her teens and him in his early twenties at the time. She told him, "Financially, we're about to have a child, we can't afford to get married." Once the social stigma of a nonmarital birth would mean a couple couldn't afford *not* to get married; today, the stigma of marrying with one's finances in disarray and the more pressing economic obligations of parenthood looming meant Erica and Joe were "priced out" of marriage.

In addition to hoping their finances will improve as they get older, couples expect that they will be more willing and able to "settle down" as they age out of the irresponsible behavior they see as common in young adulthood. Jim, thirty-five, says that while early on in his relationship "we had big spats and I left for the night or something," things have been different in the past year since he and Steffy married. "We agreed that we were grown up, and that's all kid stuff there, so let's find another option. . . . There's no saying, 'I'm leaving.' There's no walking out. There's get mad and get over it." It is important to note that there are certain relationship behaviors parents defined as immature: breaking up and getting back together, walking out in a huff, going to spend the night at Mom's in response to an argument. The expectation Jim and Steffy now hold for themselves is that they'll behave like adults, eschewing these volatile ways of managing conflict. For them, embracing productive conflict techniques is a marker of adult, rather than "kid," relationships.

We see how these relationships can evolve over time—and with maturation—from Norene, twenty-four, who is having her second child with Dave, twenty-nine. Right around the time she got pregnant with their older son, now three, the two split up. Norene explains why, laughing at her own youth: "I wasn't in the right [mind-set], I wasn't ready to settle down. 'Cause I was young and I wasn't ready to settle down, so I was still trying to be with him but also do what I do . . . so it didn't work out." Here we see how the self-centeredness of emerging adulthood—

wanting to "do what I do"—conflicts with the requirements of a committed relationship. The couple later reunited once Norene saw herself
as more grown-up—a change brought on by the baby's arrival—and saw
Dave show interest in being a father.

Marvin, thirty-six, looks back at his younger self with a wry eye, glad
that he waited to take on the roles of partner and parent until he got
older. Like Norene, Marvin had been together with his current girlfriend, Cara, years before, only to see the relationship end, for reasons
he attributes to their youth. Now back together and on solid footing,
the duo knows they have become different people, with a more mature
approach to their union. This time around, Marvin says, "We just came
together at the right time. I was in school [getting a bachelor's degree],
really really settled by now. . . . I wasn't gonna regress back to going
to the pool hall and drinking beers three nights a week anymore. . . .
I was looking for a career." Once their finances are right, the two plan
to marry, a choice Marvin thinks would have been ill-fated when they
were younger, due to their emotional, not financial, situation. "I don't
think you should [get married] when you're young, 'cause when you're
young, you're stupid. No matter how smart you think you are. . . . And
when I was younger, I was like 'Man, I know everything. I can do that.
I'm twenty now. I'm twenty-one! I've reached the apex of knowledge.' I
was stupid and reckless." He explains that this translates directly to how
a person approaches a romantic relationship:

> I think that if anything . . . you have a better chance of making it if you're
> more mature, 'cause you're willing to stick at it a little more. When you're
> younger, you're kind of stupid and more selfish. . . . You're really imma-
> ture. You still got that fire in you, so you still do a lot of reckless stuff. . . .
> So you don't really think about the consequences of what you do. You
> don't plan for the future. I think you have a better chance of making it
> work when you get older.

Here, Marvin perfectly captures how the cultural expectations of young
adults (that they aren't settled down, are irresponsible, and make rash
decisions) conflict with the role expectations of spouses, as committed
to one another and thoughtful about the future. That is, simultaneously

taking on the roles of young adult and partner risks role malintegration, with the demands of each in contradiction with the other.

The dangers of settling down young are captured in Hailey's description of her first marriage, at age nineteen, to her high school boyfriend, who is the father of her older son. "We were together for eight years, from the age of fifteen to twenty-three. And I sort of woke up one day and went, 'Oh my God! I'm a wife and mother? Where did my childhood go, where are my teenage years?' and I rebelled. We got a divorce. Did a lot of partying, living it up." Hailey is the poster child for Marvin's warnings about young people getting married. Her story also illustrates how our conception of young adulthood, as a time for drinking and partying, does not fit with the "confines" of marriage; after all, Hailey felt that to be a young adult—to truly act her age—she needed to divorce. She solved the malintegration of these roles by throwing off the confines of one. Unlike Marvin or Hailey, who are now in their midthirties, for so many of the young people walking into Family Expectations, the transitions to adulthood and partnership are simultaneously pressing issues. The joint and potentially conflicting nature of these transitions creates a risk for social poverty, by undermining their success in fulfilling their new roles as the expectations for and ability to fulfill the various roles and relationships—partner, friend, parent—may be ill-defined or clashing.

Becoming an Adult and a Parent

Parenthood forces people to contend with becoming adults,[6] a process that some see as good for making them grow up. But it also feels more complicated to become an adult and a parent at the same time. Hailey says that it's precisely because she's older and more mature with her second child that she's better prepared to be a parent than she was at twenty-one, when her older son was born. Just as she felt that her roles as wife and young adult were in conflict, so too were her roles of mother and young adult:

> I was always there [with my son], but I wasn't there. I mean, mentally, emotionally, I don't think that I was there. And I think with my age now, it's ten years later, I'm very stable financially. . . . [A]nd I do have the

tools that, you know, emotionally I want to be there for this child and not send it to the babysitter or whatever because I want to go party that weekend. So I just think that being there emotionally and knowing how to deal with this little person, this baby, it's just gonna be huge because I've learned so much in the last ten years.

Hailey feels that her previous attempts to simultaneously be a parent and a young adult were malintegrated roles; now, comfortably settled in adulthood, she is confident she'll do right by her baby this time around. Notably, she does not just say she's in a better financial position, but also a better emotional position, to be a parent.

Ashleigh, twenty, saw the adoption of the parent role as a welcome way to move out of the young adult role. She describes the conversation she had with boyfriend, Mark, twenty-one, before she got pregnant. "I was like 'We need a baby right now.' He's like 'No, we don't! Not on a KFC budget. No.'" Mark, a KFC employee, ultimately lost that debate. Ashleigh explains that she wanted a baby because "I was tired. I mean, yeah, normally nineteen-year-olds aren't like 'I want a family and I want to be married. . . .' I got tired of the wild life. I got tired of, you know, doing the bad thing. I wanted to try something right for once." As a high school dropout finding little success with employment, Ashleigh saw a child as the force she needed to propel her into adulthood. And, to some extent, it worked. She has left behind the "wild life" for the role of stay-at-home mom. "My priorities are taking care of [our daughter], make sure [Mark] gets what he needs, and my schooling. Yeah, my schooling's at the bottom of the list because I have him and her to think about first." This order of priorities, with her own pursuits as last on the list, is a hallmark many associate with adulthood, in contrast with the self-centeredness of the young adult years. The way Ashleigh resolves the potential malintegration of these roles is by prioritizing the roles of mother and partner over those of student and young adult.

Taleisha, twenty, is juggling work and single parenthood, now that her boyfriend, Darrell, isn't living with her and their baby. Although she wants to return to college, she's also hesitant because she's not sure she can successfully fulfill the roles of mother, employee, and student. She says she might reenroll in school in a few months—or a few years, once her baby is in kindergarten:

I really want to spend time with her while she's young, because I barely get to spend time with her now because with me working now she's always over my mom's house, well until I get off work, but by the time we make it back home, it's really, she's ready to go to bed, and then we got to get up and do it all over again.

Being so focused on her daughter hasn't just affected her educational plans. We hear from Taleisha how parenthood has led her to leave behind a central concern of young adulthood: her relationships with her friends. She explains that she's comfortable with her decision to prioritize time with her daughter over time with her friends:

I was just lying to them, like "Oh, OK, I'm gonna go out, I'm gonna go out," and then when it came time for us to go out I'd be like "I can't find a babysitter," you know, just making up excuses, but it's really 'cause I don't want to go out. Really, I'm in a place where I couldn't even enjoy myself if I was to go out. It's just not for me anymore. I'm just a mom now, and I'm so focused on her in my life.

Taleisha doesn't just take this as a natural part of life; rather, it's a marker of growing up and becoming an adult. She says, "I'm so proud of myself too." When young adulthood and parenthood conflict, men and women can feel they are left with a choice, as Taleisha was: maintain friendships or fulfill the parent role. Were they to enter parenthood at older ages, when their peers had also "settled down" more, socializing with friends might not be in conflict with being a parent. Chatting with other moms and dads as you push your kids on the swings or watch them splash through a sprinkler means you can integrate your roles as friend and parent. But when your friends don't start their night out until the time of your newborn's midnight feeding, the two roles don't mix. And so, these young adults are left to either lose social resources by estranging themselves from their friends or falling short in bonding with their children. That is, these role conflicts can create a risk of social poverty.

Becoming Partners and Parents

While some roles—like emerging adulthood and partnership or parenthood—seem to conflict, others are more mutually reinforcing. None of the couples in this study got pregnant from a one-night stand; rather, all pregnancies occurred in the context of a romantic relationship, with partnership paving the way for parenthood, albeit typically unplanned. Likewise, it was not uncommon to hear parents describe the birth of shared children as solidifying their relationship.

As mentioned earlier, parents often explained that one of the life experiences they most wanted to give their children was that of growing up with both their parents in a loving and healthy household—they saw this as a social resource. An investment in their own relationship, therefore, was a guard against their children's social poverty. Aaron, twenty-three, explains that their two young children have been a huge motivation for him and his wife, Illisha, to treat one another better: "Constant conflict and a lot of arguments around the kids, that's not good for them to see because that's all they're gonna think about and that's gonna mess [them] up." He describes their children as being a big reason for their recent decision to get married: "We love each other . . . and she don't give up on me and I don't give up on her, [and] especially for the kids, you know, instead of being separate and you both going all different places, rather [than] be around the kids. They need a father figure and a mother and it's best to see them together instead of separate."

Role theory reminds us that not all role transitions are created equal. Particularly relevant to the young parents in this study, role theorist Wesley Burr points out that tackling multiple role transitions simultaneously can be quite challenging, since so many norms and expectations change all at once.[7] This may be why these role transitions could be easier to navigate for those who take them on one at a time and in the traditionally normative order, with parenthood following the securing of adult roles—including stable employment and finances—and a committed partnership.[8] By the time the transition to the parent role occurs, the normative pathway would have people already transitioned out of the student role and into the employee role, out of the emerging adult's exploratory role and into the more stable adult role, and out of the single role into the partnered role. In contrast, when the transition to parenthood occurs before some or all of these are fully accomplished, the parenthood role asks that these other role transitions be tackled simultaneously.

We hear about the difficulties this can create in couples' stories of trying to successfully accomplish what is expected in their various roles. Hailey and Evan, both thirty-three, had begun their relationship during a time when each was acting young, partying and drinking often. Once an unplanned pregnancy forced them to sober up—Hailey literally and Evan figuratively—they discovered that the relationship dynamics they had developed during their "fun" time were not functional for a couple planning on marriage and parenthood. Hailey says they suddenly realized, "Hey, we never really communicated. We never talked. All we did was get mad and say 'OK, we're done. I'm leaving.' . . . I had to grow up and talk about my feelings. I needed to say 'This isn't OK,' but I need him to be a grown-up and say 'I hear what you're saying.'" Even though they'd identified the problem, solving it is no easy task, given their shaky foundation. Hailey's repeated use of the phrases "grown up" and "growing up" speaks to the triple role transition each was tackling: in addition to thinking about making a permanent commitment to one another and becoming parents together, they had to leave behind their more carefree early days to behave with the maturity of their actual ages.

For other couples, the demands of roles associated with emerging adulthood—like student—made it all the more challenging to fulfill the roles of partner and parent when taken on at the same time. Ken, thirty-six, and his wife, Laila, three-three, are go-getters when it comes to education, each already having a college degree under their belts. Laila, however, hasn't been able to convert her degree into a well-paid job, so when she unexpectedly got pregnant, it didn't make financial sense for them to pay for child care for a newborn, so she stayed home with the baby; she recently returned to work as a nursing assistant, hiding her advanced educational credentials from her employer to secure the job. They are able to make ends meet on Ken's IT shift work plus the extra from Laila's job, but they want a more comfortable life for themselves than their cramped, dark apartment currently provides, so Ken is enrolled in a master's program in engineering. He takes classes all morning and then works until ten o'clock at night. Laila's job is on the overnight shift, while Ken is home with the baby, then she sleeps until he needs to leave for class. The result, they explain, is that any attention to their partnership has fallen by the wayside. Juggling the demands of the student, employee, and parent roles is so taxing that there is no time or emotional energy left to be a couple. Laila says, "I'm like a roommate because you don't see each other. You don't communicate much, you just eat, sleep, and take care of bodily activities. Eat, sleep, go to school, go to work. So it's hard and financially it's hard because, you know, the baby has needs." While the relationship had thrived when they were working, going to school, and building their bond, the added demands of parent-hood were too much, pushing their relationship onto the back burner where, as Ken notes, it can be difficult to "keep that flame." That is, the demands of multiple, simultaneous roles raise the risk of social poverty, even if juggling so much at one time is a financial necessity.

The story we hear from Ken and Laila, one of the more financially se-cure couples in the study, shows the potential incompatibility—the role overload—of the time-intense labors of completing school, beginning a career, building a young relationship, and taking care of a newborn. Attempting these various role transitions simultaneously often creates stress and steals precious resources from the couple's relationship, leav-ing each partner with a shorter temper and feeling less emotionally sup-ported, possibly eroding the long-term possibilities of the union. And while stresses and strains in the transition to parenthood are common across all parents,[9] the changes to the partnership may be less threat-ening for those whose relationships are more firmly established before the child's birth. That is, having the key social resource of the romantic relationship firmly in place prior to the transition to parenthood means that the stresses of parenting present less of a risk of social poverty (just as having a fuller bank account means that a financial shock presents less of a risk of financial poverty).

Men's Transitions

In walking through this year of transitions with the parents in the study, I saw that fathers seemed to struggle more mightily with these changes than did mothers. While mothers certainly faced challenges, the cultural expectations of them were distinct from those for fathers. For example, Darrell and Darren describe their difficulties overcoming their criminal records to get jobs and, therefore, to find a permanent place to live, maintain their relationships with their girlfriends, and live up to their own expectations for a man, a father, and a partner. William Marsiglio and Kevin Roy, fatherhood scholars, describe role transitions for low-income men as likely to "move in fits and starts,"[10] which we see from both first-time father Darrell and father of four Darren.

Even as these men often fail to provide economically for their children, to call them "deadbeat dads" would miss the point. They want desperately to fulfill the traditional male provider role but have great difficulty doing so. And these difficulties can eat away at their willpower and commitment to fulfill their roles. Low-income young men are less likely to achieve educationally and move up the career ladder; they are seen as less "marriageable" and are less likely to keep up with their child support payments.[11] Taking on the roles of student, employee, partner, and parent, therefore, all represent opportunities to fail.

Role theory also leads us to expect that transitions may be particularly stark changes for low-income men.[12] Social scientists Lawrence Berger and Sharon Bzostek explain that "to the extent that the identity associated with the (resident- or nonresident-, biological- or social-) father role encompasses that of breadwinner or economic provider, disadvantaged men's struggles to provide economic support may impede the identity verification process for these men and their (current or prior) partners and/or children. This, in turn, may adversely influence family functioning and relationships."[13] As we heard from Darren, continuing to tackle the provider role with gusto is awfully hard when efforts are unappreciated and there's little hope for gainful, legal employment on the horizon.

Cordell, twenty-one, is immensely proud of his ability to support his girlfriend during her pregnancy. He explains, "I let her do what she can, but mostly I really don't be worried about what she can do, since I'm a man, I feel like I got to do, financial-wise, I take care of everything. That's what it is. . . . I love her so much that I just got to make it happen." His girlfriend, Lauren, twenty-three, says, "Cordell works and I just like . . ." Cordell jumps in to explain, "Do a little job." Lauren accepts his characterization of her work and continues, "Do a little job, and I pay the bills out of his [paycheck] and [mine] just stays in my bank account. That's it." While Cordell feels that the financial weight is on him, he also says that knowing there's some money in the bank from Lauren's paychecks "takes a little weight off" of him. As Cordell sees it, being the economic provider during Lauren's pregnancy and after the baby is born is part of being a "man," and it's an expression of how much he loves her.[14]

Cordell's role expectations were common, but, unlike him, some other fathers were frustrated by their inability to fulfill the demands of these roles as they desired. For men like Cordell, to be able to provide for their families on their earnings alone created feelings of worth and accomplishment, allowing them to find satisfaction in their roles as partners and parents. Conversely, for men like Darrell and Darren, failure in these roles led to frustration and disappointment in themselves. In some cases, this failure can be damaging to their romantic relationships, either from their partners' aggravation with them or from their own withdrawal in light of their failure.

Sociologists Kathryn Edin and Timothy Nelson engaged in an in-depth exploration of how disadvantaged men think about fatherhood.[15] They found that failing to fulfill their perceived roles as fathers and partners, as well as the reactions of partners and other community members to their failure, led some men to distance themselves from these roles, as they were in effect pushed away from their children and girlfriends. Other researchers have established that a lack of role "verification"—that is, the affirmation by others that one is fulfilling a role—and feelings of conflict over one's role-based identity are associated with poorer relationship quality, acrimony, and breakup.[16] This means that perceptions of one's success in the roles of partner and parent matter a great deal for the future of these relationships.

One of the avenues through which difficulties with role transitions create relationship problems is by eroding trust. As discussed in chapter 1, trust is built on a basis of expectations that are shared and fulfilled. As these young parents grapple with taking on new roles, partners can be left to wonder what to expect of one another. When he goes out with his friends, will he be thinking like a responsible family man or like a twenty-one-year-old boy? Such matters can be difficult to accurately anticipate when the man in question is both a twenty-one-year-old—trying to figure himself out and get established—and a father who talks of marriage with his girlfriend. Problems with trust and role transitions originate from the same forces—ambiguity of meaning, a lack of shared expectations, and instability. A troubled relationship, riddled with mis-trust, could make it more difficult to have the salience of this partner identity win out when in conflict with others. That is, a lack of trust could make role transitions more challenging.

These roles of partner and parent are intimately tied together, with greater father involvement linked to higher-quality relationships be-tween the parents.[17] The father's involvement during the transition to parenthood—taking part in doctor's visits for prenatal appointments or offering emotional and financial support to the mother, for example—is predictive of his involvement as a father after the child is born. Further, unmarried parents who are not living together at the time of the child's birth are particularly unlikely to stay together over the long term. And once fathers separate from the mothers of their children, their likelihood of remaining deeply involved in their children's lives plummets. While, in theory, our social norms may allow for partnership and parenthood to run on separate tracks, in reality they often remain a "package deal."[18]

Role Transitions and Family Expectations

The present and two preceding chapters introduce an important lens through which the Family Expectations program should be evaluated: as a resource for helping parents deal with role transitions and avoid role overload, ambiguity, and malintegration. As sociologist Leonard Cot-trell explained, the ease of role transitions is affected by "the degree of importance attached to and the definiteness of the transitional proce-dures used by the society in designating the change in the role."[19] Young, unmarried new parents may particularly need assistance because they are not using the social rituals that our culture has created to mark and ease role transitions: living on your own and supporting yourself finan-cially, having a wedding, having a baby shower, and so forth. While in many ways Family Expectations cannot substitute for these rituals, it could serve as an alternative mechanism through which parents can develop shared expectations and a sense of ownership and understand-ing of their new roles. By helping put in place these pieces, the program could play a part in addressing a cause of social poverty; couples could build stronger relationships and, from the other workshop participants and staff, gain a sense of community support for their relationships and receive verification of their parent and partner identities. As we have seen, when undertaken successfully, the transitions to parenthood and partnership can be mutually reinforcing, thereby strengthening the couple bond and the partners' ability to parent together, increasing the likelihood they can give their kids the family life they desire.

While the curriculum may focus on concrete communication techniques, we can look for deeper messages embedded in the program about who a father is or whether and how communication is an important part of a romantic relationship. In the absence of social rituals and norms for guidance, the program has the potential to reintroduce role expectations and transition guidance as parents adjust their self-identities and expectations of one another in their new roles. Particularly as they undertake an array of potentially destabilizing life transitions, this support and direction feel essential for those wishing for more secure relationships. The program's guidance offers to imbue their romantic unions with the key qualities—such as trust and understanding—they need to feel like real social resources. As a subjective experience, social poverty is dependent both on partners' expectations for one another and on the potential for their relationships to deliver on these expectations. Therefore, gaining a clearer set of expectations and raising the likelihood that partners can fulfill them is a potential pathway through which parents may feel Family Expectations is addressing their current needs. They are looking to Family Expectations to help them cultivate social resources for themselves and their children.

5

Family Expectations

Looking for Support

Tiana, twenty, and Stefan, twenty-one, have been together for the past four years. They did break up for about five months a year or so back, when their relationship collapsed under the weight of Tiana's struggles from being bounced between her father's, grandmother's, and foster mom's houses. Now, they say, they're stronger than ever and looking ahead to having their first child, a little girl, due in a few months.

We meet for the first time at the Family Expectations building. It's after hours, so the offices are closed, but we occasionally hear the cleaners in the background. It's far quieter, though, than it would be had we met at their house, where Stefan and Tiana live with his parents, brother, and grandmother. While they'd prefer to live on their own, this arrangement does allow the two to mostly make ends meet, splitting the bills evenly between their wages from her day care work and his hours at a grocery store.

Tiana looks young, with bright blue eyes and light freckles running across her nose. She has dyed black hair with lighter brown roots. A small green stud twinkles just below her lower lip off to one side, and when she talks, her tongue ring flashes. She's wearing a sleeveless blue tunic shirt over a distinctly pregnant belly. The straps are twisted up and interwoven with a tiny metal chain. Bright pink bra straps stick out from under the shirt.

Stefan has light blue eyes and a pudgy face. His hair is dyed blond, with darker blond roots; the top is long and floppy, and the sides are shaved close. He has piercings in his eyebrow and ear. He's wearing a metal necklace that has a cross-like symbol on it; this symbol is repeated in a tattoo on the inside of his forearm. He's wearing a black Insane Clown Posse T-shirt and baggy jeans with ragged ends and thick black skater-style sneakers. He has a black bandana tied around each wrist.

The two pride themselves on being different from everyone else, from how they look to how they act—they excitedly anticipate embarrassing their daughter in her teen years by reenacting knight-versus-dragon swordfights in the living room. In their shared differences, they find a deep comfort. Tiana says of Stefan, "He's my lifeline. He talks me through everything. . . . My personality completes his and vice versa." A life without Stefan, Tiana explains, "just doesn't make sense." In her words we can hear what an incredible social resource she has in Stefan, and so it is deeply important to her avoiding social poverty that they make their relationship last this time around.

Given her past, Tiana says, it's hard for her to trust that their relationship will go the distance. She's seen too many people, from parents to past boyfriends, walk out on her before. As she and Stefan look ahead to making a family life for their daughter, not repeating the past is a huge motivator. Tiana explains, "I think we pretty much have a moment every single day when we see his parents together or we talk about my parents and we're like, 'We are never going to be like that. Never.'" Stefan says he was open to coming to Family Expectations because he's always up for anything new and any opportunity to learn. For Tiana, the stakes feel higher: "Just learning to be happy with each other. Make it good for your child. I mean, that's really what we're in this whole thing about is for [our daughter]."

When they had arrived the first time to tour the facility, one look around sold them on the program. Stefan recalls thinking to himself, "You sit in Lay-Z-Boys [recliners] and watch a presentation and everything and they feed you? I'm cool!" Tiana laughs as she describes her first reaction to seeing the facility: "Can we move in?" While they are clearly motivated to build a strong family for their daughter, the program's well-appointed spaces and meals made Family Expectations feel like the right place to try to do so. But the people really mattered too. As Tiana explains, "It just seemed like they made things comfortable. I've taken parenting classes before for work and you're like 'Man, I don't want to be here.' But they made it feel really comfortable. When we first came in they were showing us everything and he was talking to us like he'd known us all our lives." Though the pair pride themselves on being social outsiders, feeling accepted, welcomed, and comfortable in a space was a draw.

When we first met, they had already attended a few workshop meetings, and Stefan was enjoying himself. He tells me:

> It's real fun. It's able to get a couple out, away from the hustle and bustle of life, away from their kids, even if their kids are in [the child care center], it gets them secluded, so they feel safe and away from all the stresses, able to just let go, even if it's just for an hour and a half. It's nice just to spend that time alone.

Tiana doesn't just want to escape stress; she hopes that Family Expectations will help them learn to cope with it too, especially because they're about to be parents. "Something as small as a glass of milk is like catastrophic to me when I'm stressed out, so learning how to deal with stress and put it to good use around [the baby] is what's important to me right now. 'Cause I'm not functional when I'm stressed out." Tiana knows life will spill many more "glasses of milk," and so she's banking on Family Expectations to provide them with some tools so such mishaps are not "catastrophic." And it's essential to her that Stefan is by her side through all this. After we're done with the interview, they stand up close, face to face, *almost* kiss, and then leave.

In this chapter I describe how couples like Tiana and Stefan find Family Expectations, why they say they want to attend, and the incentives and assistance that allow them to do so. I then lay out the parents' perceptions of the program's core components—workshops, educators, family support coordinators, and additional activities—as they are just beginning to participate. The present chapter focuses on what it's like to take part in Family Expectations—the *structures* of the program; the two subsequent chapters explore how participants experience the lessons of the program—its *content*—and see their participation as impacting their lives (or not), as well as what the existing research says about the efficacy of these programs. Using the social poverty lens, we can see how parents view Family Expectations' offerings as bringing the opportunity to strengthen or create badly needed social resources—what Tiana feels she needs for life to "make sense."

Beginning Family Expectations

Couples find their way to Family Expectations through a variety of paths. Some parents contact the program after hearing about it from friends, family, or acquaintances; Tiana and Stefan, for example, learned about it from her boss at the day care center where she works. In addition, Family Expectations' community relations and intake specialists are tasked with getting the word out about the program through prenatal care providers and childbirth classes; social service agencies that serve pregnant women and parents of young babies (e.g., the WIC program, which provides food assistance to pregnant woman and children under the age of five); and local advertising (e.g., family-related publications or baby stores). Although the program is not means-tested—anyone can participate regardless of income—the recruitment techniques are designed to draw in a predominantly lower-income group of families.

The program's advertising speaks to the family changes prospective participants are experiencing. For example, it uses slogans like "Grow as a couple as you grow as a family" to attract participants. "Having a baby is an exciting time, but it's also stressful. We all face challenges in our relationships. Family Expectations gives couples the tools to be successful during the exciting and challenging moments in a relationship," reads one headline.[1] This description conveys how the program attempts to normalize both the difficulties of partnership and parenthood and the idea of seeking help with these challenges. Notably, it does not mention marriage as part of its efforts to draw in couples. This is not false advertising; marriage is not a focus of the program once couples get through the door either. What couples are actively experiencing, therefore, is not "marriage promotion."

After their initial contact with the program by phone, couples visit for a facility tour and intake assessment, which determines their eligibility. Partners must be at least eighteen years old and willing to participate in the program together.[2] There is a domestic violence screening process, which takes place with partners in separate rooms during their visit; drawing on the advice of domestic violence organizations, Family Expectations staff discuss questionable cases to decide whether a couple who reports domestic violence may participate in the program or should be referred to other services instead.

Among the couples in this study, thirteen (42 percent) learned about Family Expectations from a family member, friend, or acquaintance; eleven (36 percent) through a social service agency; four (13 percent) through direct contact (e.g., Family Expectations staff at a baby expo); and three (10 percent) from a brochure or advertisement. After having experienced what Family Expectations had to offer, parents often reported referring someone they know to the program or being willing to do so (sometimes they didn't know anyone who was eligible to participate at the moment). Joanne, twenty-four, asked the program staff for Family Expectations posters to hang up at the massage therapy school she attended. Denelle, thirty-five, says with a laugh, "Even when I catch a cab, I give a brochure to the cab driver to give to his kids." Notably, even couples who had dropped out of the program continued to refer others to it. Twenty-three-year-old Lauren said that although the program wasn't for her, it could work for someone else, so when she learned her friend was having a baby, she encouraged her to check out Family Expectations.

Family Expectations staff report serving approximately 2,000 parents each year.[3] Although the present study focuses on unmarried participants, these parents make up just over half of participating couples; the others are married when they enroll. Across marital status, however, Family Expectations couples tend to be socioeconomically disadvantaged. The average annual family income is less than $20,000; one in four participants have neither a high school diploma nor a GED; and four out of five have incomes low enough that their child's birth is funded through Medicaid (putting them at an income level of 200 percent or less of the federal poverty line). Participating parents tend to be young, with 44 percent under the age of twenty-four. The program draws a racially diverse group: 31 percent black, 46 percent white, and 23 percent Hispanic or of some other race/ethnicity.[4]

Participation Assistance and Incentives

Relationship education curricula had originally been used with predominantly middle-class audiences, who paid to attend weekend workshops to strengthen their marriages. In response to welfare reform's call in 1996 for programming to strengthen romantic relationships among lower-income couples, plans were made to adapt these original curricula for a new constituency. However, there were concerns that getting lower-income participants in the door and attending consistently would be challenging. Between transportation difficulties, a lack of child care, and an array of other pressing obligations demanding their attention, regular program participation among low-income couples might have been rare. In response, Family Expectations attempts to overcome the obstacles that may prevent couples from attending and to offer further incentives to make consistent attendance a priority.

Parents can receive help with transportation and child care, as described in the introduction to this book. Parents have to sign up for on-site child care in advance to ensure the proper child-adult ratio, and they receive a pager when they drop off their child, allowing staff to contact them if necessary (such as if a baby needs to be nursed). The price of breaking down barriers to program participation looms large, constituting a substantial portion of program costs.

In addition, couples receive an array of incentives for participating in Family Expectations. Many of these rewards come in the form of Crib Cash, a currency that is the tender of the on-site "store." Couples receive Crib Cash at regular intervals for completing a certain number of hours of the program. While some spend their Crib Cash as it comes in, buying an item or two during their office visits or workshops, other couples save their Crib Cash, using it to buy larger items or waiting until a certain time (such as when their baby is born) to spend their "money."

The combination of participation assistance and incentives is a boon to financially strapped families. Carley, a first-time mother in her early twenties, explains:

> Sometimes I've gotten that ten-dollar gas coupon and been like almost on empty, you know, from running around that week, and that gets me through the week. And we've gotten stuff from their little store.... [W]e really wouldn't have the cash to go bulk up on diapers, but . . . since we take the classes . . . we don't have to stress about diapers and wipes because we have the money on our Crib Cash card to do that, and it's just been beneficial in so many ways. Just taking a lot of stress off us.

Like Carley, many parents describe using their Crib Cash to buy diapers and other basics; some explain that they have a crib, car seat, or baby activity mat thanks to their Crib Cash. Miranda, twenty-seven, says, "That was how we got all our baby stuff." Her boyfriend, Carl, twenty-four, explains, "We had this car seat and stroller picked out . . . since we first started in there. . . . We finally got it about the eighth or ninth class. We had to save up our Crib Cash."

For Mackenzie and Wayan, in their early twenties and already parents of two little girls, their Crib Cash proved essential. When their third baby was born early—a complication related to Mackenzie's cancer that doctors had discovered during her pregnancy—they weren't prepared to bring the baby home, and some of the baby items they already had on hand wouldn't work for their preemie. Both out of work, they didn't have money to spare, but they did have Crib Cash. So, Mackenzie says, "When she was born, we didn't . . . have all the stuff set up, but we had Crib Cash still and came up here and got her . . . a swing type thing 'cause she can't sleep in a bed 'cause she's so little." Couples find that they have resources—like Crib Cash and gas cards—just at a time, with the arrival of their new baby, when they're less likely to have income and more likely to have expenses.

Furthermore, for low-income parents who may otherwise rely on hand-me-downs, gifts from family, and baby items from the infant crisis center, the ability to buy items such as new toys, books, baby seats, and humidifiers with money they earned through their program participation feels good. Because they've done something to get the Crib Cash and because it's coming from people they like and feel supported by, these purchases don't leave people feeling like supplicants. As with the other aspects of Family Expectations, the way in which the program is delivered plays an essential role in couples' positive experiences with it.

Like the leather recliners and framed photographs on the wall, the participation assistance and incentives could be seen as frivolous expenditures—the Family Expectations program certainly could be financially leaner, and a more substantial proportion of program expenses could be spent on direct couple services. However, the way in which couples experience these "frivolous" features of the program begs the question of how essential it may be to attend to the program's atmosphere as a component of a social service program, akin to having a knowledgeable staff and a culturally sensitive curriculum. The environment—flickering fluorescent lights, curling linoleum floors, and banged-up metal folding chairs versus restored exposed brick walls, knit throws, and well-maintained flower beds surrounding the entrance—makes a difference. A few of the couples specifically contrast the nice setup at Family Expectations to other programs. Cara, a mother in her thirties with a toddler and another baby boy on the way, says, "The whole environment of it was . . . maybe this feeds into my snobbishness . . . , [but] it wasn't all cheap and generic, like I thought it would be." Trenton, twenty-nine, compares Family Expectations to the Department of Human Services, which runs the state's cash and food assistance programs, when he jokes, "Why aren't they running DHS?!"

Critics could point to the need for incentives as evidence that couples don't actually want to come to Family Expectations, that they have a transactional relationship with the program—attending only to procure goods. And, at first, as they are getting to know the program, couples do talk quite a bit about the baby items and gift cards they are looking forward to receiving as incentivizing their interest and program attendance. However, after they have been more extensively involved in the program, the way they talk about these incentives changes. First, the incentives are mentioned much less; while they were commonly discussed during the first round of interviews, fewer than half of the couples (twelve of twenty-eight) mentioned them during the second round of interviews, just three months later.[5]

Second, particularly during the later rounds of interviews, incentives were generally discussed as a "bonus" rather than as a reason to attend in and of themselves. In fact, some parents are critical of others who, in their opinion, are there "just to get some money" rather than "genuinely trying to learn how to be parents," as Darren, a twenty-nine-year-old father of four, puts it. A year after enrolling, he explains that the way he saw the incentives changed as he started to participate in the program:

> Of course, I went for the hundred bucks, two hundred bucks. [But then] I lost sight of that when I got there. You know, I forgot all about the money. That was weird for me. But, yeah, it helped me out. It did help me out a lot. You know, I understood that [my girlfriend] was going through her own set of things. . . . We loved that place.

This shift in the discussion of participation incentives is indicative of the increased value couples attach to the relationship lessons and their personal relationships with staff. Prior to participating, they can more easily recognize the value of the financial incentives, while the value of participating in a relationship education program is harder to gauge. Once they are involved in the program, these incentives become worth relatively less to couples as other aspects of the program gain a more concrete, and valuable, worth in their eyes.

Why Do Couples Come to Family Expectations?

Couples are drawn to Family Expectations by a combination of factors. They feel they aren't on stable ground or sure they can achieve the family dreams they have for themselves. This feels particularly pressing because they are bringing a new baby into the world, with the fresh start and all the positive possibilities for the future this implies.

Parents often gave several, related reasons for choosing to participate in Family Expectations.[6] Primary among these was a desire for an improved relationship, described by twenty-three couples (74 percent). Although Robert, a twenty-one-year-old first-time father, and his girlfriend, Elyse, have been together for several years, he says their relationship could still use some work. "If it's something that can help me understand her and her personality and emotions a little bit better, and how to cope and deal with those little situations . . . , that's what I'm expecting to get out of this right now. 'Cause, I mean, sometimes I just can't figure her out." Like Robert, other parents commonly expressed a desire to communicate more effectively and experience less conflict in their relationships.

As we heard earlier from Tiana and Stefan, the need for such relationship improvement was often discussed in the context of having a baby and creating the right environment in which to raise a child. Experiences of parental separation, divorce, conflict, and abuse in childhood were quite common among the parents, leaving many desperate to spare their own children the experiences they had suffered while growing up. It was only in one of the thirty-one couples that both partners were raised by their stably together parents.

Additionally, eleven couples (36 percent) described a desire to be better parents as motivating their participation in Family Expectations; these were more likely to be the first-time parents who were anticipating a dramatic life change with the arrival of their newborn. As Lauren puts it:

> I think when you're young, having a baby brings on so many different challenges and emotions, and I think it's nice to have somebody who helps you break down the way that you're feeling and stuff. I like that. And also just like [finding out about] all the different resources that are available to you [in the community] that you had no idea that were available to you.

Other reasons for program participation were less common: six couples (19 percent) described wanting to find friends or peers who were going through the same experiences as they were (i.e., building a family); five (16 percent) said the financial incentives (e.g., items for the baby) drew them in; and five (16 percent) explained that they hoped to experience personal growth (e.g., grappling with trust issues from childhood) as a result of their participation. Overall, between those drawn in to strengthen their relationships, to give their children a good family life, and to find friends with whom to share their experiences, nearly all couples were arriving at Family Expectations' doorstep trying to find an answer to social poverty. In their hopes for the program, we hear about the possibilities they saw in Family Expectations for meeting their social needs in various ways—bolstering a partnership, developing an environment of strong ties in which to raise their children, and creating new friendships or feelings of shared experience. Therefore, we can examine the Family Expectations program to see the extent to which it fulfills the goals participants—rather than academic evaluators or journalists—have for it.

Gender Dynamics in Participation

It was typically women who were initially more interested in and who followed through on having the couple participate in the program. It did not take long, though, for the men to get on board. The initial visit to the facility and the intake interview were generally all it took to get men interested in and, for many, even excited about the program.

For some couples, the woman said she wanted to take part in Family Expectations and her partner was happy to oblige. Some men described their initial willingness to go as something they were doing to make their girlfriends happy. Dave, a twenty-nine-year-old father of two, with another on the way, thought to himself, "There must be something that caught her eye, so I'll support her and I'll go." Other men, however, were a bit more resistant at first.

Marvin, thirty-six, has raised his girlfriend's son since the boy was born, and the couple is now expecting their first child together. He explains, "I was very skeptical. . . . I was thinking it's gonna be some third-rate program. We're gonna go into some auditorium and listen to some seminar. It's gonna be boring . . . rehashed stuff you can probably hear on the nightly news type of thing. Totally worthless, but maybe we can get some financial gain out of this." After he did the intake interview and got to know the program better, his thinking changed. As he tells me, "It sounds like an incredible [program]. . . . I think that their, the way they're trying to help you deal with, you know, handle your relationships and stuff, and how to communicate, how to resolve differences without getting into shouting, and how to raise a kid together and the importance of that. I think it'll be very helpful."

Some women take a more surreptitious route to getting their partners involved in the program. A few told stories of how they decided they were interested but knew their partners would give them grief about going; thus, they just signed up for an intake interview and let their partners know about it on the scheduled day. Denelle told Otis they were going once the cab was on its way to pick them up. He says he thought that in the program "people gonna be in my business, 'cause I'm to myself. I mean my parents can't pry stuff out of me. Once I got talking to . . . [Family Expectations intake worker] John, he put it down. He brought it to us the right way." Otis, who'd been reluctant to get in the cab, was immediately won over.

Notably, men can and do articulate what they hope to get out of the program beyond these financial incentives and the chance to kick back in a recliner. For many, these are general wishes, like learning more about babies, relationships, or better ways to communicate. Others are more specific, describing how it is important for them to learn to better cope with stress, particularly given the new baby, and to learn how to be closer and stronger as a couple. A few even explain that they see taking part in Family Expectations as a make-or-break, last-ditch effort to save their relationships. Luke, twenty-two and with his first child on the way, describes what he hopes to get out of the program: "Something. Something to change our relationship. Something. . . . Just how to get along with each other, really. 'Cause this is the last . . ." He trails off, leaving unsaid the seemingly imminent breakup on the horizon.

Conventional wisdom may have it that men would not touch any type of relationship class with a ten-foot pole. And conventional wisdom is correct—but only at first. Men are not likely to find out about these programs or pursue becoming involved, but they are willing to follow their female partners' lead.[7] Men who participate in these programs are not some rare breed who enthusiastically take part in relationship classes. They are won over by what the program has to offer and interested not only in the incentives but also in the hope the program gives for strengthening their relationships and helping them learn to be better fathers.

Hopes for Participation

These young people are drawn to Family Expectations by the desire to create a firmer foundation for their family lives. Many are struggling—personally, financially, as a couple—and the program seems to offer a way of anchoring and improving their lives. Taleisha, twenty, and her boyfriend, thirty-one-year-old Darrell, wanted to have a baby. Taleisha felt ready for the challenge, and Darrell thought that at his age, it was high time he had a child. Yet, the reality of making their relationship last and raising their daughter together has proved daunting. Taleisha looks to Family Expectations to provide some clarity and direction:

> I would say [I'm looking to get] more of an understanding about relationships and parenting. 'Cause if we was going through it on our own, we be like, "This ain't supposed to happen. Is this normal?" But if you hear another couple say that they have the same problem or their kid is doing the same thing, you have more understanding, like, "Oh, this is normal." 'Cause with us both being first-time parents, I think it'd be more of an understanding that we get out of the program from other couples and the mentors and stuff like that, telling us about family life, 'cause this is both new to us. I just want the program, basically, to just give us an idea or an understanding of letting us know that, you know, we are in a relationship

and there will, we will have conflict and it's going to happen and it's not the end of the road whenever we do have conflict or an argument. That's not the end. That's just a normal thing that every couple go through. So I feel like talking to the other couples about problems or little conflicts that they have, I feel like they be looking more like we have the same argument and they still together so that don't mean we have to leave each other and break up just because of a little argument.

Lacking social resources—a community of friends and family to provide this sort of guidance, Taleisha makes clear that she is searching for social norms and is hoping the program can provide what its name promises: a set of *expectations* for *family* life. Like many others, this couple doesn't have confidence, based on their previous relationships and what they've seen of romantic relationships from others, in their own ability to recognize what is normal, acceptable, and healthy. And even though she is able to say in advance that conflict is a normal part of a long-term romantic relationship, she is looking to have this sense reinforced by program staff and other couples. As we heard from Stefan and Tiana at the start of the chapter, a central lesson they took away from their parents was what not to do in a relationship, which is far from a comprehensive guide to building a family life together.

This experience of searching for norms was not unique to young, first-time parents like Taleisha, however. Trenton, a thirty-nine-year-old father, has a daughter in elementary school, with another baby on the way. He felt like he did everything right the first time around to guarantee him the happy, stable family life he desired: he got married, worked hard, and brought home his paycheck. Yet, here he is divorced, seeing his daughter only on weekends. In his winding way of talking, he explains that his disillusionment and confusion have left him hoping Family Expectations can show him the way forward with his current girlfriend, Ann:

I don't know how, what a stable family structure looks like. [Growing up] it was just my mother there, she did a good job, never wanted for anything, but it was just us there. So, OK, someone to help us work on things. . . . [I]f you can realize while you're going through it that you're at a crossroads and how you go about things, I think it helps.

Like Taleisha and so many others, Trenton comes to Family Expectations looking for guidance.

In part, couples are looking for the sorts of concrete relationship techniques that make up the Family Expectations toolbox (detailed in subsequent chapters). Yet, at a deeper level, many are searching for a sense of what is right, what is normal, and what is expected. The program offers, in a sense, an antidote to the consequences of social poverty. Trenton did what he figured was expected of him, but with his limited knowledge—never having seen how a father and husband acts in a family—and in light of his previous failure, he comes to Family Expectations searching for a guide to navigate future "crossroads."

In more culturally restrictive eras, such direction was more readily available, as chapter 1 discussed. This was, at best, a double-edged sword. Couples like Trenton and Ann may not have existed or, at the very least, would have struggled with social ostracism in previous eras—her first child never had a father in the picture, Trenton is divorced, they are an interracial couple, and they are living together and having a child outside of marriage. The norms against nonmarital cohabitation and childbearing, interracial relationships, and divorce have relaxed or disappeared; but so too have socially set expectations for what each partner is meant to contribute to a relationship and how each should behave. This gives Trenton and Ann more freedom to create their family life according to their own wishes, but they are left to do so without the guidance or expectations offered by social strictures. Like so many others, they feel like they're wandering through a forest without a marked path or a map. They hope that Family Expectations can show them the way forward.

Couples' Experiences with Family Expectations Services

Workshops

Couples enjoy their time in the Family Expectations workshops. The workshops are frequently described as "fun," and couples respond strongly to the program staff and workshop leaders, who are viewed as friendly and warm. Stefan and Tiana, whom we met at the start of the chapter, so enjoyed their time at Family Expectations that they volunteered to be a host couple, allowing them to continue attending even after their year in the program was up. Tiana says, "We weren't ready to leave. . . . You make good friends." Stefan gladly covers up his floppy hair with a hat and dons plastic gloves and an apron to serve meals to the newest Family Expectations couples. Even though the other participants from their time in the workshops wouldn't be there, Tiana and Stefan wanted to remain in the warm environment Family Expectations offered, with its friendly staff and feelings of fellowship among new parents. For the pair, this felt like a valued social resource to hold onto.

Stefan and Tiana's enthusiasm for the workshops was common among couples. In fact, the reactions of women whose relationships ended during their time in the program are particularly telling. Hailey, a thirty-three-year-old mother of two, married and divorced Evan during the year she was involved in the program. Family Expectations did not save their relationship as they had hoped it would. As their relationship soured, so too did Evan's feelings about the program. Hailey reports that he started hating to go and described it as "ghetto" due to the presence of visibly low-income couples in their workshop. But, even after they separated, Hailey felt she was getting so much from the program that she continued attending on her own.

For Ciara, a twenty-one-year-old mother with a toddler and a newborn, it was, in part, her ex-boyfriend's reaction to Family Expectations that brought her some clarity about their relationship, encouraging her to leave an unhealthy union. She says that before breaking up with Drew she made many attempts to make their relationship work. She explains, "We tried Family Expectations, and he stopped going to the workshops and I still went. It . . . disappointed me when he stopped 'cause I really enjoyed those classes. It's fun. And then I set up counseling for us and he never showed. And then, just tried talking to him, he didn't want to listen. So . . . I tried." Going to a relationship class by yourself might be intimidating, but like Hailey, Ciara describes having a positive experience: "Everyone was still supportive and I just made up excuses why he couldn't come and I still wanted to be there and learn. I liked it. I'd do it again if I could. . . . I learned a lot. Like just . . . about myself. And I learned a lot about what Drew wasn't and what good people are." Being around the supportive staff and seeing how other couples interacted with each other was eye-opening for Ciara:

The good people are like everybody that's there. The educators are amazing and couples I met are, I don't know if they're like in love for real or
they were putting on a front like me and Drew. There are single moms in
there sometimes. Single moms now. Just a good atmosphere. I think that
was my place to escape to.

We hear in Ciara's words what a social resource this was for her, being
surrounded by positive, supportive people. Ironically, in a relationship
education program, she found an "escape" from her relationship.

Besides Evan and Drew, a few other participants were less enthused
about Family Expectations, even though their relationships didn't end.
Cordell, twenty-one, and his girlfriend, Lauren, twenty-three, stopped
attending their workshop after their baby boy was born, with three of
their ten sessions remaining. Although they enjoyed meeting with their
family support coordinator, Cordell felt uncomfortable with other couples' open displays of emotion and revelations of personal information
in their group workshop.[8] This coincided with a particularly trying time
in their own relationship, as they struggled over trust issues. Because
Cordell didn't see their problems getting resolved while participating
in the workshops, he felt frustrated to be spending so much time on
something that didn't seem to be effective. As part of withdrawing from
Lauren, Cordell also withdrew from the program. And while their relationship survived this tough time, their participation in Family Expectations did not. By the time they were back on more solid footing, more
than six months had passed since they had attended their last workshop,
and they weren't trying to go back.

Overall, twenty of the thirty-one original couples (65 percent) completed their workshop sessions; in addition, five other couples completed
all but one or two of the workshop sessions as of my last contact with
them, meaning that approximately four out of five couples in my sample
received all or nearly all of the curriculum.[9] This far surpasses participation rates among the programs included in the federally funded Building
Strong Families (BSF) study of relationship education programs for unmarried parents, which included more than 5,000 participants. Across
all eight BSF sites, only 55 percent of couples even attended one workshop meeting, and less than one-third of couples completed half or more
of their workshop hours. At Family Expectations during its participation

in the BSF study, 73 percent of couples attended at least one session, and 45 percent completed 80 percent or more of program hours.[10] After the conclusion of the BSF study, the participation rates at Family Expectations rose. In 2009, the year in which I began data collection, more than 81 percent of couples attended at least one session after enrolling, and 62 percent completed at least five workshop sessions. In this way, the couples in the present study are quite similar in their attendance patterns to the general Family Expectations population.[11]

Educators

Couples are enthusiastic about their workshop educators.[12] They find the educators entertaining and feel that they care about them as people; parents' reasons for liking the educators are more personal than professional. They generally do not emphasize educator characteristics like being knowledgeable or well prepared, but rather being funny, caring, and personable and making them feel comfortable. This again highlights the relational element of what encouraged couples to continue participating in Family Expectations.

Zach, who is in his early twenties, describes his educators this way:

> Fred was kind of laid-back, but cool, always trying to kick it and just hang out. Greg was always cracking jokes and making fun of somebody and picking on somebody. He was a clown. That's for sure. You know, they were cool. They were all, on a personal level, not necessarily just trying to instructor you. They would try to get to know you on a personal level.

For Zach, as for many others, it was important to feel that the workshop educators knew him—he wasn't just a person in the audience but instead had a relationship with them.

Necie, a first-time mother in her early twenties, was pleasantly surprised by the educators: "They opened up, and, I mean, I just think they made me feel comfortable. I thought it was gonna be a case of where I didn't feel like being there or it wasn't gonna get my attention and they kept me, they kept me paying attention and most people can't." People like hearing personal stories from educators, and they enjoy the workshops' interactive nature. What Necie and Zach emphasize is the importance of the bond they felt with their educators to their buy-in to the program.[13] Educators, they say, cared about and were vulnerable with participants, sharing with them and letting participants learn from their own foibles and struggles. Family Expectations, therefore, was not solely addressing their feelings of social poverty in terms of their romantic relationships, but in their ties to others as well.

The features parents describe disliking in their educators are annoying voices or boring presentation styles (like reading directly from their notes, rather than speaking freely), but there seem to be more "funny," "cool," and "awesome" educators than "boring" ones. Men seem to particularly like the male educators, and women also seem to prefer the male educators when they do list a favorite by name. This may be because the male educators were more often described as the "funny" ones and because both men and women liked having constructive male role models.

In some ways this is a classroom-like environment with teachers standing up front and written materials distributed in binders, but couples rarely compare attending Family Expectations workshops to being in school. As Zach notes, they do not "instructor you." The result is that couples find material is accessible and "real," applicable to their daily lives and relationship problems. The next chapters will explore whether and how parents make use of these workshop lessons.

Family Support Coordinators

POSITIVE EXPERIENCES

Couples can form long-lasting relationship with their family support coordinators, with whom they meet throughout their year of program participation, away from the group workshops.[14] During these meetings, family support coordinators work with couples on setting and pursuing goals (around budgeting, education, employment, etc.), reinforce lessons from the workshops (such as communication techniques), and offer information on services in the community that the couple may need (e.g., WIC or low-cost medical clinics). In addition, these meetings give couples a more private space than the workshops provide for talking about some of their personal and relationship struggles, all with a mediator present. In addition, parents said family support workers were nice, someone to talk to, understanding, and nonjudgmental.

Ruby is in her late twenties and has few friends other than her boy-friend, Anthony; she has a strained relationship with her family, who has custody of her older kids. Given the couple's dire financial circumstances and Anthony's unmet financial obligations to his older daughters, his parents were also less than thrilled to learn they were expecting a new grandbaby. However, Ruby describes her family support coordinator as being "like a grandfather" when they first took their newborn in for an office visit. She explains, "He just took several pictures of all three of us together and then she grabbed my finger and he's like 'Oh! I have to take a picture of that!' He's just funny." For Ruby and Anthony, their family support coordinator's excitement over their daughter's arrival contrasts with the negative reactions of their own families. This illustrates how Family Expectations creates social resources for couples who are often lacking such supports. In their interactions with their family support coordinator and other Family Expectations staff—unlike in interactions with their families—their identities as parents and as a family are affirmed.[15]

These relationships between couples and family support coordinators are important because they build trust, allowing the couple to open up about their needs and family support coordinators to better target their support. Wayan, a father to three with his girlfriend, Mackenzie, was won over by their family support coordinator's interest in how they were doing. Wayan has been struggling for years to gain steady employment, an issue about which his family support coordinator has been helpful. He says, "For me, I think [our family support coordinator] sold me that she really cared about how we was doing and stuff. She always asked about it. You know, did you find a job? Help you try and find a job and all that stuff. That's what I really liked about her." As for Ruby, Wayan's family support coordinator is stepping up where some others in his life have not. Whereas he feels his father, who raised him, never taught him many skills related to finding or keeping a job, his family support coordinator has been offering such support. Beyond information about possible job programs and training courses, there is an important psychological element to this assistance. Wayan clearly doesn't feel stigmatized by his family support coordinator for struggling to find employment, falling short of his goal of financially supporting his family. Rather, Wayan describes her as "somebody out there on your side, trying to help you get ahead." The descriptions couples offer of their relationships with their family support coordinators are certainly quite different than those we might expect to hear about other caseworkers, such as those from the welfare office; the former are marked by support and trust, while the latter commonly involve mutual suspicion.[16]

NEGATIVE EXPERIENCES

Some participants dislike their family support coordinators, such as when personalities or expectations clash. Laila thought her family support coordinator wasn't very responsible; in her view, he didn't do what he said he would, he wasn't prompt in getting them information, and he was disrespectful if she called him out on these things. After she complained to a supervisor, the coordinator's behavior improved. Carley initially disliked her family support coordinator, with her disdain evident during our first two interviews. By the third interview, however, things had changed. She explains, "I love her. She's awesome. At first I didn't like her because she was honest. I was like 'Will you just shush already?' But I think that she's very nice and helpful, really just sometimes you need someone who sees [your relationship] from both point of views, even though I was only wanting to see it from mine."

For Ashleigh and Mark, however, their issues with their family support coordinator never got resolved. After missing a class when Ashleigh was sick, the pair was unsure whether they could attend the subsequent class or not. When a call to their family support coordinator went unreturned and the next class came and went, they basically wrote off the program. By the time the coordinator got back to them, they had already decided they were done. As for Laila, Ashleigh, and Mark, when couples did complain about their family support coordinators, issues most commonly focused on communication breakdowns (e.g., not receiving a promised follow-up e-mail or a delay in returning a phone call).

Staffing turnover did interfere with some couples developing the sorts of relationships with their family support coordinators that others found beneficial. While not common, a few couples described having two or sometimes three different family support coordinators during their time in the program. Such couples did not describe the types of personal and trusting relationships I heard about from others, or they saw such relationships with their first family support coordinator interrupted by his or her departure. This may be particularly problematic given the more intense nature of couples' investment in the program in the beginning. With participation fading after the workshops are over (discussed later), parents seemed to feel less of a reason to build a relationship with a new coordinator when their contact with the program was already waning. Abby, a twenty-two-year-old mother, explained that being assigned different family support coordinators contributed to their never finishing the workshops (with one session remaining):

> They kept changing [our family support coordinator]. . . . [W]e just said, "OK, y'all keep changing it and we're having our own situation," so we kind of just left. . . . I don't know if they're going through, have a lot of changes right now or what, but it was kind of frustrating because it was a really good program and we were getting a lot out of it. . . . I saw three different [family support coordinators]. One of 'em, she had to go on maternity leave, which is understandable, so I met with a new one and then she was gone, so I met with her supervisor and . . . we got a letter saying that we had another one and I never met her.

Issues with communication and staff turnover could be seen purely as operational matters. However, when we view them through the lens of social poverty, we see how important these factors can be to shaping participants' experiences in their programs.[17] Because family support workers are building relationships with participants—and this is an aspect of the program that parents very much enjoy—even seemingly small missteps, such as a phone call that is not returned, can be deeply disruptive to parents' participation. Their buy-in to the program occurs, in part, through their personal relationships with staff. And like their relationships with one another, the development of trust is key and is quickly undone by (in)actions that communicate a lack of investment in the relationship by the family support coordinator. Program management should be seen as part of—rather than apart from—curriculum, recruitment, and retention efforts. It is part of building the social resources participants value.

RESOURCES AND REFERRALS

Beyond the personal side of these relationships, the other major feature couples list in describing their family support coordinator meetings is the information they receive about programs and services in the community. These run the gamut from referrals to programs that provide assistance with résumé writing, job training, and additional parenting courses, to charitable and government services that offer free car seats and food or utility payment assistance.[18]

Abby describes how her family support coordinator "helped me get set up with a WIC office, so that, she helped me find one close to me. . . . But there was like a three-page list of clothes, food, shelter." She remarks with a laugh, "That was neat too, because like I know you can, if you're out here looking for resources, you can kind of run around in circles."

One family support coordinator explained that, for many couples, she and her colleagues serve almost as "Google," acting as a search engine that can explore the overwhelming amount of information out there and return those "hits" that are most relevant to a couple's expressed needs.[19] Although couples are happy to have this information that is specific to their interests, they don't necessarily make use of the information family support coordinators provide.

There are several reasons for the disconnect between the amount of information family support coordinators provided and what couples actually used. First, some information couples expressed interest in was not needed at that time. For example, a couple may want to know more about pediatricians but still be months away from their child's birth. Second, some couples do not do a great job pursuing the services in which they are interested. Couples receive phone numbers or websites from their family support coordinators, and it is their job to call these numbers or go online and apply for programs; some don't follow through. Third, family support coordinators approach couples' use of information with the attitude that it is important for couples to do for themselves.[20] That they do not make calls or fill out applications on behalf of couples is a deliberate approach to case management. They have decided couples should learn how to secure assistance and services for themselves, particularly given the relatively short period of time they participate in Family Expectations. Family support coordinators may provide support, encouragement, and reminders, but their intent is to empower couples to act in their own interest. Staff have decided there is a worthwhile trade-off between the amount of services couples access in favor of their learning to do so on their own.

In line with the way parents experience the setting and friendly environment—as welcome program participants, not recipients of government assistance—these resource referrals don't leave people feeling stigmatized. One reason a few couples didn't follow up on referrals is because they didn't want to get help from programs that are meant for those they see as more disadvantaged than themselves; there certainly is an underlying shame associated with receiving such help. However, while some of the programs themselves (e.g., public housing) may place a black mark on their recipients, receiving a referral to them within this context doesn't seem to. Lauren says, "I don't think this makes you feel like you're in a bad circumstance to be aware of those things." And her boyfriend, Cordell, concurs, "They make you feel like you doing right, and they're gonna just help you with more to get to your goal."

In rare cases, in which a couple is experiencing deep financial distress, family support coordinators can request flex funds from their supervisor for specific expenses; all expense requests approved by the supervisor also must be OK'd by the CFO of Family Expectations' parent company. Requests are only granted for expenses that are expected to be onetime or short-term (e.g., funeral costs); the funds are not meant to replace or supplement regular monthly budgets. For example, one mother in this study who called the police after her drunk boyfriend hit her found herself unable to pay the rent after he lost his job when he missed work while in jail. Her family support coordinator said that Family Expectations would help pay her rent for the month on the condition that her boyfriend did not live with the family while he was searching for a new job and getting help (he had begun attending Alcoholics Anonymous meetings and a local church and was seeking counseling for himself and their family).

Mackenzie received money from her family support coordinator to address an array of pressing issues. She and her boyfriend, Wayan, had to borrow his cousin's car to get around; without money to pay for gas (the condition under which they were allowed to borrow the car), they'd been unable to go get recertified for their food assistance. Family Expectations provided a gas card as well as a gift card to Walmart so they could get recertified for their benefits and buy some clothing for their girls; with both of them out of work, they hadn't been able to provide even the basics. Family Expectations also covered the cost of Mackenzie and their daughters getting their birth certificates from the state—necessary for enrolling in school or getting a driver's license. Although the actual dollar amounts of these expenditures were fairly low (a $10 gas card, a $25 Walmart gift card, and three $15 birth certificates), all of this made Mackenzie feel incredibly supported by the program. "It's like they've been there, done it, even though, you know, sometimes they haven't." As with receiving the resource referrals, the personal relationships with family support coordinators and the program atmosphere seemed to keep couples from feeling stigmatized for receiving financial assistance. This was seen as help from a trusted source, rather than a government handout. And unlike a loan from kin, this came without any expectation of reciprocity or the emotional burdens of borrowing from family.[21]

After they finish their workshop sessions, couples describe family support coordinator meetings as mostly checking in on the status of their relationship and whether or not they need anything (e.g., referrals to community agencies). Few describe this as a time when they are engaged in any kind of extensive work on themselves or their relationships in the context of the program. For many, once the workshops end, their participation in the program wanes; others, however, remain involved by participating in additional activities.

Additional Activities

As couples conclude their time in the workshops, many express disappointment that this part of the program is ending. For the remainder of their time in the program, their participation may consist of periodic meetings with their family support coordinator and participation in activities that are usually onetime events. These events are not with the same group of couples with whom they took the workshops, nor are they led by the workshop educators, so they are focused on content, as opposed to an opportunity to continue these relationships. These include events such as mothers' luncheons, salsa dancing, presentations on car seat safety or lead poisoning risks, family play dates, and couple date nights. Additionally, at any time in their involvement with the program (even prior to the completion of the workshops), fathers can take part in a "Dads' Boot Camp."

Overall, mothers in this study take part in an average of 104 minutes of extended activities during their year in Family Expectations, and fathers complete an average of 87 minutes of extended activities. However, these averages mask substantial differences between those who don't participate and those who do: among those who take part in any extended activities, the average number of minutes completed is 321 for mothers and 300 for fathers (the equivalent of about five hours). While those who do participate seem to enjoy these activities, they don't discuss them with the same excitement and enthusiasm as they do their time in the workshops. These tend to be less emotionally intense experiences. For example, Norene, a twenty-four-year-old mother of three, attended a mother's luncheon and liked hearing the other women talk about their lives; it was nice to know about other people's struggles and ways of coping. But she didn't take away key lessons about child rearing as she did from her time in the workshops, which had left her feeling like a more knowledgeable parent.

After the workshops are over, a limited group of people remain actively involved in Family Expectations (e.g., taking part in a variety of the extended activities). Couples do not prioritize these activities the same way they did workshop participation. Many seem to feel the program is "over" after the workshops end, and the completion celebration they have during their last workshop session seems to reinforce this perception.

What Family Expectations Offers

In learning about parents' experiences, we come to understand why they are interested in attending Family Expectations in the first place: the various sources of ambiguity in their lives leave them searching for a firmer relational foundation for their families as they look to the future with their new babies. Couples see Family Expectations as offering the possibility to lay this foundation. The program resonates with parents, and their experiences with every aspect of the program—from the physical environment to the staff to the social atmosphere—are quite positive. Couples participate extensively in the services the program offers and benefit financially from the incentives and participation supports. Further, couples gain the opportunity to have a date night, away from the stresses of home and parenting; the program carves out a time to focus on their couple relationship just as the demands of parenting an infant may be a distraction from it. That is, we see the program's potential to offer social resources in the form of relationships and interactions with staff and peers, while also helping couples build more social resources within their own unions and families. The question remains, however, whether all these positive experiences and special time together create any real changes in couples' relationships and actual, rather than hoped-for, social resources. From a policy perspective, it is important to create a program parents like, will attend, and view as well run. But without improving the quality of couples' relationships, the way they parent their children, family stability, and their feelings of social poverty, the program may not be not worth its cost. I turn to these questions in the next chapters.

6

Learning Skills

Building Trust and Communities

The house where I drop off Joanne and Matt after the first time we meet is a run-down, single-family home that's white with brown trim and the front door propped open. Matt goes up the steps first and then turns around and reaches out his hands; in a practiced motion he pulls Joanne up the steps. Her pregnancy has caused her legs to swell, making it hard for her to walk. Nonetheless, the two are overjoyed about the baby on the way. Matt describes the pregnancy as the best thing that's ever happened in their relationship, and they playfully bicker over who was happier when they found out Joanne was pregnant. Both had worried that health problems might mean they couldn't have children, so the pregnancy was a hoped-for surprise.

Joanne and Matt, both twenty-four, met at a job training program and had been together for more than three years before she got pregnant. Neither of their job training programs led to a career—Joanne is on a break from a new certificate program in massage therapy, and Matt receives disability benefits related to his mental health issues—but, Joanne notes cheerfully, "We got a relationship out of it."

Three weeks into their relationship they got engaged, and as soon as they finished with their job training program, they moved in together. Now, several years later, they still describe plans to marry and are making small payments toward a ring for Joanne. This long wait between getting engaged and married was part of their plan, not evidence of initially hot feet turning cold. Matt explains, "If you stay together for three years, live together for three years, it's all easy sailing. I want to know how she lives, what's her living like, want to know . . . what makes her tick, what makes her not tick. How far I can go with this, and how not to go." With the end of their three-year waiting period in sight, their views of marriage are contradictory yet representative of how our culture simultaneously embraces and eschews marriage. On one hand, Joanne says that since they're already living together, "marriage is just another day," and Matt describes getting married as "paperwork." On the other hand, Joanne says being married will make them a "better example" for their child, and, in response, Matt tells her, "You're my soul mate, that's why I'm getting married."[1]

Joanne is short and blonde, with blue eyes, light-colored eyebrows and eyelashes, and freckles covering her face and arms. When she talks I can see the shine of a tongue ring in her mouth. She's wearing khaki pants that are baggy and look long for her. Her oversized, light blue polo shirt has a small food stain on the chest and several sizable holes in the left sleeve above the ribbed cuff. Matt, who has a slender build, is wearing a black mesh sleeveless shirt and a green baseball hat with a white Superman logo on the front. He has a sparse mustache and goatee. When he takes his hat off briefly, his light brown hair looks thin and fine.

The house where I am dropping them off—their car is broken so I offered a ride from the Family Expectations office—belongs to Matt's parents. But his parents are dependent on Matt's income to get by, with his dad having his own disability claim denied twice, and his mom unable to work after years of injuries in her job cleaning houses. In addition to Matt's parents, there are eight other relatives living with them, straining the budget and their privacy in the overcrowded house. A year later, when we meet for the last time, they have moved far away from the city to a trailer park where Matt has some friends. Here they are happy to be sharing the trailer only with their infant son and Joanne's mom.

Their new town features an odd contrast of industrial businesses and green fields full of grazing cattle. Their trailer is whitish gray with green trim. There is no car out front (theirs is still broken), but there is a small boat sitting in the driveway. Joanne greets me at the door. Their son, Billy, is in a baby chair surrounded by a tray with rattles and other baby toys attached to it; it allows him to bounce up and down, testing his legs. He's very content entertaining himself in his chair throughout the time Joanne and I talk. He's wearing a camouflage onesie and has a little bit of blonde-red hair on his head. He smiles and laughs easily when I make faces at him or play peekaboo.

The house is clean and tidy. The walls are heavy with decorations. There's a small box containing multiple sets of graduation tassels; a wedding photo from Joanne and Matt's recent nuptials and a framed wedding invitation as well as a laminated version of the invitation are pinned to the wall; and greeting cards congratulating them on the wedding are taped up next to the invitations. A small fish tank with a goldfish swimming around in it sits in the kitchen, contributing its swishing water sound to the quiet of the room. Joanne's bouquet of silk flowers from their wedding is in a vase on the kitchen counter. Her mother's wheelchair is also in the living room.

Although Joanne and Matt got married a few months back, neither wears a wedding ring. They're doing OK but are both feeling stressed by the recent transitions they've undergone—having a baby, moving out of his parents' house and into their own place, and getting married. Their arguments seem to stem from each feeling the other is not adequately pulling his or her weight around the house. Joanne is occasionally frustrated that she, or her mother, do most everything with Billy, while Matt is irritated that Joanne doesn't help with the housework. Financially, they are making ends meet, despite continuing to support Matt's parents financially, by combining some of Matt's disability check with Joanne's mother's disability check. Joanne is still not working, nor has she returned to school. Although she says she'd like to be working and providing better for Billy, she has no concrete plans to return to work or school anytime soon. She's unsure if she'll finish her massage therapy program at all because, she now says, working in that field was never what she truly wanted to do. I hear strong echoes of the emerging adult culture as Joanne describes her fluctuating plans.

When they argue, their fights tend to escalate to yelling and swearing and are ended when one of them starts crying or they take some time in separate parts of the house to cool down. They talk things over afterward. They both turn to Joanne's mother to sort through their relationship problems, and she seems supportive of them working things out, trying to take an unbiased position as she offers advice. They also have a network of friends who are encouraging of their relationship; in fact, it was their friends who urged them to finally get married, helping to pay for what they call their "Dollar Tree" wedding, in reference to the store where they bought most of the supplies for their ceremony in a local park. Their other social assets—supportive friends and family—boost the social resources they find in their relationship.

A year ago, when we first met, Joanne and Matt had enrolled in Family Expectations. And just before they got married they had attended a weekend workshop offered by Family Expectation's umbrella organization, entitled "Forever. For Real." They saw Family Expectations as affirming much of what they already knew they should be doing to make their relationship work—like taking a time out during arguments. But now, with their move and their lack of transportation, they live too far away to make it to the Family Expectations' offices. Nonetheless, they continue to see it as a trusted organization they would turn to if it were offering courses for their next phase of life: parenting a toddler.

Like Joanne and Matt, other parents are enthusiastic about their time in Family Expectations. But the central question remains: Does this enthusiastic participation translate to real changes in their relationships and their social resources? After all, the intended purpose of programs like Family Expectations is not to provide an enjoyable customer experience but rather to strengthen couple relationships to improve the quality of the family's life and their children's well-being. In understanding participants' assessments of the program's impact on their lives, given the looming threat of social poverty so many are facing, we come to see the program's influence on their lives in a new way—one that stands in contrast to the conclusions of previous research.

Relationship Education Research and Criticisms

Among academics, there have been two main types of criticisms of relationship education programming in recent years.[2] The first takes issue with the limited impacts found in program evaluations, critiquing what the programs are doing and how well they're doing it. These studies have been primarily survey-based and quantitative in nature. The second takes issue with the existence of these programs, critiquing their underlying ideologies; research in this area has tended to be qualitative, relying on interviews, observations, and content analysis. I discuss each in turn.

Quantitative Research

Previous studies of relationship education programs have mixed results, with many studies finding beneficial impacts of program participation, and others finding limited or no effects.[3] Several meta-analyses, which combine data and findings across studies to estimate effects, have found positive impacts, although the sizes of these effects have been small to moderate.[4] Most studies of relationship education programs have used samples that are more socioeconomically advantaged than the couples in Family Expectations, which can raise questions about the generalizability of their results; however, there are some exceptions.

In a meta-analysis restricted to studies of lower-income couples in relationship education programs, results were positive but smaller than those found using more advantaged samples.[5] A study using the large sample of low-income couples from the Building Strong Families evaluation found stronger intervention impacts on relationship quality among the more disadvantaged couples (compared with those in the program who were relatively better off); there were no effects on relationship stability.[6] One evaluation of a couple relationship education course with a diverse sample found that participants reported improved relationship quality and lower depressive symptoms, among those in unstable relationships.[7] Finally, some studies have found that relationship interventions for low-income couples can promote fathers' involvement with their children, over and above any effects on the union.[8]

Nonetheless, there has been hot debate among academics about whether or not relationship education delivers on its promises when it comes to serving low-income populations. Family studies professor Alan Hawkins and colleagues have argued that the evidence suggests an "optimistic" outlook: although impacts have been modest, they have been positive, and given that these evaluations are of first-generation programs, the data indicate how relationship education for low-income individuals could be strengthened going forward.[9] In response, critics like psychologist Matthew Johnson have argued that the positive impacts Hawkins and others have found are so small and scattered among null findings that they may well be "noise."[10] Further, Johnson suggests that additional basic research is necessary to better understand whether and how factors like being a person of color or having a low income affect marital function; he asks if it's possible that the "marriage model" used as the foundation for many relationship education curricula does not hold with nonwhite, economically disadvantaged populations, thereby explaining the programs' limited impact.[11]

Past research has also demonstrated the need to distinguish between short-term and long-term impacts of program participation. Some studies of relationship education programs have shown that their beneficial impacts can fade over time;[12] couples may slide back into their old habits or may encounter new challenges they're not prepared to overcome. Other studies, however, show that positive outcomes can take time to emerge—even up to five years.[13] Consequently, in this and the next chapter I describe the ways parents saw the program affecting their relationships approximately three months and twelve months, respectively, after they enrolled in Family Expectations. Because the most intense participation tends to occur during the first few months after enrollment, as couples take part in the workshops, the way the program could affect their relationships may differ from a year after they enrolled, when they are involved only occasionally, if at all.

Qualitative Research

Sociologists Melanie Heath and Jennifer Randles have both offered extensive qualitative analyses of relationship education programs; both conclude that these programs play a role in perpetuating inequality by endorsing dominant cultural values and narratives. Heath's take is sharply critical, driven by a focus on the heteronormative values such programs promote.[14] Heath presents relationship education programming as an on-the-ground embodiment of the "marriage movement," which advocates for the value of "traditional" marriage in society. She therefore asserts that these programs share the same ends as legislative efforts to restrict same-sex marriage.

This use of the "marriage promotion" umbrella term as a lens for studying relationship education leads Heath to miss the fact that many of these programs are guided more by the work of psychologists and family studies scholars, who focus primarily on developing relationship skills, than by the ideologies of legislators or conservative thought leaders who might wish to convince participants of the value of marriage.[15] Though their initial embrace by policy makers was often values-driven, the programs themselves often have far less to say about couples' marital status than about their ways of communicating, managing conflict, and working together as parents. Heath chooses to "maintain a critical distance" from the perspectives of the program staff and participants whom she interviews, leading her to reconceptualize, rather than accept, their experiences and stated motivations.[16] In developing her conclusions, Heath puts her sociological assessment of the programs in the foreground, with the point of view of participants in the background.

Randles's take, in contrast, allows the views of relationship education program participants and staff to play a more central role in shaping her book's narrative; unlike Heath's "critical distance," she accepts and reflects on the perspectives of those she observes and interviews. She describes how couples enjoyed and found value in the lessons taught, though they struggled to implement some of these lessons to strengthen their relationship dynamics. However, Randles critiques the "rationalized romance" that she says many relationship education programs promote, arguing that it offers an inaccurate view of intimate relationships because this approach maintains that they are shaped by partners' skills and efforts, a claim with which Randles disagrees. But this was not the predominant view among the participants she interviewed and observed. In treating this skills-based approach to relationships as being applied from "above" (by government policy, family studies researchers, curriculum developers, etc.), Randles misses that it may be culturally responsive. That is, participants themselves may actually desire the rationalization of romantic relationships; it could be terrifying to feel unbound, directionless, and lacking control over the outcome of a relationship in which you are deeply investing. We saw this, for example, in the previous chapter, as parents express a desire for guidance and clear expectations for their relationships.

Randles is quite pessimistic about the ability of relationship education programs to overcome the challenges presented by participants' financial struggles, particularly how these struggles may place stress on their romantic unions.[17] She rightly identifies the challenges of developing and maintaining a strong relationship in the face of financial stress. However, it seems fatalistic—and it ignores variation in relationship outcomes among lower-income couples—to argue that poor economic circumstances will inevitably overwhelm romantic commitments and thus render any attempt to improve relationship skills irrelevant or misguided.[18] Randles asserts that the government offering any kinds of skills training, rather than just economic resources, is a way of buttressing a neoliberal system that perpetuates inequality by "reinforc[ing] individual parental responsibility over reliance on state services for meeting children's needs."[19] It is not clear why the government taking on child-rearing responsibilities is preferable to the government assisting parents in having the capacity to do so themselves, or if there's any evidence to indicate that parents want to be relieved of this responsibility.

Fundamentally, Randles's argument can provide only a partial understanding of these programs because she uses an economic bar to evaluate their success. If a program does not improve couples' finances, it is necessarily a failure in her book. She assesses the program she studied as falling short because it "did not convey how parents raising children in poverty were supposed to convert love into the money needed to provide for children's physical needs."[20]

This manner of critiquing the program ignores that love is valuable in and of itself. It treats parents' love and care of their children as a luxury item, available only to those who are in a comfortable financial position. This is precisely the approach that the concept of social poverty, guiding the present analysis, seeks to counter. While Randles is quite right to recognize the wide-ranging financial challenges low-income families face, her exclusive use of an economic lens for analyzing the program inhibits our understanding of what she sees in her data. She describes the participants' overwhelmingly positive response to the relationship education program, saying, "Most eloquently articulated without my prompting in the interviews how the classes helped reduce loneliness and blame."[21]

Without the guiding framework of social poverty, existing work on relationship education leaves us with a puzzle: researchers, like Heath and Randles, are critical of these efforts at intervention—arguing that they assert unwelcome values or focus on emotional needs that are not critical for, or relevant to, those with limited incomes—yet participants embrace these programs.[22] It is important to understand and critically analyze the heteronormative ideology of some programs' approaches. It is important to recognize the challenging financial context in which many program participants live and try to construct their emotional lives. But we cannot properly evaluate or construct public policy without a recognition of how those directly affected by it are perceiving and interacting with it. In the present study, I seek to make sense of participants' experiences in the programs; it is only in doing so that we can understand why individuals choose to invest time in these programs, despite the flaws outsiders, from journalists to researchers, see in them.

Short-Term Consequences of Family Expectations Participation

In the present chapter, I describe parents' responses to Family Expectations about three months after they enrolled in it, when they were still, by and large, involved with the program; many were just finishing their workshop sessions at this time. This allows us to see their understandings of the curriculum and larger program experience. In the next chapter, I discuss parents' views of Family Expectations a year after they first enrolled. All had far less, if any, involvement in the program by that time. Their perspectives at that point give us insight into the ways they saw the program as shaping their relationships, or not. Throughout, we can see that parents' judgments of Family Expectations are grounded in their desires for strong, supportive, lasting unions—a desire to avoid social poverty.

Three months after parents enrolled in Family Expectations and we first met, I interviewed each couple together to find out how they were doing and what their experiences had been like in the program so far. Of the thirty-one couples I originally interviewed, I was able to reinterview twenty-eight (90 percent of the original sample).[23] Approximately one year after couples had initially enrolled in the program, I reinterviewed them, talking to each partner separately; this was an intentional approach in anticipation that some would have broken up by this time. For this third round of interviews, I was able to meet with twenty-four couples (77 percent, or 86 percent of the twenty-eight couples interviewed at round two) and to get information about the relationship status of another four couples. Over the year and three rounds of data collection, between individual and couple interviews, I conducted a total of 192 interviews.

In terms of their employment situations three months after enrolling, twenty-three parents were working full-time and five part-time, and twenty-eight were unemployed, disabled, or out of the labor force.[24] Fathers were more likely to be employed than were mothers (many had just had or were soon to have a baby), with sixteen men employed full-time and three employed part-time, compared with seven women who were employed full-time and two part-time. In five couples, both partners were working; in another five couples, neither partner was working. Couples' monthly incomes ranged from $25 to $2,400, with an average of $1,445. In terms of their relationships, none of the couples had broken up permanently (although there had been some churning), and four couples had gotten married since the first interview.

Lessons Learned: Romantic Relationships

Couples report they learned new information, typically about relationships, during their time in the workshops. The lessons teach concrete tools for dealing with conflict and communication in productive ways, including the "speaker listener" technique and "time out," as well as general messages about communication. Overall, the couples viewed these techniques positively, seeing them as offering the potential to help them feel more understood by their partners and to experience less conflict in their relationships. Both of these outcomes would make them feel more secure in their relationship as a social resource, protecting against social poverty.

SPEAKER LISTENER

The speaker listener technique prompts couples to take turns while talking through a difficult issue, with the speaker explaining his perspective while the listener paraphrases what she hears to guard against misunderstanding and to stop her from merely responding with her own point of view, instead of truly hearing what her partner has said.[25] Twenty of twenty-eight couples brought up learning this technique during the second round of interviews (three months after enrolling); at the third round of interviews, only ten couples mentioned it by name. Speaker listener is more "controversial" than any other technique taught in the workshop, with some couples saying they would find it annoying or even something that might escalate a fight if their partner repeated back what they were saying. Some do not always seem clear about the purpose of the paraphrasing and think they need to literally repeat what is said word for word, as opposed to paraphrasing what they hear. However, people are able to absorb lessons about communication from this technique, even if they reject the tool itself. For example, it can serve as a reminder to listen to a partner or to take turns speaking.

Ann and Trenton, both in their late twenties, understand the speaker listener technique better than most, to their benefit. Trenton says:

> That speaker listener technique, they call it, worked, 'cause they were saying like when people argue they really don't listen to what people are saying, they're too busy thinking of a rebuttal and keeping score in their own head. "Oh yeah, well, I remember . . ." And then they're waiting to say that, so they're not really hearing what you're saying. And paraphrasing and stuff like that, so I think it helps. It just made us stronger, you know . . . it made us stronger in each other, our foundation, our family structure.

Ann explains that they do not use the technique as they learned it in class, not taking it so literally. Trenton adds that they just "take the time to actually listen." The result, Ann says, is that "I don't blow up as easily like I used to. I stop to think and listen." The message about communication has had an opposite, but equally important, impact on Trenton. "I don't hold it in until I can't no more," he says, and describes how he has been working on opening up more to Ann.

Even those who do use the technique describe being uncomfortable or finding it difficult at first. This technique does not come naturally to people, despite the specific practice they do in class. Because it is more difficult or does not immediately resonate with people, many drop the technique or adapt it greatly. As we see for Ann and Trenton, these adaptations can still improve communication skills.[26]

TIME OUT

Time out encourages couples to take a break before a conflict gets too heated and to set a time to return to the discussion once emotions have cooled, as we heard from Joanne and Matt at the start of the chapter. In interviews, eleven of the twenty-eight couples mentioned learning this technique during the second round of interviews; by the third round of interviews six couples mentioned it by name, with another three describing "walking away" or "taking a break" during arguments. It seems that few couples take a time out in the way it is taught. It is uncommon for partners to set a time to reconvene and talk through the issue, as they are taught to do in their workshops, although some couples do have an implicit understanding that this will happen at some point. Some do not even say that they are taking a time out; rather, one partner will just walk away.

Carley and Nick, both in their twenties and with their first child on the way, had struggled with their communication prior to Family Expectations. Nick explains that he would try to take a break during a discussion, but Carley would continue pushing the issue. The lessons on time out have helped Carley understand that taking a break could be helpful and have made Nick see the importance of returning to the discussion later. He says, "Setting a time to come back to things and talk about it really helps." This has produced a big change in how Carley handles their disagreements. She explains:

> 'Cause then I don't feel like I have to chase him. 'Cause if he doesn't set a time, "But when? But I want to talk about it. . . ." 'Cause I feel like I'm never gonna get to talk about it ever, like I'm just gonna hold it in forever and I'm gonna explode. So him saying, "Listen, I really can't talk to you now, but can we talk tomorrow morning before I go to work?" or "Can we talk in an hour? Let me have a beer and relax and then we can talk about it" or whatever, and it kind of, I feel like I know that we're gonna talk about it, so I don't have to sit there and eat myself alive trying to figure out how I can get this out of my system. . . . I don't feel the urge to follow him around the house harassing him over it. . . . Even if it's not at that moment, I know that I'm going to be able to get this out of my system and we'll probably talk about it a lot more calmly now that he has that little bit. And it also gives me time to think about it. "Maybe I'm coming at this the wrong way . . ." and I'll play it in my head for a little bit and try to think, "Oh, maybe I'm being a little bit harsh. Let me try it this way." And then we can come back and usually we can work it out after that. Even if the problem's not solved, at least I feel heard. I feel like I got it out of my system and I can just relax about it. And that was my big thing, is I felt like no one heard me. And yelling doesn't get me heard any better either, so taking that break's very beneficial.

While Carley lets things cool down, Nick knows how important it is for them to come back to a discussion later, so that Carley will continue to feel comfortable temporarily letting an issue drop. Although people use time out with various modifications, generally those who discuss time out understand the fundamentals of this technique—you stop before things get really heated, and you revisit the issue later. Couples experiment with time out to learn ways to disengage and avoid escalating a conflict. Afterward they revisit the issue to talk it through or realize they had been having a silly argument that got blown out of proportion and can be dropped.

COMMUNICATION

Couples also discuss learning more general lessons on communication, beyond the specific tools discussed earlier.[27] These include thinking about how what you say will be perceived by your partner (e.g., saying something in a way that is not mean), paying attention to what a partner says as a way of showing care, sharing feelings with a partner, not letting an argument get off track (e.g., by letting the argument extend to new subjects or incidents from the past), and not involving outsiders in your arguments.

Robert, twenty-one, describes how the program's lessons about communication changed how he responds to his girlfriend, Elyse:

> Then one thing that I know that I had to work on too that I saw from the class was definitely when she's talking to me or whatever and she thinks something is more of a big deal than I do, and I just take it as like, you know, it's not really that big a deal and I won't listen or pay attention to her or anything like that. I realized that I did do that, so I was like, "OK. Maybe I need to stop and actually take what she's telling me as important. Maybe it's not that important to me, but it is to her, so maybe I need to take the time to sit down and listen to what she has to say." So I know that class right there was definitely for me. I needed to hear that.

People describe a variety of specific ways they applied lessons about communication to their relationships. Robert, for example, primarily views this "technique" as one that helps him be more attentive. As Cara, thirty-two, notes, for her "the most helpful thing is to just be more aware of [my boyfriend] and his feelings." This is reflective of lessons from the workshops that teach couples to identify and avoid patterns of interaction that are associated with relationship distress. They are taught about communication "danger signs" and how these can negatively affect their relationships. Couples are more conscious of the importance of how they communicate with each other and more thoughtful about employing healthy (or at least not as damaging) ways of talking through problems or sharing emotions.

It is clear in people's descriptions of how they use Family Expectations lessons that it is a trial-and-error process. Ennis, in his early twenties, describes how he and his girlfriend, Akira, would try out techniques from class, adapting as they went. "Like that listener speaker thing that, we tried that. It feels funny. . . . At first we was doing it the way they showed us, and now we just taking a little bit here and a little bit there and putting it in something we'd feel comfortable with." Couples do not practice the workshop lessons or discuss together how they will implement them; rather, they try them out as situations arise, with most adapting the techniques to meet their needs and comfort levels.

Beyond the specific tools or techniques, the implicit and explicit lessons about strengthening the relationship and caring about a partner through healthy communication come through for couples. It makes them more conscious of how they talk to and respond to one another, from tone of voice to eye rolls, from guarded silence to pushy escalation. Though seemingly small, such changes in a relationship could be essential to cultivating trust by making the relationship a safer place to be vulnerable. With trust, a relationship can serve as a resource—protection against social poverty.

Additionally, the Family Expectations lessons provide couples with labels and formulated ideas that help them to identify, better understand, and work to correct dynamics in their own relationships. We see this in how Robert was able to identify how he reacted to Elyse when she raised "unimportant" concerns. Tiana and Stefan, both in their early twenties, explain how learning about the concepts of "dodgers" and "chasers" helped improve their communication. Tiana, who realized that she was a dodger, explains, "I don't like to talk. I get too flustered and I'm not comfortable with it." Prior to the program, Stefan was a chaser. He says, "I used to be like 'Tiana, Tiana, Tiana . . .'" This has slowly started to change. As Tiana has realized she needs to open up more, Stefan has not been so dogged in his chasing. She explains:

He would have to bug me for days to figure out what's wrong with me and now it only takes him a couple minutes before I'm like, OK. . . . Once we started, you know, really paying attention to what each other were saying and what our different needs are, it made it easier for me to understand that I was a dodger, and I need to learn how to communicate so I feel comfortable enough to let him listen to me.

Course material resonated with couples, speaking to the concerns they had about their own relationships, frequently about couple communication. Although few directly transfer course lessons into their daily lives, many are able to adapt tools through trial and error, to take away general communication lessons, or to better identify and respond to their negative communication practices. Like a pitcher cultivating his fastball or an author developing her writing style, couples' adaptations of communication skills are not necessarily problematic. The mechanics of holding a baseball, proper grammar, and communication techniques are not of primary importance, so long as the outcomes are good. For many couples, at the point of the interviews, the result is still a work in progress as they try to figure out new ways of communicating and to overcome bad habits, but some note important changes in how they deal with conflict and talk through problems. The lessons couples highlighted learning during their time in Family Expectations emphasize the importance of micro-level interactions in contributing to social poverty or building social resources. The difference between a few days versus a few minutes of Tiana's stony silence, as she avoids disclosing her worries, with Stefan pestering her to do so, can fundamentally change the couple's day-to-day experience of their relationship—whether it is primarily a source of comfort or conflict.

Lessons Learned: Parenting

Participants were much less likely to note aspects of the sessions that had to do with parenting, with the couple-focused lessons having more apparent resonance. In part, this may be due to how many participants are not new parents; in sixteen of the original thirty-one couples, one or both partners had a child prior to their most recent pregnancy. Nonetheless, thirteen of twenty-eight couples do mention lessons about parenting in their discussion of Family Expectations during the second round of interviews; with more of the parents in the full swing of parenting their new babies by the third round of interviews, it's perhaps not surprising that a larger proportion of parents—fifteen out of twenty-four—describe learning lessons about parenting in Family Expectations.

The parenting lessons couples describe learning usually involve fewer major behavioral changes compared with those learned about relationships. Some men make note of parenting lessons, sharing interesting tidbits they had not known before. For example, Zach, twenty, offers up a factoid he learned: that "a baby can swim as soon as it's born." Lance and Kristina, both twenty, just had their first baby. While Lance found it useful to learn to distinguish the meaning of different baby cries and how to swaddle, Kristina notes, "There wasn't too much stuff [about parenting] that I didn't already know. Some of it was common sense, but it comes natural, usually, to moms." Parents' hopes for the future focus on providing a good life for their child, but most focused on building a better relationship with each other, rather than new parenting techniques, as the way to get there.

Couples' Beliefs about How Family Expectations Changes Their Relationships in the Short Term

Couples describe a variety of ways their relationships have changed during their participation in the Family Expectations workshops. By the second round of interviews, of the twenty-eight couples, nineteen describe seeing a positive change in their relationships as a result of participating, two say they have seen no change, and two explain that they have not been able to sustain the positive changes in their relationship and have lapsed into their old ways.[28]

Couples describe an array of changes: less bickering, taking time outs, being better able to discuss issues without arguing, disagreeing without being mean, letting go of small issues, identifying problems in the relationship, doing activities together, being more confident in the relationship, feeling like more of a team, building greater trust, praising kids more, being more appreciative of one's partner, using the speaker listener technique, raising issues as needed, helping out more at home, keeping arguments focused on the issue at hand, spending more time with a partner's child, both partners participating more in parenting, learning more about one's partner, being calmer, having fights that no longer get physical, attending to one another's feelings, being less clingy, scheduling couple time, and planning together for the future.

We see how these changes play out and what they mean to couples in the following exchange between Ann and Trenton, who have struggled with two main concerns: Ann's trust issues and Trenton's reluctance to open up and share his feelings. Three months after starting the program, Ann says, "Well, my trust issue, I've seen it change. I've seen it change in myself. . . . It's gonna be there always just because we're only human." She laughs and explains, "I've experienced too much. Stuff [still] happens, but it's not as bad as it was. And I actually think about his feelings more now than before." Trenton interjects, "Instead of saying I don't have any." Ann smiles in acknowledgment of her tendency to do this. And Trenton adds, "I just don't show 'em all the time." Ann explains, "Then I stop and I think 'Oh, well he's, hello, everybody's different.'" She then smiles again as Trenton says, "You could have been holding the weight of the world on your shoulders up until the person [says] 'What's the matter?'" Ann describes how this has affected how she feels in their relationship: "It's made . . . [our relationship] more open for where I don't feel weird about being open. 'Cause that's the beginning you're like 'How the hell do I tell this person what I need to tell him without feeling like an idiot?'" Trenton summarizes how this has changed their relationship: "I don't think we even argue now. 'Cause there's no reason."

Although Ann and Trenton have not left behind the problems they carried into Family Expectations, they have been learning to manage these issues. Ann's lack of trust is easing, and at the same time she is becoming more understanding of Trenton's ways of communicating. For his part, he is starting to see the benefits of opening up to Ann a bit more. On the one hand, changes like these are not a fundamental overhaul of the relationship. On the other hand, they make people feel more satisfied with their relationships and more hopeful about the direction the relationship is moving. They play a role in strengthening the relationship as a social resource, with partners feeling closer to and more supported by one another.

As discussed in chapter 1, due to both broader cultural changes, including the deinstitutionalization of romantic relationships, and personal experiences, with many of these young parents not having seen well-functioning unions while growing up, couples often lack shared norms that could create a foundation for their relationships. This lack of shared norms can translate into conflict, as partners' expectations of one another may not align, and their ability to interpret the meaning of one another's behavior is weakened. This can erode trust and dedication, weakening key social assets.

Brianna, eighteen, and her boyfriend Zach, twenty, are living with his mother and having their first child. When they started Family Expectations, their arguments often ended in Brianna shutting down emotionally and refusing to talk and Zach going out to smoke, walk around, or hang out with a friend. After their time in the workshops, they are still responding to conflict in these ways. But to interpret this as nothing having changed in their relationship would be a mistake. They now label these behaviors as their ways of taking time outs, and, even though it annoys the other when one of them does it, they both think it's useful in helping them deal with conflict. Brianna says, "At Family Expectations, they said . . . when you get so angry, take a time out. . . . So I just let him walk away and calm down and I give him a few minutes and then go talk to him or he comes and talks to me." Family Expectations didn't teach them to take time outs; rather, the workshops taught them to label the behaviors they were already engaging in as time outs. As a result, rather than deriding one another for their different ways of managing conflict, they now view their actions as positive ways of dealing with arguments. Establishing this norm—time outs are a way to take a break and cool down during conflict, and doing so is beneficial—transformed the way they understood one another's behavior. Rather than undermining the relationship, their ways of managing conflict now help to maintain the union.

Another way the workshops helped couples establish shared expectations and relationship norms was by showing, through the group workshop setting, that conflict and struggles were common and a part of every relationship. That is, in easing social poverty by offering a community of families going through similar transitions, the program provided a framework to help couples better understand their relationships. Abby, twenty-two, says, "It was exciting to see a lot of other people going through the same things we were and you know, you get feedback from them. . . . 'Oh, I never looked at it like that.' So it was just neat."[29]

Abby was also enthusiastic about the communication techniques they'd learned, but with her boyfriend, Darren, living with his mom while she remains in a transitional living facility across the city, they've not managed to use them. Abby feels emotional and vulnerable; she's just had the baby and is adjusting to motherhood again—it's been a couple years since she had children around after her older two were removed from her custody when her now ex-boyfriend attacked her in front of the kids. Right now Abby feels disconnected from Darren, and the Family Expectations communication skills seem of little help. "I felt really distanced. . . . We're still together, but physically we're apart and it's really hard to actually sit down and say OK, this is how I need to say it. Usually it just comes out and not always in the best way."

Nonetheless, as with seeing that other couples also went through struggles, her time in the workshops has helped Abby to view her relationship differently. In the workshop, Abby explains,

> we were talking about trust and forgiveness. . . . It really did change my outlook on a lot of things and . . . it was like common sense, but to hear them say it. . . . To trust somebody is to know that they're doing what they have to do to make the relationship better. . . . Usually when you think about trust you think can you trust that person to not cheat on you. That's just like society's main thought. Trust is just knowing the other person is doing what they can for the better of the relationship and that was really neat.

When I ask her what that realization made her think about her relationship, she says:

> It made me feel really good . . . because my emotions are crazy right now, it seems like he's not here for me, but I think he's out there working two jobs and doing what he's got to do and makes time to come down here and he's helping with his mom, you know, helping with his son out there. . . . I know he sacrifices a lot. He doesn't get to go out. He doesn't get to do much, and he's pulled between being here with us and helping out his family and working, and it made me feel really good to look at it like that. To know that I can trust him with anything, you know, whatever he's doing he's doing for the better of our relationship, so that we can be together.

As for Brianna and Zach, Family Expectations offered Abby a way to reinterpret her struggles with Darren and his absence that was positive, affirming his feelings toward her and his commitment to their shared future. Rather than simply feeling lonely in her relationship, Abby was able to see that Darren was contributing to the relationship, even when he was physically absent.

Hannah, eighteen, and Luke, twenty-two, are having their first child. The two of them have a very rocky past, marked by domestic violence (with her being violent toward him) and frequent churning (breaking up and getting back together). The change in their demeanor and behavior toward one another between our first and second interviews was remarkable. When we first met as they were starting the Family Expectations program, they couldn't make it through our interview without arguing and rolling their eyes at one another; the tension in the room was thick, making it one of the more uncomfortable interviews I'd had. By the second interview, three months later, it was like a weight had been lifted off of them. As they waited for the baby to arrive, they were living together (Hannah had previously been living with her mother), and they said positive things about one another and didn't argue while I was at their house. Not wanting me to get the wrong impression about their transformation, Hannah noted, "One thing to know is not everything's been like instantly peachy. . . . We still have rocky times. . . . It just is like progressively getting better." They explain that the Family Expectations program came at just the right time for them, allowing them to get on this better path as they were preparing for the baby. Luke says, "I think we're both growing up, 'cause we got together young. She was sixteen and I was like eighteen or nineteen. . . . So we're growing up, and we're starting to learn better ways. So this is probably a good time to be learning this stuff so we're not already too set in our habits." Hannah describes how it takes practice and trial and error to learn these new ways of communicating with and treating one another, and it is clear that they see their participation in Family Expectations as facilitating their transitions to adulthood, parenthood, and partnership simultaneously, as it offers new expectations for how they should treat one another and ways of acting to fulfill these expectations.

Like Hannah and Luke, during the first round of interviews, most couples report that they are interested in Family Expectations, at least in part, because they have relationship problems, typically with communication. Usually, they are not participating to strengthen an already strong relationship but to address problems that they are having difficulty figuring out how to remedy on their own. For most couples, the program felt like a reasonable response to the needs they brought into it. The changes parents described seem to indicate that they are starting to move their relationship in the right direction. While the workshops certainly did not fix all the problems couples faced, they offered tools partners used to begin to work on their issues, and they helped couples believe that their problems could be successfully addressed.[30] For some, learning the mechanics of particular communication skills was less important than the framework Family Expectations offered for creating shared expectations and ways of deciphering relationship events and behaviors. Although there are stories of amazing transformations, with couples turning around damaged, unstable relationships, this is not the typical outcome. Rather, the average experience is one of a couple making smaller changes, being a little slower to anger, a little quicker to let trivial matters go, and a little more sure that this is the kind of relationship they want to show their children, one that could be happy and lasting. These nudges help push their relationships from the deficit to the asset category. We see suggestions here for why couples believed in the power of Family Expectations—they felt they were gaining tools they could use to shore up their relationships, thereby protecting themselves from social poverty.

7

Relationship and Parenting Changes

Making It Work

This last round of interviews brought me to Steffy and Jim's house. The couple, both thirty-five, lives there with their new baby and Jim's two preteen daughters, when they're staying with him. Since Steffy's brother died earlier in the year, her three young nephews have also stayed with them several times a week. And now they have one more houseguest: Steffy's mother just retired and is staying with them until she moves into an RV, currently parked in their driveway. With so much hustle and bustle around the house, Steffy and Jim take turns talking with me in the RV.

Jim's hair suggests he rolled out of bed recently. Above his white socks, his ankles look like they're rubbed raw; he has scabs left by his work boots from the construction site where he's apprenticing to be an electrician. He's wearing a simple gold wedding band. Steffy shuffles back and forth between the house and the RV with her pink socks stuffed into hot pink flip flops. She's wearing a gold engagement ring and a gold wedding band. Her hair is parted in the middle and pulled into a low ponytail. There are noticeably more gray hairs all along her part than there were last fall. Her brother's death has been hard on her, sparking the return of her mental health struggles. Nonetheless, Steffy and Jim feel like their relationship is moving in the right direction, and they credit Family Expectations for giving them the tools to stick together through the trying times the last year has brought.

Steffy is reluctant to leave the baby overnight, so they've not yet gone on their honeymoon, but they make sure to spend one-on-one time together. Jim describes how, every night before bed, they used to take turns answering questions from the friendship jar Family Expectations gave them. More recently, they've been reading Stephen King books together, with each taking turns reading aloud to the other every night. Stephen

King may be the king of horror, but for Steffy and Jim, sharing his frightful tales is a way to carve out space for and reinforce their bond.

In the past, their disagreements would escalate to name-calling and yelling. They felt like they didn't know how to fix their problems. Now life's struggles haven't gone away—far from it—but they feel better prepared to handle them. They take a time out before things get too heated, and they try to really listen to one another when they talk through an issue. Steffy shares that they've even taught these techniques, which they learned at Family Expectations, to Jim's daughters to ease their squabbles. Steffy describes her brother as having been her best friend, and she wants her stepdaughters to have just as much of a social resource in one another as she had in her sibling.

As for Steffy and Jim, participating in Family Expectations was not a regular part of life for most of the parents when we met this last time, about a year after they'd first enrolled in the program. However, many believe the program's impacts continue to reverberate in their relationships and parenting. Some struggle with implementing what they learned, inhibited by issues ranging from mental health and trauma to deep financial needs; a few have broken up. While they still view their unions as works in progress, they continue to find value in the lessons they took away from their time in the workshops, crediting the program with their relationship improving or even lasting this long at all.

Relationship Changes

Positive Growth

On their face these may appear to be tales of troubled lives, as couples struggled with imprisonment, addiction, financial hardship, and unemployment. While critics have argued that relationship education is a pointless exercise in the face of such difficulties, the cases of the couples profiled here, and others like them, call such criticism into question. The parents themselves saw value in the program, despite—or because of—their challenges. There were couples who described seeing clear and encouraging growth in their relationships over the course of their year in Family Expectations, even amid such struggles.

Twenty-eight-year-old Ann, a mother of two who gets by on her disability check, has been left to parent alone after her boyfriend, Trenton, thirty, was sent to prison on nonviolent charges just a few months after their son's birth. Ann and Trenton had contended with her trust issues and his difficulties sharing his thoughts and feelings when they had entered Family Expectations. Ann has seen positive changes in how they talk with one another, pointing to the speaker listener technique, which they had adapted so they were comfortable with it, as particularly important:

> That does help us 'cause it makes us stop and think and realize if we're hot, if we're mad and steamed up about something, instead of just blurting something, stop and think and realize, just look over the situation more. . . . It helped us because now we put the shoe on the other foot, instead of talking or doing things that we feel is right, we always got to remember about the other person and how they feel. . . . It makes everybody happier 'cause then we know what's going on with each other and ain't nobody walking around bottling up and exploding at any moment.

Interrupted by her baby starting to fuss, she goes over to check on him, then finishes her thought. "Happier life. Happy relationship. There's no fighting. There's no arguing. It's perfect. You can't beat that."

Such a glowing evaluation of their relationship is remarkable, given that their communication is now quite constrained: Trenton is in a prison ninety miles away, and Ann doesn't trust their jalopy to make it there and back, so they haven't seen each other since Trenton left for court the day of his sentencing. With limited income from her disability benefits, Ann can only afford to pay for collect phone calls from Trenton a couple times a month. This has left them writing letters nearly every day, with Ann tucking a few photos of their infant son inside each of hers, and Trenton trying to weigh in on parenting decisions from afar— asking that she shampoo the carpets before their little one starts scooting around on the floor, for example. Despite these challenges to maintaining their bond and communication, Ann feels more positive than ever about their relationship, which she credits to Family Expectations:

> With my childhood, I don't care what anybody says, it affected me and that's my problem now is trust issues with him, but they've gotten a lot better since we went through Family Expectations. . . . I shouldn't be ac-

cusing [him] all the time. . . . Doing all that crap all the time and worrying . . . I don't get to enjoy life. . . . So I've learned to control it and just
learn that not everybody's bad and out to do me harm.

Family Expectations also helped change the way she evaluated Trenton and their relationship. "Nobody's perfect. I got to realize that I will
not find the perfect person, because there is not one. So if I find a guy
that's 95 percent good, then I'm gonna stick with it. Even if it's 85 percent good, it's better than, way better than 50 percent," she says with a
laugh. Coming from Ann, who had made it to her late twenties without
a single serious relationship—having always kept men at arm's length,
this is a notable change. We hear in Ann's story the social poverty she
was experiencing—"everybody's bad and out to do me harm"—and the
social resource she now feels she has in her relationship with Trenton.

Denelle was a thirty-three-year-old mother of a teenage daughter
when she met forty-year-old Otis, a father of four. After becoming a
mother at a young age and abandoning her youth for the responsibilities of parenthood, Denelle had seemingly reentered adolescence in recent years, partying and allowing her apartment to be a raucous circus,
with friends and acquaintances alike coming by at all hours of the day
and night. A year into their relationship, Otis had had it; he felt enough
ownership of the apartment by that point to put his foot down, saying that the constant stream of visitors had to end. At the same time,
Denelle, whose nearly two decades without another child had led her
to believe she couldn't conceive, discovered she was pregnant. Although
the household quieted down, Denelle and Otis's fights did not. Nor, apparently, did her drug use, which was discovered when their daughter
was born prematurely with drugs in her system. Child welfare authori-
ties intervened and placed the child with Otis's sister while the couple
went through court-mandated drug testing, Denelle saw a counselor,
and Otis volunteered to attend parenting classes (in which, he proudly
reports, he was the star student).

During our first interview when Denelle was still pregnant, the tension between the two was palpable, as little slights quickly escalated, despite my presence. At the second interview, after three months in Family
Expectations, they had seen some improvements but were still struggling to treat one another decently. Denelle would blow tiffs into major

arguments and mistrusted Otis's friendships with other women, while Otis pushed aside Denelle's requests for more attention. By the third interview, though, things felt different. The baby had been placed back in their care, and Denelle now respected Otis's time outs, no longer insisting their arguments spill out into the common areas of their housing project, where she had previously followed him as he tried to cool down. "I stay in here and be with the baby and I calm down. I have to be calm for the baby. . . . We communicate more. We used to didn't." She credits the speaker listener technique for part of the change in their communication. Her court-mandated therapist has reinforced this Family Expectations technique, giving Denelle a key chain she uses: "You put it in your hand and be like, 'It's my turn to talk.'" Another change in how she communicates, she notes, is that she tries to "not be so loud with it. You know, 'cause he'll calm his voice down and be like, 'Why you yelling?' and it make me think, 'Calm down. Calm down. Don't have to be so upset.'" Denelle and Otis still have a long road ahead, as they are nearing the end of their involvement in the child welfare system, which will also mean an end to the court-mandated drug testing and counseling. But both are feeling far more positive about their relationship, and the quality of the home life their daughter is experiencing is far better than the loud fights and tension she would have been met with a year before. While their financial circumstances haven't improved much, they feel like their social resources have.

Illisha and Aaron's relationship has a quiet strength; both twenty-three, the couple feels like each has the other's back, and they get support for their relationship from their families. Over the year that we meet, the rough edges of their relationship continue to get smoothed out—they argue less, they get married—despite the fact that their sources of stress increase: they have their second baby, and they both lose their jobs. They credit Family Expectations with playing a role in their ability to weather these storms. The workshops offered them a much-needed date night away from their very energetic two-year-old daughter. They both appreciated that the other men in the program, both participants and staff, gave Aaron the opportunity to be around men—role models, they say— who were more family-oriented than the friends he used to be around. They do learn a few new strategies for improving their communication, especially on Aaron's side of things. As he explains, "Speaking calmly and if not, then go take a break and then come back instead of going all day angry and going to bed angry and waking up angry. . . . [And] thinking about your words instead of just splurging out. . . . I can talk and get a little off my chest."

Illisha has seen this change in Aaron—it has moved their marriage closer to her definition of a good relationship, which requires "trust and communication." Recently, she's noticed that "he'll speak up and say whatever's going on. He'll want to get it out, clear the air. . . . I think it makes it better just so we won't be holding a grudge and wanting to bring it up every time you get an attitude and want to fuss about it. I like it." This is not to say they don't get into arguments anymore. Rather, they've started to take time outs, so "it's not to a point where anybody's getting so upset that it's gonna go past raising our voice," Illisha notes. After taking a break, "eventually we'll just get over it and discuss it. What are we gonna do from there on forward. Just get over it."

Illisha and Aaron's relationship isn't perfect: their finances leave them struggling, and Illisha's not totally satisfied with their division of labor at home—Aaron spends too much time playing video games, in her opinion. But none of this has shaken their fundamental commitment to one another and their children, as they see positive growth in their relationship. After their son is born, Aaron switches to the computer version of his video game so that he can play in the living room where the rest of the family spends time, instead of being isolated in the back room with his gaming system—a small step, but one Illisha appreciates. And perhaps a bigger benefit for them, beyond particular communication techniques, is the affirmation Family Expectations gave them that the work they're putting into their relationship is worthwhile and that they're approaching things the right way—it's like a stamp of approval that makes them evaluate their relationship and the effort they put into it more optimistically. With her parents divorced and his never having married, having such guidance is quite valuable to them, they say. In altering their daily interactions, the program has helped strengthen the position of their relationship as a social resource, with it providing more support and emotional sustenance than before.

Two Steps Forward, One Step Back

Others couples have experienced two steps forward, one step back as their relationships developed over the course of their year in Family Expectations. Carley and Nick are both twenty-one; they get married and have their first child during the program. My initial interview with them was quite difficult, as Carley would rarely allow Nick (or me) to get a word in edgewise and was quick to sharply criticize whatever Nick did say. This may have been, in part, due to the fact that she had to stop taking some of her medications during pregnancy (taken for mental health reasons), and she was trying (ultimately unsuccessfully) to quit smoking. Over time, however, she seems more appreciative of Nick and more cognizant of her own shortcomings. That said, they are still a long way from handling conflict in a way that doesn't damage their relationship; their arguments spiral out of control fast, and Carley still threatens to and does leave when they have an argument. Nick is particularly troubled by her willingness to throw around the word "divorce." Although they both express strong ideas about commitment consistently across the year, they have trouble acting in ways that would support their goal of staying married. About six months after finishing the Family Expectations workshops, Nick decided they needed more assistance than the program could offer, and they had several sessions with a marriage counselor, over Carley's resistance.

Despite their many challenges, their relationship does seem more functional than at the program's start a year earlier. Carley explains:

> I'll be honest. There are still those blowups that are absolutely ridiculousness. But I think we've done better at communicating. And after the blowups, we can oftentimes come back to the conversation and say, you know, "That's not what I meant, and I hope that's not what you meant." I still say things that are hurtful and that I probably shouldn't say, but I think it's just something we're gonna have to work on. It's our first year of marriage and having a baby and . . . all these other things, so it's been, it's been different learning about each other. . . . You know, I'm working on the not threatening to leave because I know that that's a trigger for him.

In addition to trying to change her behavior, Carley has gained a new understanding of what to expect from relationships, which impacts her commitment to her union. She tells me:

> I've learned that . . . you don't quit just because he calls me this or I call him that or I throw something across the room or I call him a dirty name or I tell him this or he tells me that. I don't like you at this moment, but I'll like you in twenty minutes. And that's something I've had to learn. Just because you've had a fight doesn't mean you're over, doesn't mean you're done, doesn't mean you quit.

She credits their time in Family Expectations with some of the changes in how she behaves and thinks about their marriage:

> A lot of our communication came from Family Expectations. . . . Maybe we don't use the exact style, but a lot of it. "Why don't you just give me a break?" is actually a time out. . . . [O]ne thing that did work was, what's it called? I don't even know what it's called. Oh, [statements like] "I feel like this because . . ." Because I would always say you, you, you, and it had nothing to do with him. Technically it did, but if he didn't feel like I was accusing him it was much more easy to communicate about things. . . . Or this morning he was tired and he just blew up at me. Instead of chasing him, that's what [Family Expectations would] call it, by calling him 'cause he was on his way to work and he was running late, I blew it off and he came home and I cooked dinner and everything was fine. So it wasn't worth blowing up or chasing him over. . . . I thought, "Well, there's no need to chase him about this. He's just tired." . . . 'Cause before it was just based on emotion that I would chase him, and now I can think, "OK, he's just having a bad day. If he's still like this when he gets home, then we'll talk about it."

Taking time outs and recognizing that their "dodger-chaser" dynamic wasn't getting Carley the kind of reaction she wanted from Nick led to more productive ways of managing conflict and helped Carley to interpret Nick's behaviors in a more forgiving light.

For Nick, the lessons from Family Expectations about how fighting in front of children can affect them have given him even more motivation to improve their relationship. As he says, "It's important to have better communication, teaching us better communication, because we can't be living in a hectic household with a child who's learning everything you say and do. [T]hey taught us, constantly recognize, don't forget, he's right here." Carley and Nick clearly still have a ways to go before they're able to model good conflict management techniques for their baby son, but they nonetheless see themselves moving in the right direction, thanks in part, they say, to Family Expectations. The change in Carley's thinking has been particularly important, as she is owning up to and working to avoid those behaviors that can undermine the quality of the key social resource their relationship represents to them.

Limitations on Family Expectations' Impact

While Ann and Trenton and Carley and Nick could see Family Expectations' lessons bolstering their relationships, others find themselves struggling to actually implement what they learn. Hailey and Evan, both thirty-three, seem surprised to have found themselves where they are— attempting a serious romantic relationship with a baby on the way. Both have sons in junior high school and had been dating casually for only two months when Hailey got pregnant. Their nights out drinking and going to concerts were quickly replaced with discussions of whether and how to combine their family lives. But the union never seemed to find solid footing. Breakups were frequent, but temporary. After one reunion, the couple decided to marry and move in together. This legal commitment did little to calm their volatile fights.

The couple did try to save the relationship, adding marriage education classes at their church to the Family Expectations workshops in which they were already involved. While the two programs were complementary, Hailey and Evan were unable or unwilling to put into practice the lessons they had learned; by the third interview, Hailey had moved into her mother's house, taking her older son and the baby with her, and was in the midst of an acrimonious divorce. She tells me:

> We did use [those communication techniques] for a little while, but then stuff would get escalated and it would just go over the top. And, I mean,

I'm not a little princess either. I wouldn't use the tools either, once it got escalated and I felt like he wasn't listening to me, I would go over the top too.

Although they had learned how to take time outs, their arguments got heated so quickly, they often were unable to think clearly enough to take a break from the fight—they had trouble switching from pushing the gas pedal to the brake pedal once an argument got going.

Hailey says that before moving out of Evan's house, she saw the Family Expectations materials sitting on a shelf. She remembers thinking to herself:

> "We should have put that into effect. We should have just stopped and done it instead of letting our tempers escalate." . . . Take twenty minutes, take a break, breathe, go walk around the block, whatever, then come back. I think if we both would have really used that, and I was probably worse than he was about that because I'm the type of person, I need to fix it right now. But the thing with him is that he would use that every single time. "Oh, I need a break." And then he wouldn't come back to it. So I think if we really would have set a time, "OK, in thirty minutes we're gonna talk about this, but let's cool down," that that would have helped us a lot. A lot of nasty things wouldn't've been said. I think that's probably the biggest thing.

Unlike Carley and Nick, who used the labels of "dodger" and "chaser" to identify, understand, and address some of the conflict dynamics in their relationship, Hailey and Evan couldn't figure out how to make sense of the forces at work in their relationship and implement some ground rules to govern how they related to one another.

Other couples saw factors external to their relationship as impinging on their ability to implement some of the techniques they learned in Family Expectations. Abby and Darren find it nearly impossible to carve out the time or physical space to communicate in the ways they've learned from Family Expectations. Since Abby left the transitional living facility with their baby daughter, they've spent time living with her mom, with Darren's dad, and in motels. Living with family in close quarters has made it very challenging for them to focus on their relationship. They learned from Family Expectations about the importance of communication. But, as Abby explains, it's hard to make this happen:

> We're just starting to, you know, recognize, OK, we need to take a time out. . . . And we run and we stay at a hotel and we shut everybody out and we sit and talk. . . . We have to do that to be alone because we've been staying with his dad. But we get somewhere where there are no distractions. His mom will take [the baby] if she can, and we just, we just sit down and be like "OK, look . . ."

Obviously, finding child care and getting a motel room in order to have a discussion is prohibitive of Abby and Darren actually using the communication techniques they know on a daily basis. This means that the reality of their relationship, Darren says, is far more troubled than what they want for their daughter:

> Usually we just fight 'til we're tired and then make up later, you know, and it goes, kind of works itself out, but sometimes we can't just take the time out, you know, calm down, and one of us will end up going somewhere or saying something that the other don't feel like they can take back and it gets out of hand. I try to keep my main focus on the baby, you know, what she needs. That's pretty much why we're still together. We want what's best for her. You know, we love each other. It's not like we don't care about each other anymore, but it's all the stress built up.

Darren describes how they don't deploy their techniques from Family Expectations at the right place and right time to successfully resolve their arguments, with their efforts often not in alignment. "I'll use some of 'em and she didn't know how to use 'em then and she'll do the same. She'll try to use that technique when I'm fired up and I don't even want to talk to you. Just let me be." Nonetheless, Darren says:

> What we learned does help because . . . it reminds us. . . . She'll come back and say something nice . . . out of character. And I appreciate it and I do the same for her. . . . And she's done a wonderful job with [our daughter], you know. She watches her real closely. She . . . has a relationship with her.

She's not just there with the kid. She bonds with her. She got a lot of that from Family Expectations. . . . They try to teach you how to be parents together, you know, and she's learned a lot from it. . . . We both learned a lot from it. We just haven't learned to apply it right now.

Between their financial stress, living situation, and personal demons (discussed further in this book's conclusion), they sometimes feel like they have the will to implement what they've learned, but not always the way.

It's clear in the story of another couple—Mackenzie and Wayan—that these external factors matter. Both in their early twenties, this couple adds a second and third child (separate pregnancies) to their family and gets married during their year in Family Expectations. For much of the year they are living with Wayan's cousin's family, in a house that is crammed full, with the couple and their children sharing one bedroom. Eventually, they move in with Mackenzie's grandmother when the woman requires around-the-clock care. On top of the stresses of becoming her grandmother's caregiver, they had the surprise third pregnancy, during which doctors discovered Mackenzie had cancer; Mackenzie had to leave her job. Wayan also lost several jobs because their car was so unreliable he often couldn't make it to work. While their families are helpful in some respects—providing baby items and housing—in other ways they are a major strain as they question and try to undermine the couple's relationship.

Still, Mackenzie and Wayan are quite happy with how their relationship has developed over the year. Wayan reports they're arguing much less, which he credits to a combination of learning to take time outs and the newfound ease of actually doing so now that they're out of his cousin's house:

We'd just fight it out about it and stay in the same room. Now, get out of the room for a minute and when we all cooled down then, you know, go back. . . . When we're at our cousin's, we didn't have no kind of privacy, you know, it's like somebody was always there. So now it's like you go into the other room and chill and then come back in there. . . . I see things a lot different than I did back then. I felt like nothing was going right. And when things ain't going right, we always mad. . . . [B]ut now, you know what I'm saying, we're taking our time with it and when we have a problem, talk about it now. We didn't do that last year. . . . I mean, when it gets like that [with us arguing], a year ago I would have been all over her, but we fight a little bit and then when I see I ain't gonna win . . . I'll go outside or take a walk or something to get out there because I know if I stay, it's gonna be worse in the end. I don't want none of the kids to see us like that.

Mackenzie describes their new ways of dealing with conflict as a "relief." It means they're "not always stressing 'cause we're fighting and if we're gonna leave each other." Mackenzie and Wayan are armed with skills from Family Expectations and the space to use them, and so their relationship has weathered their trials and tribulations far better than Abby and Darren's. While Mackenzie and Wayan emerge from the year stronger, more positive about the future, and married, Abby and Darren are just barely holding their relationship together. While the physical space to implement these relationship techniques is only part of the story, it seems to be an important one.

Financial circumstances are one factor that makes progress difficult, but this is a challenge that some couples are able to weather. Ann and Trenton, Denelle and Otis, and Illisha and Aaron all face deep financial difficulties, yet they all see their relationships emerge stronger for their year in Family Expectations. Certainly, improved material circumstances can enable couples' use of the tools they learn at Family Expectations, as Mackenzie and Wayan's story illustrates. But money isn't where this story begins or ends; rather, parents like Hailey and Evan or Abby and Darren bring an explosive combination of personal circumstances—like addiction, felony convictions and related employment difficulties, and mental health issues without health care, as in Abby and Darren's case— that the Family Expectations intervention by itself may not be adequate to overcome, an issue I explore in greater detail in the next chapter.

Changes in Parenting

In recounting changes in their family lives, most parents focused primarily on Family Expectations' relationship lessons, but some described learning new information and techniques around child rearing. Norene, twenty-four, and Dave, twenty-nine, are notable in this regard. They are parents to four children between the two of them; while Dave's oldest son lives with his ex's mother, Norene's five-year-old, Donny, their shared three-year-old, Ricky, and baby Melody live with them. They were initially more interested in Family Expectations for the parenting aspects of the program, and indeed these seem to be what they focused on most in the workshops. A major takeaway for them was to be more supportive and verbally affirming of their kids—that is, to be more of a social resource to their children. From their perspective, though, this is also a way to build their relationship as a couple. Norene explains that they hadn't changed much about what they did as a couple: "I mean, we focus on each other, but we need to put more focus on our kids. But I think if we do that with the kids, you know, together, then I think that'll help us." And Dave clarifies by adding, "Bond us."

Specifically, Norene says she learned about safety practices with the baby and about how to feed Melody a healthier diet with more fruits and vegetables. They received referrals to a speech program for the middle boy and a summer reading program that helped get the oldest's literacy skills up to grade level. The change in the parenting techniques Dave uses are perhaps more fundamental. He explains:

> I was raised different, you know, always getting yelled at, and that's how I was seeing things, and I guess that's how I've always been so far until I went up there and seen . . . you can do it differently. I took that step and I've been using it here. Ricky, I guess, I'd been getting on him so much there at the end that, you know, he wouldn't come to me, he'd go to his mom. But now that I've been going up [to Family Expectations], I come back and I noticed that I tried to change. . . . I do other things a different way and now he's coming up to me, talking to me more, so I'm like, I've learned a lot. . . . I try not to yell at him. That's my biggest thing. I noticed that, like I said, I got a real short temper. . . . There's not to a point where I want to beat him or anything, but if he does get out of line I'll give him a little slap right there on the butt. . . . But lately, getting onto him, I have him sit out on time out or have him lay down and take a nap 'cause I know that there's times where he's tired, you know. If he gets out of hand, he won't get to play his Wii. I'll take the Wii from him, 'cause I know he wants to play that.

Dave was raised by his grandfather, who was heavy-handed when it came to discipline. Dave often felt judged and unsupported by his grandfather. These ideas from Family Expectations about how to parent are new to him, and he seems gratified that he and his son have been getting closer as he's tried new ways to keep the energetic preschooler from getting out of hand. In building his father-son relationship, Dave is trying to pass along a social resource, rather than social poverty, to the next generation.

When Mackenzie and Wayan had their first child, now two, Wayan took a backseat when it came to parenting, deferring to Mackenzie. Even though he had a good deal of experience taking care of children, a role he stepped into with his siblings after his mother's drug addiction drove her away from the family, he still felt like there was a lot he didn't know. As he learned about parenting in Family Expectations and the important role a father can play in his children's lives, Wayan wanted to step up more when their second daughter was born. He tells me:

> When we had her I didn't have patience at all. She crying, I'm like "Here Mackenzie. Here. I don't know what to do." But once we had our second child, that's when we came up [to Family Expectations] and they showed us how to control, you know what I'm saying, your patience and how to be patient and all that, so once [the baby] was here, you know, I was more laid-back and know, like in certain situations, how to handle it.

Wayan's growing confidence as a father is apparent. During our interviews, I often see him take the lead on caring for the baby or entertaining their preschooler.

Although she had been the parenting authority in their relationship, Mackenzie was also open to learning more about parenting. As the arrival of their daughter's "terrible twos" meant frequent tantrums, Mackenzie and Wayan disagreed on how to handle these fits. First Mackenzie refused to let Wayan spank the girl for acting out. When this approach didn't work, they both resorted to spanking her. Once they were in Family Expectations, though, they learned about some new approaches—necessary since the tantrums hadn't ceased. Mackenzie explains, "Now I'm sitting her down, talking to her, showing her that's not the right thing, . . . so like me and her's on a more better page. . . . She's starting to listen a lot better to me. . . . Like me yelling makes her yell louder and me yelling over her." Being able to avoid these yelling matches has been a welcome relief for Mackenzie and Wayan (and presumably their daughters too).

Taleisha, a twenty-year-old first-time mother, viewed Family Expectations as a relationship program, not a parenting program, but still found herself feeling more prepared and calm about life with a newborn thanks to the workshops. She explains:

> I was able to not get so stressed out as other new moms do. I would see my friends, they'd be all stressed out because their baby's crying, and I'm like "She's probably hungry" or "She just bored" because I was able to read my [Family Expectations] book and know. And [my baby] was doing everything right off the book. . . . I go through there and look at the little section on the baby and be like "Look, Baby, it said she'd do this at this age and this is why she's doing it" because she goes and rubs her hands through the carpet to find the littlest bittiest crumb and put it in her mouth and I'm like, I read that. . . . I love, you know, having all these extra resources that I can refer to so I don't freak out and be at the emergency room all the time and there's nothing wrong.

While Taleisha doesn't describe changes in her parenting behavior coming from her time in Family Expectations, as Dave, Wayan, and Mackenzie do, she has a greater understanding of child development and clearly feels more competent as a mother and less stressed as a result. These parents are likely better positioned to support their children's development.

Attributing Outcomes to Family Expectations

Breakups

Could Family Expectations have done more to "save" the relationships of the four couples in this study who broke up? One of the four couples never took part in the workshops but did stay in contact with their family support worker for many months. They had been on shaky ground all along, which may have been why they didn't actually commit to doing the workshops. Their series of excuses for why they hadn't begun the workshops sounded increasingly dubious. By the last interview, they had not been in touch with each other in five months. Their commitment to one another and to creating a family life together had been relatively weak from the beginning. Family Expectations could not, and perhaps should not, have "saved" this relationship. This case points to a central flaw in evaluating relationship education programs with a central focus on whether they boost the proportion of participants who stay together after enrolling: it is a distinct possibility that staying together is not the best outcome for some.

The second of the four couples—Hailey and Evan, profiled earlier—met, got pregnant, broke up, got back together, got married, and are now set to divorce all in the past eighteen months. There has always been a great deal of instability in this relationship. Evan was very marriage-averse—having refused to wed his older son's mother throughout their decade-long relationship—while this was Hailey's third marriage. They struggled to use Family Expectations tools when they were angry; they weren't good at heading off fights before they escalated. Adding to their stresses, around the time of their baby's birth Evan had lost his job and wasn't making, in Hailey's mind, an adequate effort to secure a new one, though they were making ends meet financially with Hailey's income. Another consistent issue in their relationship revolved around how to combine and reshape their families—both had preteen sons from previous relationships. Hailey felt she and her children took a backseat in Evan's mind to his older son, and he asserted that his son should come before Hailey. This made Hailey feel as though Evan wasn't willing to really make space in his life for the new family they were trying to build. In the month or so after she moved out of their house, they had several fights, typically via text message, and he had not seen the baby or contributed financially. Throughout these ups and downs, Hailey stayed in touch with her family support worker, but Evan did not; the worker has offered resources as Hailey navigates a divorce and looks ahead to going back to college.

Hailey and Evan may be a couple who were destined for breakup—with or without Family Expectations—as an accidental pregnancy only two months after they started dating had led them to a far more committed relationship than the two had intended. But their inability to put the brakes on once a conflict started raises questions about whether the way the time out technique is taught needs to be modified. Some people may lack the emotion regulation functions necessary to identify and act in the moments of a conflict before a fight spirals out of control.[1] Further innovation from curriculum developers in adapting this technique or the way in which Family Expectations participants are instructed in it may be necessary.

In the third of the four couples who broke up, Ciara, a twenty-one-year-old mother of two, said that her boyfriend, Drew, was unwilling to try to institute the tools they learned in Family Expectations or to try any of the others things she proposed to fix their relationship, including counseling, so she eventually gave up. Drew had lost his job and wasn't making an effort to help support their family; Ciara said he had begun wasting the income from her job and her older son's child support on drugs. They also had ongoing disagreements over how he dealt with her older son, with Ciara claiming Drew's expectations for the preschooler's behavior were unrealistic and his reactions to misbehavior too harsh. Since they split up, things have been very up and down between them— one day he'll be trying to win her back and the next he'll be cursing her out; she has no interest in getting back together. He has not contributed financially to the baby, but has seen him on occasion.

Ciara really loved Family Expectations, and Drew's lack of interest in the program was one of the signs to her that she couldn't make the relationship work. Ciara described Family Expectations as her "place to escape to" during and after the breakup. It seems a notable compliment of a program for couples if it can provide a sanctuary to an individual during a breakup. In fact, Ciara's family support worker helped her plan her breakup so that she knew she'd be able to leave safely. Ciara recalls:

> She helped me get sole custody of [the baby]. She helped me have an escape just in case he decided to snap. Like I knew who to call, I knew where to go. So she helped me a lot. . . . We talk about, you know, everything going on. If I'm stressed then I get to vent. . . . I definitely get to vent and I get to see where my budget's at and see how I've progressed.

In her worker, Ciara has found someone who provides emotional and practical support—a key social resource. While critics of relationship education have expressed concern that such programs would encourage or strong-arm women into staying in unhealthy relationships, Ciara and Hailey have had the opposite experience, using Family Expectations as a resource to help them through their breakups.[2]

The last of the four couples, Necie, a twenty-two-year-old mother of one, and Leonard, twenty-three, has broken up for long periods of time in the past. Although he thinks they will get back together and get married one day, she is very unsure of what might happen and seems to be jerked around by his whims. Despite how their relationship has played out, both have positive views of the Family Expectations program. In fact, Necie describes the two months or so that they were going to the workshops as the best time in their relationship. They were communicating, and she felt like Leonard was really committed to their future. It's not clear what made Leonard pull away again after the workshops. One of the negative influences Necie sees is Leonard's group of friends, who are not family-oriented, she says. He's also been very reluctant to commit to the relationship. While some fault for this may lie with his friends, his incomplete education and limited income seem to have left him feeling like he's not ready to fulfill his responsibilities as a partner or father. The future of this relationship still remains to be written, it seems. However, it raises the question of whether Family Expectations staff are equipped to help parents transition into coparenting roles while negotiating the romantic side of their relationship (e.g., that one partner may want to get back together). As research on young adult relationships in general and the unions of unmarried parents in particular suggests, there can be a good deal of churning and fluidity.[3] Family Expectations may need to build lessons for navigating tumultuous times and ongoing transitions in romantic and parenting relationships.

Marriages

Is Family Expectations the reason the couples who got married did so? Generally not. All who married entered the program either engaged or with plans to marry. Program participation was probably decisive for Mackenzie and Wayan, though. Their family support worker has played a large role in their lives, helping to sort out employment, transportation, housing, and child care for date nights. Additionally, although this couple had been saying they wanted to get married for a while, it was their worker offering that they could get married at the Family Expectations facility that seems to have pushed them from talk to action. Another couple, Steffy and Jim, whom we met at the start of the chapter, also credit Family Expectations with helping them stay together and proceed with their plans to get married.

Some politicians and activists support programs like Family Expectations based on their advocacy for the "marriage movement"—promoting the idea that people need to be taught to value and pursue marriage. Presumably to the chagrin of such supporters, Family Expectations does not engage in such explicit promotion.[4] Unmarried couples and even single mothers feel welcomed and supported by the program's staff. While there is an implicit positive value placed on marriage—couples are congratulated and given a small wedding present by the program when they marry, and the workshop educators are all married—those taking alternative relationship paths do not feel stigmatized. The program does not push marriage, and this is probably key to couples' positive valuations of it.[5] Evaluating the program based on how many marriages it produces would seem to miss the intent of what's happening on the ground.

Preventing Breakups

Did Family Expectations prevent any breakups? I could not say decisively yes or no. There are couples who say they would have been much worse off in their relationship if it hadn't been for their time in the program. These couples say their communication has improved—fights escalate less severely or less frequently—and they're happier and more stable in their relationships, but it's not clear if they would have actually broken up absent the intervention. But because social poverty is about feeling lonely, not being alone, such changes are essential in and of themselves, in parents' eyes.

Both Steffy and Jim, whom we met at the start of the chapter, have survived a bruising divorce in the past, and they are committed to making a better family life and romantic partnership this time around. More than anyone else in the study, they take the time to think about and consistently practice the techniques taught at Family Expectations, and they're seemingly the better for it, with Steffy crediting the program with saving their relationship. "If it hadn't been for Family Expectations to teach me to not be such a bitch, we might not have [made it]," she admits. From their time with the program they learned about "how to talk to each other." "That was a real big deal. Mainly the listening for me, because I can talk," she says with a laugh. She continues:

> When it came to something that upset me, I didn't want to hear it because I wanted to be right, obviously. So, yeah, it's taught me how to be able to say I'm wrong and not cry, and I can apologize and not feel like an idiot. . . . Mainly it taught us how to talk to each other. Especially when we were fighting, because we didn't know how to do anything but holler, you know, and name-call and all that stuff. I look back now and that was just so stupid. It's so much better like this.

The result is a family life that has fulfilled Steffy's dreams:

> I don't know where I'd be without [Family Expectations]. I mean, I can tell you, if we hadn't found 'em, we wouldn't have been together because we wouldn't have known how to work it out at that point. So, yeah, Family Expectations, they kind of saved my life because I don't know where I'd be. Now that I have what I have, I don't know where I'd be without it. So I'm really grateful.

Even other couples who end their year in Family Expectations with their relationship as far more of a work in progress than Steffy and Jim credit the program with saving their relationship. Denelle's boyfriend, Otis, credits Family Expectations with creating the changes in their relationship that were necessary to keep him from leaving. Even though he has four children from three other women, he had never really been in a relationship with any of the mothers of his children. This time he's trying to do things differently, and it hasn't been easy. The lessons from Family Expectations have been helpful, he says, because they're a reminder about "just sticking with it, talking about it, instead of just giving up and just leaving, sit down and talk about it. It might be an hour or two after, but talk about it." He's started to believe that a couple can get through tough times and that arguments can be solved. The result, Otis says, is that "I'm here! I'm telling you, I'm here," as he indicates the apartment—and seemingly the life together—that he and Denelle share with their baby girl.

From a researcher's perspective, I can't conclusively state the counterfactual—that in the absence of this program these couples would have broken up. But from the perspective of Steffy, Otis, and others like them, Family Expectations gave them the tools to communicate more positively and resolve conflict more productively, as well as a belief that sticking with it and working on a relationship is normal and the way to build the family lives they desire. The program helped to address their risks of social poverty, bolstering their relationships so they feel their unions are, on balance, social resources rather than sites of conflict. The program might not have kept them together, but it helped them build a relationship they wanted to keep.

An Overview: One Year Later

When they first enrolled in the program, eighteen couples (58 percent) were romantically involved but were neither engaged nor had concrete plans to marry, seven (23 percent) were engaged, and another six (19 percent) described concrete plans to marry, although they were not formally engaged. One year later, four (14 percent) were no longer romantically involved, 13 (46 percent) were still together but without plans to marry, five (18 percent) were engaged, and seven (25 percent) were married. While examining these relationship statistics is far from the only—or the most important—way of evaluating the program, doing so allows us to compare it to other quantitative research in the field.

Among the couples in the Building Strong Families (BSF) study, at the fifteen-month follow up survey, 24 percent were no longer romantically involved and 17 percent were married. In terms of relationship status, then, the Family Expectations couples' outcomes more closely achieve the goals of the intervention than do those of the BSF couples. The results in my study are comparable, however, to those of the BSF sample from Family Expectations, in which 19 percent were no longer romantically involved and 25 percent were married fifteen months after enrolling in the program.[6] Further, we can compare the relationship status of parents in Family Expectations with that of the unmarried parents in the Fragile Families and Child Wellbeing study, which is nationally representative of nonmarital births in American cities. Among the unmarried Fragile Families couples, one year after their babies were born,

42 percent were no longer romantically involved and 9 percent were married.[7] Compared with the Fragile Families couples, the more stable romantic relationships among the parents in Family Expectations are not surprising. First, these couples wanted to take part in a relationship education program, indicating a level of commitment to making their relationships work that may not be present among all unmarried parents. Second, participation in Family Expectations may have helped to solidify their relationships.

Among the couples in the present study, even within seemingly static relationship categories ("married," "no longer romantically involved"), there is a good deal of messiness.[8] A married couple may reveal that they recently had a time when one moved out for a few days, or a member of a couple that is no longer romantically involved might describe them as being on an extended break, as opposed to really broken up. Overall, relationship instability is not uncommon, but most couples are still trying to make their relationships work.

The year of couples' program participation coincided with the height of unemployment in Oklahoma following the Great Recession. This was reflected in the experiences of the couples I got to know, as many struggled with employment throughout the year, sometimes ending in a worse situation than the one in which they'd started. A year after enrolling in Family Expectations, twelve parents were working full-time and seven were working part-time; twenty-nine were unemployed, disabled, or out of the labor force (including two who were imprisoned). Ten fathers were employed full-time and another three part-time; two mothers were working full-time and four part-time. In only three couples were both partners working, while in eight couples, neither was employed. In line with these declines in employment from the previous round of interviews, couples' monthly incomes had also declined, ranging from $0 to $2,200, with an average of $1,065.[9] This is to say, improvements we see in couples' relationships, by and large, cannot be attributed to improvements in their financial situations, since money troubles were a constant or worsening worry for most.

Understanding the Results of the Building Strong Families Evaluation

The Building Strong Families study was a federally funded, randomized controlled trial of several relationship education and parenting curricula across eight sites in the United States. Approximately 5,000 unmarried parent couples were recruited; half were offered the opportunity to take part in group workshops, receive support from staff, and get referrals to other services (e.g., WIC), while the other half served as the control group. The sites varied in the curricula used and the type of organization running the intervention—from universities to nonprofit organizations to for-profit companies (like Public Strategies, which runs Family Expectations).

Most of the sites chose to use the curriculum Loving Couples Loving Children (LCLC), which John and Julie Gottman had adapted from their commercially successful program, Bringing Baby Home.[10] Family Expectations was the only site that used the Becoming Parents Program (BPP), supplemented with relationship education content from the Prevention and Relationship Education Program (PREP). Because these programs were being targeted at low-income, unmarried couples, a new audience for them, they were instructed by the federal funders and evaluators to adapt the form and content of material to meet the needs of this population. These curricula differ, in part, in their structure. For LCLC, participants met in small groups of four to six couples for approximately twenty weeks, receiving a total of forty-two hours of workshop time. At Family Expectations, participants met in groups of twelve to fifteen couples for six to ten weeks, receiving a total of thirty hours of workshop time. The curricula also differed in their content. Compared with Family Expectations couples, those who participated at LCLC sites received less exposure to topics around communication, marriage, infants/children, finances, and stress and more exposure to topics around conflict and affection. LCLC sites also differed in that the curriculum emphasized group discussions of couples' current issues; this is closer to a group therapeutic approach than in Family Expectations.[11]

Results of the study were largely disappointing for relationship education supporters and program staff. The impacts of the BSF programs were measured fifteen months and thirty-six months after couples enrolled in the study. Comparisons between the treatment group and the control group found that those in the treatment group were not more likely to stay together, nor did they report higher-quality romantic relationships. While these results held at most individual sites, there were a few exceptions, including Oklahoma's Family Expectations.[12]

At the fifteen-month survey, BSF treatment group couples from Family Expectations were more likely than control couples to still be together; they also reported better relationship satisfaction and less infidelity, a greater use of constructive conflict techniques and avoidance of destructive conflict behaviors, and more support and affection. Further, likely driven by the greater proportion of intact unions, fathers in the treatment group were more likely to be living with and providing financial support to their children than were fathers in the control group. By the three-year mark, the relationship quality differences between treatment and control couples had faded, but those who had enrolled in the Family Expectations program were more likely to still be together.

Another difference between Family Expectations and many of the other sites was apparent in the attendance rates. Overall, only 61 percent of BSF treatment couples attended at least one workshop session. In fact, at five of the eight sites, the majority of couples in the treatment group did not participate in the program at all—this is similar to most of the patients in the treatment group of a drug trial never taking the pills they're given. At Family Expectations, a quarter of couples never participated. Further, 45 percent of the treatment couples at Family Expectations completed at least four-fifths of the available workshop hours; no other site came close to having such widespread completion. While the very low participation rates at some of the sites could create the impression that couples are not interested in this service, the substantially higher frequency of participation at Family Expectations suggests otherwise.

The systems in place for getting couples through the door in the first place may be a concern. Although I did not interview couples from other programs, Family Expectations couples in my study did note the value of reminder phone calls, staff responsiveness, and the program's general environment (discussed in the introduction and chapter 5) in encouraging their participation. Seemingly minor issues like a lengthy wait from when a couple first contact a program to when they are invited to complete their enrollment documents or from when they enroll to the start of their first workshop session may deter couples from getting involved. This points to the need for a greater understanding of site-based differences in program management.

In conversations with Family Expectations staff, they were quick to note that they viewed the results from the BSF evaluation as a positive starting point but not an adequate finishing point. That is, they have continued to try to boost participation and couples' outcomes through management techniques, staff training, and curriculum refinement. Because they were starting Family Expectations from scratch at the beginning of the BSF study, they speculate hopefully that were the study redone today, findings would be far more robust, as they've learned from initial mistakes and tried to improve the program in a myriad of ways.

While the fading of the relationship quality benefits among Family Expectations participants at the three-year mark in the BSF study could be seen as a blow to the program's utility, there is an alternative interpretation: like the tetanus vaccine or learning algebra, the influences of the intervention wear off over time and may require a "booster" to have a lasting impact.[13] Indeed, as I interviewed couples a year after they initially enrolled, nearly all said they would be interested in taking part in another Family Expectations workshop to address the next set of challenges they faced in their lives. Ciara, who broke up with her boyfriend during the program, notes that it should offer more workshop series, so it could accompany her and her children throughout their lives. "Toddlers and preteens and out of the house and retirement. All of it," she says with a laugh. And Mackenzie wants to see the next generation benefit from the program like she and Wayan did: "I hope Family Expectations is around when [our daughters] get older!" Participants don't see the workshops as a onetime event that they'll never need again, which suggests that researchers and policy makers may also want to adjust their expectations. The program may help couples get on a better path (be that a life together or separately), but it's not a permanent solution to parents' challenges.

"Building Us Up Stronger"

Although the program does not articulate its mission in terms of addressing social poverty, Family Expectations seems to speak to the social needs parents have; the course lessons resonate with the communication and trust problems couples see in their own relationships, and the social support provided by the friendly and accepting program staff can be a welcome resource. Further, the workshops help parents carve out time to focus on each other and their relationship, with the program taking away the barriers—physical space, child care, and money—that otherwise stand in the way. Finally, I argue that a key benefit comes through the creation of "family expectations"; the program helps couples to label their behavior patterns, recognize that problems are common and solvable—as opposed to necessarily an existential threat to their relationship—and establish norms so that they can reasonably predict and understand how one another reacts to and approaches their relationship. Taken together, this works to address sources of social poverty in their lives, building more positive, supportive relationships. It does this by altering the qualities of their everyday interactions and their interpretation of these interactions; making relatively small changes in how couples communicated and dealt with conflict helped partners to feel safer and more secure in their unions. In this way, these were investments in resources that could keep parents out of social poverty or lift them out of its grasp.

We see many of these key features emerge for Elyse and Robert, who are in their early twenties and having their first child. Prior to the program, Robert had brushed aside issues Elyse raised if they weren't important to him. As a result of participating in the program, they say, Robert started taking Elyse's concerns more seriously, and Elyse began to see how approaching their arguments differently might get her more of the reaction she wanted. She says that before Family Expectations, when they got into a disagreement she basically didn't care how Robert was feeling: "I wanted to talk about it, you know. I just wanted to get it over and done with, so I can get everything off of my chest, so I can feel good, better. Yeah, I would follow him down the stairs, like 'What's going on? Why are you mad at me?' . . . So when we went to that lesson [on dodger-chaser and time out] . . . he's like 'You do that.' I said, 'Oh, yeah, I do do that.'" Elyse admits with a sheepish smile, "I still have to catch myself though, 'cause I still do it." I ask her how it feels now when Robert leaves to take a walk when things get heated, and she says, "I feel a whole lot better. . . . It still kind of bothers me, but . . . it helps. It helps a lot. . . . Try to remember it. . . . 'OK. I'll just stay here and he'll go there and come back.'"

These sorts of changes in behavior and in how they think about the relationship are very meaningful to Elyse and Robert. She says of their time in the Family Expectations workshops, "It helps strengthen your relationship. . . . Yeah, it's made us a whole lot better. 'Cause we probably wouldn't really even be together now if it wasn't for Family Expectations, 'cause we were having some pretty bad problems [when we enrolled]." And Robert agrees, joking:

> Well, [our relationship] was getting dragged through the mud. . . . Then after [Family Expectations], you know, we graduated from the water and started dragging ourselves through dirt. . . . While the program was going on, I mean, after every week that went on, I saw us getting a whole lot better 'cause . . . we was finally able to realize, "Hey, this is what we're doing now." . . . Now we can identify exactly what the problem was. . . . It was like Family Expectations put a phrase or a word above the problem we had. It was like "This is your problem here," so now we knew how to take care of what steps we needed to do to take care of it, so that was definitely building us up stronger each week.

Like many other couples, Elyse and Robert are not unrealistic about the state of their relationship—they're still slogging "through dirt," but they feel they're moving in the right direction as a family. Having hope that the relationship will last helps it serve as the social resource they crave.

Elyse and Robert's story is testimony to the complex ways in which Family Expectations works to affect a couple's relationship. They learned concrete conflict management techniques, like time out. But they also learned to recognize negative behavior patterns—like the dodger-chaser dynamic—in their relationship. Having "a phrase or a word above the problem," as Robert puts it, made them feel like they had a better handle on why arguments would blow up, and this made them more hopeful that they could change their relationship for the better. Family Expectations didn't solve all their problems, but it gave them some tools to experience fewer storms and to weather those that do come their way. As parents to a newborn baby, and having seen strife in their parents' relationships when they were children, the couple considers the changes both in expectations—when Robert goes to take a walk during an argument, it's just a break, not a breakup—and in behaviors deeply important as they try to build the family life they desire.

Conclusion

Escaping Social Poverty

Relationship education programs have undeniably failed to deliver on their initial promise to address income poverty. But to evaluate this policy solely through an income poverty lens would, in some ways, miss the point. Social poverty is a pressing problem for many of the young, low-income parents the programs serve. Relationship education programs draw these couples through their doors by offering a potential solution to this social deprivation.

As Richard Reeves, Edward Rodrigue, and Elizabeth Kneebone, of the Brookings Institution, write:

> Poverty as a lived experience is often characterized not just by low income, but by ill health, insecurity, discomfort, isolation, and lack of agency. . . . The main thrust of policy will be—and should be—to try and reduce the number of people who are disadvantaged on each of these and other dimensions. . . . [I]t is important to consider ways to *de-cluster* as well as to *reduce* disadvantage. These goals are perfectly compatible.[1]

Seeking to address social poverty should not be seen as a competing policy objective with successfully easing income poverty. We can both try to address multiple forms of poverty simultaneously and make it less likely that experiencing one form of poverty will mean a high likely of experiencing another. While relationship education is not an effective tool for addressing financial poverty, it seems to offer one way forward in making people feel more secure in their social resources. We might not want to spend government money that we've earmarked for economic support to this end, but that doesn't mean it's not an end worth supporting.

Twenty-eight-year-old Ann and thirty-year-old Trenton live in a small white house, located on a street of modest, single-family homes.

The decoration of the house is somewhat successful in masking its condition. The front door opens into a living room that has a TV, coffee table, and brown leatherlike couch. It's decorated with an animal print rug, photos of their children, and colorful candles. Some pictures of crosses lean against the wall, waiting to be hung. The smell of incense lingers in the air, and the air conditioner is running in the window next to the table. Upon a closer look, the flaws of the house become more obvious—a nearly three-foot section of the living room ceiling is completely falling in. When I leave later, I notice that an outside corner of the eaves is torn up and a bird's nest of straw and grass now occupies this roof space.

Ann is heavyset with a wide, round face. Her hair is brown with some bits of dyed blond remaining; it's slicked down to the sharp part in the middle and pulled back into a low ponytail. She's wearing a T-shirt featuring an image of President Obama's face. She has a tattoo of a black panther running the length of the inside of her forearm. Her light-colored, overly plucked eyebrows arch over her brown eyes.

Trenton's head is shaved, and his beard extends into a three-inch-long, thin braid. He's wearing baggy jeans (with his build, I suspect anything would be baggy on him) held up by a brown leather belt and a sharp-looking, brightly colored polo shirt decorated with green, light blue, and dark blue stripes; he wears his shirt tucked into his pants. He has a small diamond-like stud in each ear.

The couple was together for a year and a half before deciding to have a baby together. Each has an elementary school–aged daughter from a previous relationship; while Ann's daughter, Piper, lives with the couple full-time (her father is out of the picture), Trenton's daughter, Destiny, lives with his ex-wife, coming to spend the night on weekends. Although Ann and Trenton had discussed getting married, the pregnancy came along first, and they didn't feel any need to rush down the aisle.

When we first met, Ann was pregnant, which was making it harder than usual for her to get around. Years back she suffered a workplace injury that led to an unsuccessful knee surgery, difficulty standing for long periods, and limited mobility. For someone with only a GED, finding a job that can accommodate such physical limitations was quite difficult, leading her to go on disability. Trenton typically did construction work for his stepfather's company but had recently seen a big drop in income after a broken ankle meant he needed to find other work—a gig as a pizza delivery man meant there was some income coming in, but not much.

Ann and Trenton were touchingly sweet when we talked the first two times. When they looked at each other, the love in their eyes was clear to see, and they became visibly emotional hearing the good things each had to say about the other. At one point, when Ann was describing how she wished Trenton wouldn't put all his stress on himself—noting that he should remember that they're in this together—Trenton started crying. Upon seeing his tears, Ann also teared up. She reached over to touch his face, saying that she loves him, and he leaned toward her and they kissed twice.

When I return to their little white house a year later, a lot has changed. Baby Aiden has joined the family. He has generous cheeks and wisps of black hair that are curly on top. He's wearing a onesie with an elephant and the word "Love" on the front with dark-washed blue jeans and blue socks. While I visit, he's quiet and generally quite content to get cuddled by Piper or sit in his walker or on his mom's lap. Aiden has brought a lot of joy to the couple and has given Ann a positive focus in life. But perhaps the bigger change in their family is Trenton's absence from the home.

Trenton went to prison a few months after Aiden was born; he has been there for almost five months by the time we meet. Although Ann knew about the pending court case, she was under the impression that Trenton's lawyer would be able to arrange things so Trenton wouldn't have to serve time. She discovered this was not the case when Trenton didn't come home that day; she called his lawyer and learned that he'd been sentenced to three years in prison on a felony conviction. She doesn't seem to harbor resentment that Trenton didn't give her any warning, agreeing with what she assumes to be his logic, that she would just have freaked out even though they couldn't do anything about it.

Because of overcrowding in the state penitentiary, Trenton is being held in a jail about an hour-and-a-half drive from Oklahoma City. Since their car is only good enough for going short distances, Ann doesn't want to risk driving down there to visit. So they've worked hard to maintain their relationship from afar. They write letters every day or two, with Ann including pictures of Aiden with every letter. When she can, Ann puts money on a credit card so Trenton can call home, which happens two or three times a month. Through his letters, Trenton tries to be as involved in parenting Aiden as he can be, offering advice and making suggestions about all the little details of taking care of the baby. Ann seems happy to hear his ideas. She says that as soon as Trenton gets out, they plan on getting married. She thinks their lives will actually be better after he gets out because this court case and the possibility of his going to prison have been hanging over them for years, as have his payments to his lawyer. All those emotional and financial stresses will be gone once he's released. Ann says she knows they would have made it through all these difficulties no matter what, but that their relationship wouldn't be as "perfect" as it is now without Family Expectations. Despite what it costs her financially—with jail phone calls and related expenses straining her limited budget—Ann feels the financial costs are worth it because of the social resources she gains for herself and her son as she pays to maintain her relationship with Trenton.

A Multiplicity of Transitions

The young parents profiled in this book are experiencing a variety of major life transitions simultaneously: attempting to figure out their educational and career futures; establishing their own households and managing their limited finances; trying to find and hold down jobs in the face of transportation troubles and felony records; struggling to make their romantic relationships work and questioning whether their unions are worth the effort; and becoming parents. These transitions involve transforming their roles, their identities, and their daily routines. And they are often a gamble. Do you try to live on your own—like a "proper" adult—since you now have a boyfriend and child, despite your financial insecurity, or do you remain living with relatives, despite the stresses of doing so? Do you put school on the back burner to focus on making ends meet now, or do you take the risk of running aground economically now for the chance of the longer-term payoff from a college degree? Do you further enmesh your life with your girlfriend's even as you question your own ability to be the man she wants and her willingness to talk through troubles with you rather than running off to her mom's house every time you have a fight?

Struggles to achieve the traditional markers of adulthood are not experienced equally across the population, with lower-income young adults facing greater challenges. Today, across demographic groups, young adults are far more likely to be living with their parents than were their age counterparts in 1970.[2] This may be the product of struggles to complete desired transitions, rather than a preferred state. Among today's cohort of young men, earnings are lower compared with their counterparts in 1975, save for those of college graduates.[3] With limited financial means, independent living, financial responsibility, securing reliable transportation, and being an attractive marriage partner all become more difficult to achieve.

Those with less than a four-year college degree are less likely to marry and more likely to divorce than their higher-educated counterparts.[4] And it's not that they are stably cohabiting instead. It is those with a college degree who are likely to see their cohabiting unions lead to marriage rather than a breakup.[5] The lower one's educational attainment, the higher one's risk of experiencing a breakup (including both marital and cohabiting unions), over and above a wide range of other factors.[6]

However, explanations for "fragile family" outcomes—such as the frequent dissolution of cohabiting parents' relationships—that focus exclusively on economic obstacles or weakened relationship norms are missing the point. While liberals often focus on the former and conservatives on the latter, both explanations matter. Financial hardships are a clear source of stress on the family in general and the couple bond in particular.[7] However, in previous eras, couples who were struggling financially were less likely to divorce than are comparable couples today.[8] Family sociologists Kathryn Edin and Paula England explain, the growing inability of less-educated men to support a family on their wages "explains only a small fraction of the retreat from or delay of marriage."[9] It is not the case, however, that couples split up today simply because they no longer value marriage and commitment. And so, to focus only on cultural factors would ignore the omnipresence of financial factors in shaping individuals' lives and couples' relationships.

Social and economic factors are *working together* to create instability. Weathering the stresses of financial hardship is that much more difficult when a couple lacks a clear commitment and has inadequate communication skills to work through troubles. Couples who are good at coping with problems do not report increases in conflict when experiencing financial pressures; those couples, however, who normally struggle to solve problems see their relationship quality and stability disintegrate under economic pressure.[10] Such an environment is not conducive to relationship success because, without adequate relationship skills, couples are missing the fundamental elements that make trust, and therefore deep and lasting commitment, possible. In short, these factors create a context in which social poverty is a distinct likelihood, and social poverty makes it that much harder for a relationship to be maintained in the face of financial strains.

The stories of Ann and Trenton and others like them illustrate how focusing solely on economic factors limits the policy options available for supporting couples as they try to build their family lives. It is doubtful that our society will totally erase the possibility of families encountering financial hardship; after all, a tight bottom line is hardly just the province of the poor. And easing financial hardship does not automatically translate into changes in relationship behavior.[11] Few social programs that intervene to increase participants' material well-being end up affecting marriage rates, particularly for men.[12] Therefore, given the seeming inevitability of economic pressures for many couples, helping to build the skills that are compensatory and buffering in the face of these pressures may be key to their well-being and avoidance of social poverty. While improved financial circumstances would certainly do much to ease some stresses for Family Expectations participants, addressing financial poverty is not likely to solve social poverty. But there is evidence that equipping people with better interpersonal skills can help guard their relationships—a key social resource—against the destructive power of financial stress.[13]

Financial poverty matters, without a doubt. However, to assert that in the presence of financial poverty no other issues can or should receive priority fails to respect the wishes, plans, and needs of low-income people. As we hear from the parents throughout this book, securing social resources for themselves and their children is a primary concern. Consequently, we must conduct social analysis, policy, and program evaluation accordingly.

Programs' Potential to Alleviate Social Poverty

While previous research has not analyzed policies and programs through the lens of social poverty, we nonetheless can find evidence of success in addressing this need from other interventions. I offer two examples here to illustrate this point. In the mid-1990s, low-income adults in inner-city Milwaukee participated in the New Hope project; the program offered employment assistance, income supplements, subsidized health insurance, and subsidized child care. Researchers found that, even five years after the project ended, participants' children showed better educational attainment and engagement than those in the control group. They speculate that part of this effect may have been due to changes in parenting that resulted from their parents' "respectful and useful" interactions with the New Hope staff. This newfound "social support," researchers say, may have been key to improving parents' psychological well-being, which in turn shaped their relationships with their children.[14] This suggests that creating social resources may be part of having a successful program.

As a second example, Pamela Holcomb and colleagues have identified multiple ways in which men in fatherhood programs discover a salve to their social poverty. First, men chose to participate in the program because their relationships with their children were not going as they wanted; the program helped them develop the skills they felt they needed to (re)build their ties with their children. Second, participants found a community among themselves within the program; they particularly valued the camaraderie with men who shared their values around the importance of fatherhood to their identities. Third, men found program staff who supported their pursuit of these values and reinforced their identities as fathers. Their relationships with staff made them feel like they had someone to turn to, and the program as a whole provided a place where they felt like they "fit in."[15] Their participation created a variety of avenues through which men's socioemotional needs were met and their social resources were bolstered.

These examples suggest that addressing social poverty is not simply the purview of Family Expectations specifically or relationship education programs more generally. Rather, participants highly value these features of programs, and programs seem to be able to deliver, at least to some extent, in meeting participants' social resource needs.[16] Further research is undoubtedly warranted to better understand how programs can be designed to purposefully meet social needs as part of their missions; nonetheless, initial evidence—even beyond the present study—is encouraging.

Family Expectations: A Port in a Storm

Couples come to Family Expectations in need of help negotiating their life transitions. Many of the young people here are taking on multiple transitions at once, with each potentially a destabilizing force in other areas of life. With so much uncertainty, the foundations for trust and commitment in their relationships are wobbly. While the program focuses on partnership and parenthood, it is clear that these are far from the only challenging changes they are working through, as detailed in chapters 2 through 4. Added to this mix, few have grown up seeing other relationships on which they can model their own. Stories of parents' breakups, divorces, mistrust, and violence were the more commonly shared childhood recollections.[17]

Couples are unsure of what they should expect of themselves and their partners in their relationships and as parents. They aren't sure how to communicate, whether it's OK to fight and how to do so fairly, and how to protect their fledgling relationships from the stresses they are facing. They want to stay together, to raise their children as a family under one roof, but they want some guidance in securing this future. And so they arrive at Family Expectations.

These young parents typically saw their participation in Family Expectations as having benefited their relationships. They discussed two main types of benefits: the first was a set of practical tools they adapted to improve their communication, taking greater care to understand one another's perspective or calling a time out before an argument went over the top; the second was a set of shared expectations of how partners should treat one another so that the other's behaviors were no longer so mysterious, despite the lack of social norms governing the relationships of cohabiting couples and unmarried parents. Overwhelmingly, even among those who had dropped out of the program, assessments of it were positive, with parents referring their friends to the program and expressing an interest in attending additional workshops in the future if Family Expectations were to offer them. It felt like a good place, with good people, who were helping them create a better life.

Twenty-one-year-old Taleisha and thirty-year-old Darrell are first-time parents. The couple has faced triumphs and setbacks over the year they've been involved in the program. Darrell wants to be the provider in the family, but his felony record has made it very difficult for him to hold down a stable job. Securing even a temporary job felt like a win, but after each temp position ended, Darrell was left searching and scrounging. And so Taleisha has taken on the role of breadwinner, which she is happy to do, but she sees how it eats away at Darrell that he can't be the "future husband" and father he wants to be. Family Expectations offered them a model of relationships that was not so traditionally gendered as the one Darrell idealizes. Taleisha says, "I don't mind helping you because I feel like, they told us at Family Expectations, well, you're not always gonna be working. One of you might lose a job sometimes and it's up to that other partner to step up and, you know, I don't mind stepping up." But Darrell's traditional norms weren't shaken by the alternative the program presented.

Where the couple has found common ground, though, is in adopting the advice Family Expectations offered about making time for their relationship and for fun, to ensure that the stresses of daily life don't destroy their bond. At the program's suggestion, the couple has a "fun jar" from which they can draw slips of paper with free activities jotted down. Taleisha explains:

> We don't have that much money. Fun jar for us would be coming to the park, going down by the river, and walking with the stroller 'cause I do want to lose some weight, so whenever the weather's not bad, we'll go, I keep her stroller in my trunk and we'll go and just walk and just talk. . . . Go to the park or something, put her on the swings, go down the slide. To us that's fun jar 'cause we don't really go out or whatever. . . . Yeah, without talking about the kids or the stresses. Just go and have fun for that. And [Family Expectations] taught us how to do that too. Don't talk about nothing that's going on through the week or anything y'all are arguing about. Just have fun and take a load off.

It is important to them, they say, to look up from their daily struggles and enjoy the pleasure of one another's company. Taleisha continues:

> I think it makes a difference 'cause I get to kind of see, you know, he still loves me and he's willing to participate with me to make the relationship work and do, not whatever I say, but some of my little ideas and his ideas too. Do stuff together where we can show each other we don't always have to argue. There will be fun times in our relationship despite the other stress, you know.

In lives as stressful as Taleisha's and Darrell's, such a reminder is deeply needed.

Nonetheless, Family Expectations was not a magic pill that cured all their ills. Even among those couples who saw a lot of positive growth in their relationships, there were still many struggles. At our last meeting, Taleisha and Darrell were strained nearly to the breaking point. After he had to move out of her housing unit (he hadn't been on the lease), he's basically been homeless, and when Taleisha can't track him down, she gets angry, wondering whether he's with another woman. Some of the hardships couples like Taleisha and Darrell face stem from the need for continued learning and work in cementing positive ways of treating one another and viewing their relationship. Others come from forces outside the relationship—such as incarceration, arguments with kin, or financial troubles—that make the obstacles couples need to surmount that much higher.

Limitations to Supporting Families through Relationship Education

This raises the question of whether Family Expectations is a reasonable or an adequate response to the struggles these young people face in negotiating life's transitions. Their positive views of the program suggest that it is at least a reasonable response to their needs; in some cases, it's likely not enough.

CHILDHOOD TRAUMA

Childhood trauma may build barriers to participants implementing the skills they've learned. Creating shared expectations is not the same as building the capacity to deliver on them. This is certainly not the case for all participants in the program, but it is more likely among the parents served by Family Expectations than among the original target of first-generation relationship education efforts with middle-class, married populations.[18] Unmarried parents are more likely to describe traumatic childhood experiences,[19] which may make it less likely that some can successfully implement the skills they learn in the program.[20]

Trauma can influence children's development, including their executive function and self-regulation.[21] It also can affect children's physiological development, including their neuroendocrine stress responses, resulting in over- or underreactive responses to stressful situations (i.e., hyper- or hypocortisolism).[22] In addition, childhood trauma can influence psychosocial development, possibly resulting in lower self-efficacy (your belief in your ability to have some control over how your life plays out)[23] or insecure attachments to caregivers.[24] These effects can carry over into adulthood. The physiological, psychological, and emotional consequences of highly stressful childhoods, therefore, can affect romantic relationships and, potentially, the ability to enact the skills Family Expectations teaches and secure desired social resources.

Using the program's tools is dependent not just on understanding them intellectually but also on whether one has the psychic resources to implement them. For example, some parents may lack the emotion regulation functions necessary to identify and act on the moments in a conflict before a fight spirals out of control. Childhood trauma may make it more likely that partners' conflicts escalate quickly and that they have more limited abilities to follow through on taking a needed time out to halt such escalations.[25]

Hailey and Evan are more economically advantaged than the typical Family Expectations couple. When I first meet them, they are in their early thirties, and both have stable jobs with decent incomes. But within a few months of their baby's birth, Hailey had moved out and was seeking a divorce. Hailey says she recognized the value of the tools they were learning in Family Expectations, but once a fight got going, it would "go over the top" quickly, and any thought of good communication skills or healthy conflict tactics would go out the window. Were they to have behaved as they'd learned to do, Hailey believes, their marriage could have been saved.

By way of understanding Hailey and Evan's struggles to implement what they learned, their family histories may be relevant, as they both reveal having had traumatic experiences while growing up. Hailey was sexually abused, which she explains as a cause behind some of the mental health struggles she's faced since then. In addition, her mother has grappled with mental health issues of her own. Evan's father was an alcoholic, which played a role in the demise of his relationship with Evan's mom. Her next husband was physically abusive to Evan, his mother, and his siblings. As Evan puts it, "When I got old enough, I had to throw him out, or he'd probably still be kicking the crap out of her today. So I learned how to drink and how to fight from my parents."

Relationship education participants can understand the mechanics of the tools and even appreciate their value, but this doesn't necessarily mean they'll be able to implement them in the heat of the moment. And part of what is important to understand about the effects of trauma is that it can make the moment heat up much more quickly than what would be experienced by others without a history of trauma. This means that people may be less able to calm themselves down and to think clearly when emotions get heightened and also have a shorter time frame in which to accomplish these tasks. Curriculum developers in the relationship education field should contend more deeply with whether and how the cognitive, physiological, and psychosocial consequences of childhood trauma and stress play a role in mediating the effects of program participation in adulthood; they could work to include relationship education techniques that have been found effective for those affected by childhood trauma.[26] In addition, relationship education could be offered as part of a suite of services, which may include therapy for some.

MEN'S MULTIPLE BARRIERS

The stories of the most disadvantaged fathers beg serious questions about whether relationship education alone can ever be an adequate response to their complex needs. These are fathers with multiple barriers to success (limited education, spotty employment history, troubled family background, felony convictions, no driver's license, child support arrears, etc.) and who would be offered as "Exhibit A" in other studies for a lack of "marriageable" men available to lower-income women. However, these men really seem to want to do the right thing by their partners and, especially, by their children. It is very hard for them to stay on the right path when they can rarely find any success in doing so, and at times they can face trade-offs—for example, for some, being a good financial provider can most easily be accomplished by dealing drugs. Some may turn away from their roles of partner and father when they feel like they are failing in fulfilling these standards. Understandably, their female partners are not always supportive of their struggles as they are the ones left keeping it together for the kids.

When I first met him, Darren, twenty-nine, was getting ready to have his fourth child, his first with girlfriend Abby, while completing a drug rehab program. His parents had split up when he was one, but their fighting didn't stop, leaving him feeling stuck in the middle. His father then moved into a rough neighborhood. "I'd rebel. Mom'd want me in school, doing right, and I'd be like 'No.' Go stay with my dad for a while. I got involved in gangs. It was pretty rough when I was around him." After getting his girlfriend pregnant, Darren dropped out of high school, taking and passing a GED test just days later. He had two more children with other women before meeting Abby. His previous relationships with his children's mothers ended within a year or two of the children's births. And the drug trade and drug use to which he was introduced in his dad's neighborhood have had a lasting effect on him; he started selling meth around the time of his first baby's birth and has struggled with addiction as well. Now he's been out of prison for two years and is trying to stay away from his old life and neighborhood. He was optimistic about what the future held for him, Abby, and their baby.

When we meet for the last time, a year later, Darren and Abby are teetering on the brink of homelessness, shifting between her mom's, his dad's (where he had vowed not to return), and motels; and they don't have a car, making it quite challenging to go to appointments or hold down a job. Though their daughter is just cutting her first teeth, her parents' relationship is already decaying, as happened with Darren and his previous girlfriends. In light of their financial difficulties, unstable housing, and employment problems, I ask Darren how he's been doing staying sober. He responds:

Doing real well for a long time and [then] . . . I started smoking some weed. You know, to calm my nerves. . . . I get to stressing and need to get high. I used to take prescription medication, you know, Xanax and Prozac and stuff like that, but I just, I can't afford that stuff anymore, you know. They diagnosed me with bipolar and everything else, and they tell me what medications I need, but I can't afford 'em, so I go smoke me some weed. . . . With the marijuana, it's just [making me] lazy. So, I'm probably one of the least, least lazy people you know. I'm pretty motivated, and every time I get me some of that, something messed-up happens. . . . I mean, if I had, like a Xanax or Prozac, or they had me on Zoloft for a while, I would feel, I would feel calmer, but I wouldn't be lazy. . . . I get to smoking too much marijuana and I don't feel like doing nothing. I feel better, but I don't get nowhere, you know.

He tries to avoid smoking pot, he explains, despite the fact that it eases his mental health issues, but "when bad stuff happens to me and [Abby], go our separate ways, or we'll have a big fight and I'll go to cool off, that's when I want to smoke, you know, or all these bills stacking up." Darren is able to find solace in his daughter, though. He tells me:

Angel's really happy. . . . She's spoiled, you know, but that's what keeps me going. As long as she's happy, I'm all right. She eats. She don't miss a meal. She's taken care of. . . . [W]e've kind of let ourselves, our relationship, get put on hold. . . . We've had one day in the past ten months, maybe two days, that we've had [to spend together while Angel was with his mother]. And we spent one of 'em fighting. You know, it's ironic, but we did.

Men like Darren have a host of complex, intertwined issues ranging from mental health problems to addiction to homelessness to unemployment to felony convictions. Doing the right thing—not selling drugs to make some easy money when they're broke, for example—can feel like a triumph to Darren, but it's one that earns him no accolades, even from his girlfriend. Darren clings very tightly to an identity as a "good father," but his myriad struggles make it difficult for him to live out this role the way that he'd like to.[27] Relationship education alone, even if effective at teaching new skills and firming up shared expectations, faces a steep, uphill battle to change Darren's trajectory as a partner and parent.

Updates: What Has Happened since the Interviews

Some five years after I last spoke to these young men and women, I attempted to contact them again. Not surprisingly, most phone numbers were disconnected or belonged to someone new, and e-mails bounced back as undeliverable.[28] Ultimately, I was able to reach only three of the thirty-one original couples, and they were hardly representative of those I originally met. All three couples—Cara and Marvin, Carley and Nick, and Jessica and Will—were still together. I expect that those couples who were more stable were the ones whose phone numbers were still connected years later. While all still faced many of the same stresses of life—juggling educational pursuits, work, kids, and finances—they all reported feeling safely settled into their marriages, facing these stresses as a team.

While Marvin had dreamed of going to law school, already having a bachelor's degree under his belt, he ultimately put his educational dreams on hold to work and do a lot of the child care so Cara could finish community college, then college, and then enter graduate school. He is just now making his way back to his plans to pursue an advanced degree. Along the way they've added a third little one to their family, and they've moved three times. But Cara notes that they still use what they learned through the parenting classes Family Expectations connected them to; and the speaker listener magnet they received in Family Expectations has made the move onto the fridge in each of their three houses, reminding them "about taking turns and active listening," Cara explains. Although trying to juggle so many responsibilities takes a lot out of them, occasionally leaving them feeling "like roommates," Cara says, they are now married and "so very close."

Jessica and Will have also gotten married and purchased a home. Jessica balances running a small home business with taking care of their four—going on five—children, while Will works for a local utility company. Interference from family (especially his mom) remains a primary source of stress for the couple. Jessica wishes Family Expectations could have taught them more about how to deal with those kinds of issues, but nonetheless she credits the program with strengthening their relationship. "It really did teach us to work together. . . . We really did learn how to talk to each other more. . . . I've still never seen a program that's helped as much as that at getting everybody ready. It took off a lot of stress with the Crib Cash. . . . I've always recommended it for friends." And, ever since their time in Family Expectations, Jessica tells me with loving exasperation, Will has impishly teased her, encouraging her to tell him "how she really feels," harkening back to communication lessons they learned in the program.

Carley and Nick have been busy juggling work, caring for their two children, and continuing to pursue college degrees. The duo still struggles to keep their fights from being damaging; while Carley still threatens to leave Nick when their arguments escalate, she never really has. Family Expectations has continued to serve as a reference point for them, a reminder of the healthy relationship behaviors they're meant to pursue. Nick reminds Carley to use the speaker listener technique, and Carley says, "We have that book [from Family Expectations], that binder full of papers on the bookshelf in our living room. . . . Before [Family Expectations] neither of us were educated on how to communicate; we still go back [to] that knowledge."

While far from representative of all the couples who have passed through Family Expectations' doors, these three couples all maintain that Family Expectations benefited them, particularly in boosting their communication skills. In addition, their past participation in the program now offers them an easy shorthand for reminding one another (and themselves) of the need for respectfully talking through life's inevitable challenges. All three of these couples had broken up and gotten back together at least once before enrolling in Family Expectations. The stable footing they've now found in their relationships means they have an essential social resource—one another—on which to rely.

How to Move Forward

The debate over marriage has made enemies out of those who could otherwise be policy collaborators. Those who advocate the idea of "promoting" marriage are out of step with today's mainstream American values, which embrace individuals' abilities to form the families they choose for themselves. Further, stigmatizing those who by choice or accident are parenting outside of marriage does more to fuel talk of "culture wars" than it does to fuel policy action to support parents in doing their best by their children. Likewise, those who see any support offered to couples as an insult to single parents are missing out on what many unmarried parents want for themselves: a lasting, healthy relationship with their child's other parent.

Public opinion on changing family forms shows that many eschew the duality at the heart of political debates on this topic, embracing the ideals both of marriage and of family diversity, indicating a preference for parents being married and maintaining that single parents can do well by their children. Young adults are far less concerned than older generations about rising rates of nonmarital childbearing and are far more likely to view growing family diversity as a positive change in society.[29] Views have evolved fairly rapid: while less than half of American adults saw nonmarital childbearing as acceptable in 2002, approximately 60 percent did just over a decade later.[30] However, more than two-thirds of adults (and more than half of never-married parents) say that children need to live with both their parents to grow up "happily." And more than two-thirds also say that if a couple is planning to be together for the rest of their lives, it is "somewhat" or "very" important that they get married. At the same time, nearly 60 percent of adults say that divorce is preferable to staying in an unhappy marriage.[31] Public opinion, therefore, illustrates social scientist Andrew Cherlin's argument that the United States is exceptional in its simultaneous embrace of marriage and individualism; we maintain this relationship ideal of marriage while increasingly accepting alternatives.[32] This is also embodied in the family lives of the couples profiled in the preceding chapters: pregnancy before marriage, but a desire for a future together as a family. Like the general public, they believe that children are most likely to be happy in a home with both of their parents. But like other young adults, they are also accepting of their families taking other forms.

This book offers a set of takeaway lessons for policy makers, practitioners, and researchers that includes but extends beyond relationship education programs. Here I discuss three general lessons and three that are specific to the relationship education field. As a guiding principle, I suggest that we must *take social poverty seriously*. Just because people are financially poor doesn't mean their needs for emotional closeness, intimacy, and social support should be seen as relatively unimportant. Couples did not disdain romantic relationships as a result of the financial pressures they faced, and researchers, policy makers, and commentators should not decide for them that successful intimate ties are unimportant so long as they are poor. Similarly, we can't treat money as the silver bullet for social poverty, as the many divorced and unhappily partnered individuals in the middle and upper classes can attest.[33] While social and financial poverty certainly can and do mutually influence one another, each deserves respect, research attention, and appropriate policy making in its own right.

We should construct policy through a social poverty lens. Two decades ago, sociologist Arlie Hochschild wrote, "We need not simply better schools but also better relationships between mentors and students. We need more jobs for men but also fuller support for men who try to be good fathers. We need better housing but also more mother-teen workshops, youth outreach programs, and other programs not yet devised because we haven't been thinking about 'relational poverty.'"[34] Building on Hochschild's words and the insights of the present study, this means taking steps such as those described here.

1. *Design programs to promote dignity and human connection.* Here, I offer three examples. First, education research has shown the benefits of building relationships in a school setting. A combination of emotional and instrumental support can be key to keeping at-risk youth in school; these supports need to come through relationships in which youth feel security and trust.[35] People need to feel like they matter to someone; policies and programs can be designed to nurture such connections.

Second, researchers have conducted randomized controlled trials to examine interventions that build support networks for the family caregivers of Alzheimer's patients, who are often isolated and overwhelmed by their obligations.[36] They have found these interventions are successful at building or activating such networks, and that doing so may facilitate caregivers' adjustment to their role. Notably, it is emotional, rather than instrumental, support that appears to be key to caregivers. This indicates how part of health care delivery and local programming—such as social events that cater to both patients and caregivers[37]—can include attention not only to patients' medical needs but also to their social needs and to those of the caregivers on whom the patients' well-being depends.[38]

Third, a Dutch nursing home has begun offering free housing to university students who volunteer to spend time with the older residents.[39] While the program has been lauded for addressing the social needs of the elderly, we should also recognize that young adults may similarly gain from the social connections and relationships they develop in this setting. Such creative ways of supporting young and old alike—the two groups most vulnerable to social isolation—should be applauded and evaluated. This sort of policy making may address social and financial needs simultaneously.

2. *Deliver social services in a way that builds relationships between program participants, between participants and staff, and between participants and important others in their lives.* For example, sociologist Victor Chen details how, in comparison with the devastating isolation of laid-off autoworkers in Detroit, their counterparts across the border in Canada found support in "action centers," established following a mass layoff, which were purposely staffed by some who had also lost their jobs. In addition to helping workers navigate benefit access and retraining programs, the centers provide a physical site for them to find fellowship and emotional support during their struggles with unemployment.[40] Similarly, researcher Mario Small uncovered how parents often gain essential knowledge and other resources via the relationships they develop with staff in organizations such as child care centers. This was more likely to occur when organizations incorporated opportunities—such as cookouts—for trusting informal relationships to develop between parents and staff.[41]

Programs should also be designed to build trusting relationships within participants' lives; this is key, as support from program group members and staff will likely end when program participation does, whereas strong ties outside the program can continue to buoy former participants over the long term. For example, Anu Family Services has focused its approach on building connections between foster youth and other adults in their lives (such as extended family) and helping youth heal from trauma so they can trust and invest in these relationships. The result has been a decrease in the time foster youth spend in treatment placements and an increase in the proportion of youth who are discharged to permanent homes.[42]

3. *Strengthen men's economic standing so they and their partners can have more confidence in their ability to fulfill our culture's conceptualization of a family man, while also continuing to offer alternative visions— like care work—for how men can contribute to family life.* Nearly one in

five men aged twenty-five to fifty-four and with a high school degree or less is not in the labor force.[43] Among those men who are working, wages have been falling.[44] Young men are less likely to attend college or earn a degree today than their female counterparts, and less-educated men work less than those who are more educated. Less-educated men are less likely to be married compared with their more-educated counterparts.[45] And less-educated men are far more likely to be living apart from their children than their college-educated peers.[46] Less-educated men have been simultaneously drifting away from economic and family institutions; it is to the detriment of individual families, our nation, and the men themselves to leave them unmoored. We need to bolster men's abilities to contribute to their families economically.[47] But cultural change is also necessary so that men and women feel that men's contributions to the family through child care, housekeeping, and so forth, are also valuable ways for them participate in family life, as it is unlikely that men will return to serving in a primary and exclusive breadwinner role in the American family. Recognizing men's social needs and their abilities to meet the social needs of their partners and children can alter how men are seen and treated in policies, such as parental leave and child support.[48]

When it comes to the relationship education field specifically, the insights of this book give rise to three suggestions.[49]

1. *Relationship education should be incorporated with services that address other needs, be they economic, education, or health.*[50] This can help to tackle the various transitions and sources of instability parents face as they traverse the path into adulthood. Relationship education may serve as the entry point to these other services, or these other services may serve as the entry point to relationship education. Building local coalitions of service providers who can combine resources and colocate to ease access to multiple services for parents may be productive. A social poverty perspective should inform the development of these services. This requires attention to how participants' interactions with staff, including as they are recruited and in the timeliness of returned phone calls or e-mails, as well as issues of staff turnover, may shape the social resources parents are able to build while in the program.

Since my research ended, Family Expectations has altered aspects of its programming in some ways that follow this and other recommendations discussed earlier. For example, it is now trying to partner with a local mental health and substance abuse counseling organization, as well as a local nonprofit that focuses on employment issues. The curriculum developers have built in more opportunities for couples to practice their communication skills, such as speaker listener, in the safe setting of the classroom. In the face of state budget cuts, the program has restructured, placing less emphasis on the role of family support workers and more on the workshop educators, to try to deliver the same bang for less buck. A federally funded evaluation will reveal whether these new strategies deliver; the five-year project will conclude in 2021. I encourage evaluators to include measures of social poverty in these assessments.[51]

2. *Practitioners and curriculum developers need to be prepared to serve diverse families.*[52] Not doing so only serves to maintain the connection in people's minds between relationship education services and broader cultural fights between the political right and left about who "owns" marriage and how much stigma should be attached to alternative family forms. This obfuscates the reality of relationship education on the ground—as a service that supports couples in staying together and individual partners in ending unhealthy relationships—and distracts from an empirical, rather than philosophical, evaluation of such programs.

3. *It would be ideal to reach individuals before they are pregnant or have children, and perhaps even before they have been struggling in difficult relationships.* Continuing work to reach young people in high school and higher education settings is therefore appropriate. While the effects of relationship education with teens have generally been modest, the findings are consistently positive. Researchers have found benefits of high school relationship education, with increases in self-esteem and relationship skills (such as conflict management) and decreases in relationship violence.[53] However, a discussion of romantic relationships should be not set aside as an elective to be taken in home economics (as it traditionally has been) or seen as a separate issue from learning about sex.[54] Teens need to learn to navigate romantic relationships in order to tackle the challenges of making healthy decisions around sex; likewise, the discussion of romantic relationships cannot exclude the physical part of those relationships. The result, hopefully, can be teens entering young adulthood with less social poverty, better equipped to make decisions around relationships and childbearing.

A Final Word on Social Poverty

Becoming an adult—getting established in your career, with your finances, and in your sense of self—is difficult. Becoming a partner is difficult. Becoming a parent is difficult. Doing all three at once is enormously challenging. This is particularly the case today given the relative lack of guidance—which can also be flexibility or choice—people have across these arenas. This lack of guidance has its origins in both macro-level forces—such as the weakening of norms governing romantic relationships—and micro-level ones, especially the fact that few of the young parents in this study grew up with healthy romantic relationship role models they can now follow. And trying to make all these transitions in this environment means that developing trust in a union is tricky. Trust requires dependability and predictability, as well as having a shared set of expectations for one another. These are hard to come by when education, work, finances, housing, and identities are still very much in flux. The difficulty of achieving this myriad of goals doesn't mean that these young parents have given up on this future, however. They want to create a forever family, and many feel they could use a helping hand to find their way.

Lauren, twenty-three, who just had her first child while trying to finish up college, says, "I just don't think it's an easy path to be on . . . , having a kid . . . and trying to make a relationship work." When I ask her what would be in place in an ideal world before someone had a child, she says with a laugh, "Two hundred thousand dollars in the bank, a home, what private school you want them to attend." She knows these are outlandish standards given what's possible, and continues, "But seriously, money in the bank and a strong marriage. . . . You'll still have stresses of life, but you'll have that center you can come to and just be at peace with. Knowing that you have money in the bank and a family that loves you." Even though they might not have reached this ideal, Lauren's fiancé, Cordell, says of their son, "My baby love that me and my girl are together. You can tell just by how he smiles." Though they don't have much "money in the bank," Lauren and Cordell are working to ensure their son at least does not experience social poverty—and they see evidence of their success in their baby's smile.

ACKNOWLEDGMENTS

This book would not have been possible without the essential support of so many.

Kathy Edin said "yes" to my pursuing this project before I was her student and before the project was even really possible, all the way back in 2005—but she was, of course, eventually right. And she has continued to provide indispensable guidance ever since, from talking through ideas to teaching me how to write a book to reading chapter drafts.

The National Center on Family and Marriage Research at Bowling Green State University supported my time in the field while I was a postdoctoral fellow there. As my postdoc supervisor, Wendy Manning provided guidance during that time and has since been gracious enough to read early chapter drafts. Marcy Carlson and Nils Ringe also generously read chapters and provided needed feedback. Catherine Turco has been a constant companion, sounding board, reader, and more throughout this project. Special thanks to Ilene Kalish and Maryam Arain for stewarding the book through the publication process.

I am very grateful to the Family Expectations team for opening themselves up to the scrutiny of many researchers, including me. Doing so is always a risk for an organization, and it's one Family Expectations and its staff have embraced time and again. It would be far easier for them to only do internal evaluations and to focus exclusively on metrics by which they'd undoubtedly shine, like participant satisfaction, and leave it at that. We should applaud organizations that are willing to let research play a key role in the development and direction of their interventions.

I am humbled by the openness of the parents profiled in this book. They shared their life stories, their living rooms, and moments of great vulnerability with me. I hope I have lived up to the responsibility of sharing their experiences, values, and dreams in these pages.

Finally, I owe a debt of gratitude to my family—my "forever."

APPENDIX

Introduction to the Research Project

While learning about welfare reform in college—a relatively recent policy event at the time—I was struck by the words in the legislation that included a goal of promoting "the formation and maintenance of two-parent families," a curious addition, I thought, to an income support policy. At the time, the George W. Bush administration was beginning to fund programs to achieve these goals. When I entered graduate school, I wanted to focus my studies on understanding this policy arena. I set my sights on Oklahoma, which was the country's hotbed of "marriage promotion" programming. I found I could not interview the parents participating in the Family Expectations program in Oklahoma, since it was part of a federally funded evaluation, whose researchers understandably didn't want a graduate student mucking around.

In learning about Oklahoma, though, I read about the Oklahoma Marriage Initiative (OMI), an effort started by Governor Frank Keating in 1999 with a goal of cutting the state's notoriously high divorce rate by 25 percent. And so I turned my attention to another area OMI was targeting as part of this larger goal: providing free curriculum and training to middle and high school teachers who wanted to offer healthy relationship education. My dissertation research on this topic took me to four high schools in Oklahoma and two in Florida (where relationship education was a graduation requirement for a brief time under Governor Jeb Bush). During my repeated trips to Oklahoma, OMI folks allowed me to informally observe Family Expectations workshops, even though my research at the time was focused on high schools. What I saw surprised me. The curriculum and atmosphere of the workshops did not embody the heavy-handed marriage promotion that the welfare legislation had seemingly envisioned. While the jury was clearly still out on whether or not these efforts would work, my interest in these programs was piqued further by the disjuncture between the moralizing legislative intentions and the more supportive and practical activities on the ground.

OMI, now known as Project Relate, serves as an umbrella organization, overseeing an array of relationship education initiatives around the state. Beyond Family Expectations and high school courses, the initiative includes programs targeting particular subpopulations, such as Spanish-speaking couples, black couples, college students, engaged couples, foster parents, and incarcerated people. These programs range from extensive workshops, like Family Expectations, to weekend retreats; many aim to serve couples, while others cater to individuals. Since the initiative began in 2001, these programs have served more than 350,000 people across the state, providing its services for free. Between federal and state funding, it has spent upwards of $70 million to do so.[1] The initiative aims to be evidence-informed by having a research advisory group, which meets annually to review program activities and share the latest relevant research with program staff.[2]

My timing in finishing graduate school fortuitously coincided with the end of the data collection for the federally funded evaluations, opening up the Family Expectations program as a potential site for my research. With the generous support of OMI and a postdoctoral fellowship from the National Center for Family and Marriage Research at Bowling Green State University, I had the time and freedom to travel to Oklahoma three times for extended periods over the course of a year to conduct interviews with participants and staff, and to continue my informal observations on site.

The curriculum used in the Family Expectations workshops is the Becoming Parents Program (BPP), originally developed by Dr. Pamela Jordan. In addition to the more standard-issue topics like some basics of infant development, the program aims to ready couples for parenthood by thinking holistically about the family system, mindful that parents' ability to nurture their new child is dependent, in part, on how they get along with and support one another. BPP describes its approach this way:

> There's so much to think about when getting ready for a new baby and there's never enough time for it all. Preparing an environment that is not only physically safe, but emotionally nurturing is very important.

In the rush to "ready the nursery" expectant and new parent couples often forget to prepare the most important part of the child's nest: their relationship.[3]

BPP's parenting content is supplemented with the relationship skills content of the Prevention and Relationship Education Program (PREP), designed by Drs. Howard Markman and Scott Stanley. The efficacy of PREP has been evaluated in peer-reviewed studies,[4] and it is listed on the National Registry of Evidence-Based Programs and Practices. It focuses on topics such as developing communication skills, including learning how to talk and listen to reach an understanding, how to prevent conflicts from escalating, and building a strong basis of friendship and emotional supportiveness in couple relationships.[5]

To recruit the sample for my study, after receiving IRB approval, I asked the program to share the contact information of the couples who had most recently enrolled in the program (meaning most had signed up but not yet begun participating). I contacted forty-six couples in total, among whom thirty-one participated in the interviews. Of those who did not participate in the study, five did not end up taking part in Family Expectations, six could not be contacted (e.g., phone numbers were out of service), two couples were dealing with medical issues that precluded their participation, and two couples declined to participate. I additionally met with fifteen members of the program staff—mainly workshop educators and family support workers—to discuss their views of the program. In the book, I discuss these staff interviews sparingly because the purpose of the volume is to put the participants' perspectives front and center. Program staff expressed strong beliefs in the utility and efficacy of their approach to supporting couples and families.

I conducted the first round of interviews just as couples were beginning their participation in the program (N = 31 couples); this consisted of both couple and individual interviews with each set of partners. Table A.1. lists the pseudonyms and characteristics of all respondents; table A.2. provides a comparison of the sample's characteristics against those of the parents in the Fragile Families and Child Wellbeing Study, a nationally representative sample of births in twenty US cities that oversampled nonmarital births, and the national population of young adults more generally.

TABLE A.1. Study participant pseudonyms and characteristics

Couple Pseudonym	Age	Race/ Ethnicity	Education	Number of Children*	Parents' Marital Status	Employment (Round 1)	Couple Monthly Income (Round 1)
Jessica	19	White	HS	1	Divorced	Not working	$2,200
Will	22	White	Some college	2	Divorced	Full-time	
Brianna	18	White	11th grade	1	N/A#	Not working	$1,300
Zach	20	White	10th grade	1	Divorced	Full-time	
Steffy	35	American Indian/ White	Some college	1	Divorced	Not working	$1,620
Jim	35	White	HS	3	Divorced	Full-time	
Ashleigh	20	White	11th grade	1	Divorced	Not working	$1,000
Mark	21	White	HS	1	Divorced	Full-time	
Joanne	24	White	HS	1	Never married	Not working	$637
Matt	24	American Indian/ White	HS	1	Married	Disability	
Necie	22	Black	HS	1	Never married	Not working	$0
Leonard	23	Black	Some college	2	Divorced	Not working	
Kayla	19	White	HS	1	Divorced	Not working	$700
Ryan	20	White	10th grade	1	Never married	Full-time	
Macken- zie	21	White	12th grade	3	Divorced	Not working	$0
Wayan	24	Black	12th grade	3	Never married	Not working	
Ann	28	White	GED	2	Married	Disability	$1,800
Trenton	30	Black	HS	2	Never married	Part-time	
Skye	20	White	HS	1	Married	Not working	$800
Eddy	21	White	11th grade	1	N/A	Full-time	
Miranda	27	White	8th grade	2	Never married	Not working	$2,000
Carl	24	Hispanic	HS	1	Never married	Full-time	
Taleisha	20	Black	HS	1	Married	Full-time	$900
Darrell	31	Black	HS	1	Never married	Not working	
Denelle	35	Black	7th grade	2	Never married	Disability	$1,000
Otis	42	Black	HS	5	Married	Part-time	
Erica	22	White	GED	3	Never married	Not working	$300
Joe	27	Hispanic	11th grade	3	Divorced	Not working	
Cara	32	White	Some college	2	Divorced	Not working	$1,750
Marvin	36	Black	BA	1	Divorced	Full-time	
Chantelle	21	Black	Some college	1	Married	Not working	$0
Sam	20	Black	9th grade	1	Never married	Not working	

TABLE A.1. (cont.)

Couple Pseudonym	Age	Race/ Ethnicity	Education	Number of Children*	Parents' Marital Status	Employment (Round 1)	Couple Monthly Income (Round 1)
Tiana	20	White	HS	1	Divorced	Full-time	$2,700
Stefan	21	White	GED	1	Married	Full-time	
Lauren	23	White	Some college	1	Married	Part-time	$1,850
Cordell	21	Black	Some college	1	Never married	Full-time	
Elyse	20	American Indian/ Black	12th grade	1	Divorced	Full-time	$3,300
Robert	21	Black	HS	1	Married	Full-time	
Norene	24	American Indian	HS	3	Married	Not working	$1,300
Dave	29	American Indian	HS	3	N/A	Full-time	
Kristina	20	White	HS	1	Divorced	Full-time	$1,900
Lance	20	Black	12th grade	1	Never married	Part-time	
Hannah	18	Asian	HS	1	Divorced	Not working	$2,400
Luke	22	White	11th grade	1	Divorced	Full-time	
Abby	22	White	10th grade	3	Divorced	Not working	$80
Darren	29	White	GED	4	Divorced	Not working	
Akira	22	Black	HS	3	N/A	Full-time	$1,800
Ennis	24	Black	HS	4	Divorced	Full-time	
Ruby	29	White	Some college	3	Divorced	Not working	$800
Anthony	36	White	AA	3	Divorced	Not working	
Carley	21	American Indian	Some college	1	Divorced	Full-time	$2,400
Nick	21	White	Some college	1	Divorced	Full-time	
Laila	33	Asian	Graduate	1	Married	Not working	$1,800
Ken	36	Black	BA	1	Married	Full-time	
Illisha	23	Black	HS	2	Divorced	Full-time	$2,600
Aaron	23	Black	HS	2	Never married	Full-time	
Emilia	23	White	HS	1	Never married	Disability	$718
Andy	26	White	HS	1	Divorced	Not working	
Ciara	21	White	HS	2	Divorced	Not working	$1,300
Drew	22	White	HS	2	Never married	Full-time	
Hailey	33	White	Some college	2	Divorced	Full-time	$4,300
Evan	33	White	Some college	2	Divorced	Full-time	

Respondent did not live with parents while growing up.
* Number of children for each respondent includes shared children (that is, shared children are counted for each individual's total).

TABLE A.2. Comparison of characteristics of present study sample, sample from Fragile Families and Child Wellbeing Study, and the current young adult population in the United States

	Family Expectations Sample	Fragile Families Sample*	National Comparison across Young Adult Population*
Couples	N = 31		
Individuals	N = 62		
Race			
Both partners white	12 (38.7%)	17.4%[a]	59%[b]
Both partners black	7 (22.6%)	44.3%[c]	14%[d]
Both partners other race	1 (3.2%)	38.3%[e]	27%[f]
Interracial couple	11 (35.5%)	13.0%[g]	
Participant age (mean)	24.8	23.8[h]	
Monthly couple income (mean)	$1,452	$2,212[i]	$4,758[j]
Education			
No HS diploma/GED	18 (29.0%)	43.3%[k]	8%[l]
HS diploma/GED	33 (53.2%)	36.2%[m]	24%[n]
Some college or more	11 (17.7%)	20.5%[o]	68%[p]
Mean number of children per couple[a]	2.2	2.1q	
Couples with multiple partner fertility[b]	13 (41.9%)	41.9%[r]	
Relationship status (rounds 1 and 3)			
Romantically involved R1	31 (100%)	82%[s]	
R3	25 (86.2%)	58%	
Married R1	0 (0%)		
R3	7 (24.1%)		
Engaged R1	7 (22.6%)		
R3	5 (17.2%)		
Marriage plans R1	6 (19.4%)		
R3	0 (9%)		
No marriage plans R1	18 (58.1%)		
R3	13 (44.8%)		
Broken up R1	0	18%[t]	
R3	4 (13.8%)	42%	

*Not all categories from the present study have an applicable comparison in these other data sources.
a. Figure is for individuals (not couples) and represents the race/ethnic composition of the Fragile Families sample of unmarried mothers (Carlson, McLanahan, and England 2004).

b. Figure is for individuals (not couples) and represents the race/ethnic composition of the millennial generation (Interactive: A portrait of five generations 2010).

c. Figure is for individuals (not couples) and represents the race/ethnic composition of the Fragile Families sample of unmarried mothers (Carlson, McLanahan, and England 2004).

d. Figure is for individuals (not couples) and represents the race/ethnic composition of the millennial generation (Interactive: A portrait of five generations 2010).

e. Figure is for individuals (not couples) and represents the race/ethnic composition of the Fragile Families sample of unmarried mothers (Carlson, McLanahan, and England 2004).

f. Figure is for individuals (not couples) and represents the race/ethnic composition of the millennial generation (Interactive: A portrait of five generations 2010).

g. For the Fragile Families sample, this figure is calculated independently of those for the other race/ethnic categories, and 86 percent were same-race couples (Carlson, McLanahan, and England 2004).

h. For unmarried mothers at round 1; for unmarried fathers = 26.7 (Carlson, McLanahan, and England 2004).

i. Calculated based on the household income of the cohabiting mothers in the Fragile Families sample (Kalil and Ryan 2010).

j. This is monthly household income among those in the millennial generation; therefore, this figure may include the earnings of others (e.g., parents) with whom the young adults reside (Interactive: A portrait of five generations 2010).

k. For mothers at round 1; for fathers = 39.2 percent (Carlson, McLanahan, and England 2004).

l. Bureau of Labor Statistics 2016.

m. For mothers at round 1; for fathers = 37.3 percent (Carlson, McLanahan, and England 2004).

n. Bureau of Labor Statistics 2016.

o. For mothers at round 1; for fathers = 23.6 percent (Carlson, McLanahan, and England 2004).

p. Bureau of Labor Statistics 2016.

q. For mothers at round 1; for fathers = 2.2 (Wagmiller 2010).

r. For unmarried women at round 1; for fathers, 32 percent report multiple partner fertility (Carlson, McLanahan, and England 2004).

s. Carlson, McLanahan, and England 2004.

t. Carlson, McLanahan, and England 2004.

The second round of interviews took place three months later, when couples were scheduled to be concluding their Family Expectations workshops (N = 28 couples; 90.3 percent of the original sample). I conducted couple-level interviews at this time.[6] The third round of interviews took place approximately one year after couples had begun participating in the program and consisted of individual interviews (N = 24 couples; 85.7 percent).[7] Between the second and third rounds of interviews, approximately seven months passed. During this interim, I sent holiday cards to all couples as a way of staying in contact (hopefully making me less of a stranger when I contacted them again for the third round of interviews).

I made reminder phone calls the night before each interview. Still, a few times respondents forgot about our appointment and were not home when I arrived. In nearly all of these cases, I was able to reschedule the interviews and conduct them at a later time. I did not exclude couples from study participation if they dropped out of the program because I wanted to understand their reasons for doing so. The sample size fell during the second and third rounds of interviews when I was unable to recontact some people when their phone numbers and addresses were no longer valid (with attempts made by phone, mail, and e-mail); no participants from the earlier interviews refused participation in subsequent rounds. All participants were compensated for their time for each interview. Over the year of the interviews, I conducted a total of 192 couple and individual interviews with the members of these thirty-one couples.

To conduct interviews, I offered to meet respondents at a time and in a location that were convenient for them. For most, this meant we met in their homes, so I often got to meet other family members with whom they were living, pet their dogs, and play peekaboo with their babies. Some chose not to meet at home, so we would meet at coffee shops, fast-food restaurants, local parks, or the program site. While the program is located in downtown Oklahoma City, the participants were spread out across the metropolitan area, so I spent a lot of time driving the city from end to end, thankful for its easy-to-navigate, grid-like streets. While I normally arrived empty-handed, besides my digital recorder and consent forms, I occasionally brought some muffins to an early morning interview, and I would offer to buy something to eat or drink when we met at a restaurant or coffee shop. Interviews, then, were taking place in informal settings. Children were often popping in and out (or present throughout, when they were young babies); television sets were often on (I learned after struggling through transcribing early interviews that I needed to ask that the volume be turned down); and the realities of family life, from dirty dishes to nagging about chores, were on display. I was continually humbled by the willingness of these new parents to open their homes and lives to me.

In introducing myself to the respondents, I made sure it was clear that I was a researcher, not program staff, as I did not want them to feel constrained in being critical of the program. As an outsider to the program, I treated respondents as experts on it, allowing them to explain it to me, rather than having them assume I understood what it was like to participate.

In my late twenties at the start of the research, I was a similar age to my respondents, which provided one form of common ground. My gender and race were the same as some of the respondents. My not being a parent, as well as my socioeconomic status and education, set me apart from all. Some respondents, often those with some college experience, would ask about my degree as we chatted before or after the interviews. Respondents also asked about where I was from, prompted by my cell phone number that showed up on their caller IDs (I had somehow ended up with a New Hampshire cell number on the phone I was using for the project) and by my accent, which lacks the charm of Okies' slower drawls. All said, my position vis-à-vis my respondents was clearly that of an outsider, which could limit my ability to bond with respondents but also puts them clearly in the driver's seat as the experts on their own lives, since their experiences are ones over which I have no claim. Sharing stories about our pets or the latest gossip about a celebrity whose face was splashed across their TV offered some ways of bridging our differences. And, because I was visiting new parents, there were cute babies to coo over together.

I used an interview guide to ask a set of open-ended questions, and also included clarifying and follow-up questions based on participants' responses. At each round of data collection, I asked all respondents to fill out a brief questionnaire to confirm educational attainment, employment status, and monthly income. Prior to the second and third rounds of interviews, I refreshed my memory about each couple by rereading previous field notes and transcripts so that I could ensure parents felt I was talking to them as individuals, not just running through a checklist of standardized questions; this included, for example, referring to where they worked or their pregnancy due dates as we talked. During the first round of interviews, I asked couples to talk about how their relationship had progressed over time, what their relationship was currently like (including their plans for marriage and their ways of handling conflict), and their thoughts on and experiences with parenthood. Additionally, I asked couples about the Family Expectations program, including how they had found the program, why they had decided to participate, and what their initial impressions were after they had visited the facility to enroll. In individual interviews at this time, respondents talked about the types of relationships they had seen as children, their romantic relationship experiences prior to the current relationship, their intentions and emotions around the current (or most recent) pregnancy, and what they found fulfilling and concerning in their current relationship. I also asked about their educational and occupational experiences and related plans for the future.

In the second round of interviews, I asked couples about any big life changes or events that had occurred during the intervening three months since the first interview, with many couples talking about the arrival of their baby and their experiences as parents. This also included getting an update on how things were going in their relationship; what their current educational, employment, and living situatiozns were like; and whether or not they had made any progress on the personal goals they had discussed at the first round of interviews. Additionally, I asked couples in great detail about their experiences with Family Expectations, including what they thought about the workshops, the family support coordinators, referrals they may have received to outside services, and any supplementary program activities in which they participated. I asked what they felt they had gotten out of participating so far and whether or not they had seen any changes in their relationships or parenting since beginning the program. Finally, I solicited their feedback on the program, including changes that should be made, and whether or not they recommended the program to other people.

The third round of interviews consisted largely of getting updates on respondents' relationship, employment, living, and educational situations, as well as their experiences with and thoughts about parenting. I again asked respondents how they handled conflict with their partners, as well as how they conceived of a good relationship and who they turned to for support when dealing with relationship difficulties. Finally, I asked respondents about their ongoing participation in Family Expectations, if any. I asked them to reflect back on how they believed their relationship evolved over the past year to gauge their perceptions of relationship quality, stability, and change. Those who had broken up with their partners were asked about visitation and child support arrangements and the quality of their coparenting relationship. Throughout the interviews I was able to see relationships evolve (and sometimes devolve) over the course of the year; I also was able to gain a sense of how the perspective and approach of each member of the couple fit together or conflicted, underlying the way in which the relationship progressed.

In addition to audio-recording each interview, I wrote field notes afterward, often sitting in my car between interviews. Although this was not an ethnography, I wanted to capture the atmosphere of the interview, in ways that might not be apparent on the transcript page, as well as having detailed physical descriptions of the places and people, so that I could make the interviews come alive for myself (and my readers, I hoped) when I revisited the interview data in the future.

With a limited research budget, I transcribed the interviews myself. Despite the threat of carpal tunnel syndrome, this meant I began the process of immersing myself in the data prior to formally analyzing it. While not a pleasant task, I believe this process of transcribing helped me to become a better interviewer, since I had to listen to myself conduct each interview. It also helped me get to "know" my data in a way that's only possible when you've written down every word of it yourself. In all, the three rounds of interviews produced 2,439 pages of transcript.

I analyzed the data in two ways. First, I wrote memos on each couple, which sought to distill key aspects of each couple case based on all three rounds of interviews taken together. Second, I engaged in a two-stage coding process of the transcripts. I open coded a subsample of transcripts from each round of interviews for themes related to participants' perceptions of the program and its impact, if any, on them. I then used the list of codes this process generated to code all interviews from each round.[8] I used these memos and codes in various ways, depending on what issues I was exploring in my analysis. For example, when tracking respondents' discussions of specific relationship skill techniques they learned in their workshops, I relied on the relevant codes and themes that emerged.[9]

In the book, I tried to walk the line between, on the one hand, showing the variety of experiences across couples and representing the depth of evidentiary support for the points I made while, on the other hand, not overwhelming the reader with in-depth details from each of the thirty-one couples. We learn far more about some couples (like Brianna and Zach or Ann and Trenton) than we do others (like Emilia and Andy). While all the individuals and couples have their own story and experiences, I have tried my best to represent the broader themes common across couples in these chapters. There are a variety of issues in the data that I could have explored in greater detail, such as those around mental health issues, early educational or family experiences, and parenting experiences. The necessities of producing a cohesive "story line" and a book of a reasonable length, however, precluded that possibility.

I periodically shared preliminary results with Family Expectations staff and members of the research advisory group. In doing applied research, it is important to me that what I learn can inform what is done moving forward. The program has changed in a variety of ways since I collected my data, as discussed in the final chapter of the book. In small part, this is due to staff decisions in response to the results I shared. In larger part, the program has been altered by two key policy changes. First, the state legislature decided to substantially cut funding to Family Expectations and the initiative's other programs in response to a budget shortfall, combined with ongoing scrutiny of the initiative for failing to fulfill Governor Keating's original promises to slash the divorce rate and substantially address the state's poverty rate.[10] These cuts are not limited to the state's relationship education programs, however, with cuts made in areas ranging from education spending to mental health services.[11] Second, the federal government has funded an array of relationship education programs across the country through five-year grants that require rigorous evaluation. Family Expectations received one of these grants and is therefore continuing to provide services despite the state funding cuts. The lead evaluator of Family Expectations under this latest federal grant, Dr. Galena Rhoades, has embraced exploring social poverty as part of program evaluation. I look forward to what we will be able to learn from this ongoing research about whether and how government-funded programs can play a role in influencing young parents' experiences of social poverty.

NOTES

1. I use pseudonyms for all interview respondents; some small, identifying details have been changed to protect respondents' identities.

2. Mark is not a rare exception in his wish to address their communication issues, despite the heavy presence of financial struggles. In her study of relationship education programs, Jennifer Randles writes, "Long accustomed to stretching the meager resources they did have through skillful budgeting, minimizing their lifestyles, and simply doing without, most parents did not believe that significantly improving their financial situation was amenable to techniques they could learn in a class. This contrasted with how they viewed communication. Most parents told me they could learn a lot about how to be better communicators" (2017, 185).

3. Malveaux 2002.

4. Starr 2001.

5. Work in the relationship education field is beginning to expand, including the development of relationship education programs specifically for men and women in same-sex relationships (Buzzella, Whitton, and Tompson 2012; S. B. Scott and Rhoades 2014; Whitton and Buzzella 2012).

6. Clark, Esch, and Delvac 2016.

7. Catlett and Artis 2004; Furstenberg 2007; T. L. Huston and Melz 2004; Karney and Bradbury 2005.

8. Wood et al. 2012.

9. Lundquist et al. 2014.

10. See table A.2 in the appendix for additional information on respondent characteristics.

11. Stack 1974.

12. Desmond 2012; Hartigan 1999; Miller-Cribbs and Farber 2008; S. S. Smith 2007. This is not entirely new, of course (see, for example, Howell 1973; Rainwater 1970).

13. Burton et al. 2009; Desmond 2012; Edin and Kefalas 2005; Levine 2013.

14. Alkire and Foster 2008; Blank 2008; Desmond 2015; Misra and Brucker 2017; Perkins and Sampson 2015; Reeves, Rodrigue, and Kneebone 2016; Samuel et al. 2017; Wagle 2008a, 2008b, 2014. For a summary of concerns about social exclusion and social integration for youth in the European Union facing long-term unemployment, see Kieselbach 2003.

15. See, for example, Desmond 2012; Sarkisian and Gerstel 2004; S. S. Smith 2007.

16. See, for example, Briggs 1998; Dominguez and Watkins 2003; Edin and Lein 1997; K. Newman 1999; S. S. Smith 2005.

17. In a previous article, political scientist Joseph Lewandowski (2008) used the term "social poverty." I do not adopt the meaning he offered. He used the term to describe a lack of what sociologists and others call "bridging social capital." It's not clear why he classified a lack of bridging, but not bonding, social capital as demarcating social poverty. In the article, he presented social poverty as a characteristic of a place or group of people, rather than of an individual; this means the concept does not create an easy parallel with economic poverty, which is typically measured at the individual level (with place or group-level measures of poverty then an aggregation of individual indicators). His definition would classify wealthy people who live in enclaves, separate from economically poor people, as being socially poor, which seems to miss some of the key ways that we typically conceptualize social ties to and among the powerful. Most fundamentally, this conceptualization of social poverty does not speak to the lived experience of lacking relationships that are adequate to fulfill one's emotional needs; as such, I offer an alternative definition of the term in the present study.

18. This insight about struggles with trust and feelings that perhaps only your ties to your children can truly be counted on are not unique to this book (see, for example, Edin and Kefalas 2005).

19. For reviews describing these findings, see Cacioppo and Patrick 2008; Holt-Lunstad et al. 2015.

20. Collins et al. 1993; Luecken et al. 2013; Nylen, O'Hara, and Engeldinger 2013; Stapleton et al. 2012.

21. Angley et al. 2015; Bono, Sy, and Kopp 2016; Byrnes and Miller 2012.

22. Fragile Families Research Brief 2002.

23. Teen attitudes about marriage and family 2010.

24. Heath (2012) also finds that relationship education programs that do not promote marriage are more popular among participants.

25. See also Willoughby and Spencer 2017.

26. This program description does not reflect changes in the physical space or program model that have taken place more recently.

27. See the appendix for additional information about the program's curriculum.

28. Nationally, BSF enrollment ran from 2005 to 2008 and SHM enrollment from 2007 to 2009. Data for the present study were collected in 2009–2010 from unmarried couples, meaning there is no crossover between this study's sample and the BSF or SHM samples.

29. David Kimmel, Family Expectations director, personal communication, August 14, 2017.

30. Funding from the Office of Family Assistance includes federal grant programs. During the time of data collection, this included funding from the BSF and SHM evaluations.

31. This is a description of the program model during the time I collected data for the present study.
32. Workshop content is described in greater detail in chapters 5 through 7.
33. Family Expectations has since increased its core curriculum to thirty-six hours of content.
34. Kimmel, personal communication.
35. Furstenberg 2008, 7.
36. Previous research has explored the potential for organizations to overcome limited social capital for lower-income parents (see, for example, Small 2006). Silvia Dominguez and Celeste Watkins, in their study of low-income African American and Latina mothers, write, "We saw several clear examples of mothers abandoning the dense, insular, and localized neighbor and familial-based networks described in Carol Stack's *All Our Kin* (1974) in favor of an institution-based network that was able to provide financial, child rearing, and emotional support. . . . These institutions go beyond providing the basic services advertised and are becoming important links in the women's social support networks. Some institution-based networks provide clear advantages such as reliable, high quality resources and relationships that are less stressful and burdensome in terms of reciprocity" (2003, 129).
37. Parents' relationship status five years after a non-marital birth 2007.

CHAPTER 1. YOUNG, POOR PARENTS

1. Briggs 1998; Ferlander 2004; Hawe and Shiell 2000; Hutchinson 2004; Lillbacka 2006; Lochner, Kawachi, and Kennedy 1999; Rohe 2004; Sarason, Sarason, and Pierce 1990; Stone 2001; Uchino 2004; Woolcock 2004.
2. For a review of various conceptualizations and uses of the social capital concept, see Putnam et al. 2004.
3. Bourdieu 1986; Coleman 1988, 1990.
4. For a discussion see Briggs 1998; Dominguez 2010; Mazelis 2017.
5. Granovetter 1973.
6. See, for example, Brisson and Usher 2005; Putnam et al. 2004.
7. Briggs 1998.
8. S. Cohen and Wills 1985; House et al. 1985; Weiss 1974.
9. Barrera 2000; Cutrona and Russell 1990; Uchino 2004.
10. For example, Mazelis argues for the importance of social ties because they can "alleviate . . . poverty" (2017, 20). See also Briggs 1998; Desmond 2012, 2015; Dominguez 2010; Kissane and Clampet-Lundquist 2012; Putnam et al. 2004; S. S. Smith 2007.
11. Simmel (1950) offers an examination of the intrinsic value of humans' "sociability."
12. See, for example, Briggs 1998; Harknett 2006; Kissane and Clampet-Lundquist 2012; Tigges, Browne, and Green 1998. Some scholars do explicitly recognize the importance of emotional support; for example, Xavier de Souza Briggs notes that "some of the most important support[s] we all rely on . . . are emotional and not

material" (1998, 178). However, this has not extended to developing the distinction between the functions of support that are inherently valuable versus useful for its transactional power to gain other resources.

13. See, for example, Cacioppo and Cacioppo 2014; S. Cohen et al. 1985; Holt-Lunstad et al. 2015; Steptoe et al. 2004; Thurston and Kubzansky 2009; Veenstra 2002.

14. Baumeister and Leary 1995. Material and informational support are often not perceived as emotionally supportive and are associated with an increase in depressive symptoms (Finch et al. 1997; Trobst 2000); providing material support is associated with a greater likelihood of experiencing material hardship oneself, particularly for low-income individuals and single parents (Pilkauskas, Campbell, and Wimer 2017). In the Moving to Opportunity study, researchers found that many low-income women who moved described feelings of relief at extricating themselves from material exchange relationships, but no similar sense of relief accompanied the loss of any emotionally supportive ties that were strained by their move (Kissane and Clampet-Lundquist 2012).

15. Light 2004, 145. In addition, Lin states that social capital is an "investment in social relations with expected returns in the marketplace" (2001, 19).

16. See, for example, the results of the seventy-five-year Grant and Glueck studies (the Harvard Study of Adult Development). For a summary of results on this point, see Curtin 2017.

17. Arlie Hochschild uses this term in her foreword to Elaine B. Kaplan's book on teen mothers, Not Our Kind of Girl (1997). Unfortunately, the concept is not more fully developed elsewhere. In advancing the concept of "social poverty," I attempt to do so here.

18. Note that one need not feel part of mainstream society to avoid social poverty. A high school chess player may feel estranged from many classmates, for example, but his feelings of sharing a community with other chess players at other schools could save him from social poverty.

19. Laursen and Hartl 2013; Qualter et al. 2015.

20. For example, Cutrona 1982.

21. Experiences in infancy, childhood, and adolescence can shape emotional and behavioral responses to social interactions, the ability to form trusting relationships, and expectations about socioemotional needs being met by others. Ainsworth 1989; Amato and Booth 2001; Hazan and Shaver 1987; Kim et al. 2009; Mikulincer 1998; Qualter et al. 2013; Rhoades et al. 2012; Rotenberg et al. 2010; Schinka et al. 2013; Stocker and Richmond 2007. (In contrast, some other studies find that childhood attachment is not a key determinant of loneliness in adulthood [Cacioppo and Patrick 2008; Shaver, Furman, and Buhrmester 1985].)

22. Some research shows that both individual poverty and neighborhood poverty are predictive of a lower likelihood of having someone with whom to discuss life's problems (Tigges, Browne, and Green 1998), which emphasizes how isolation is not uniquely the product of individual characteristics or choices but also of environmental conditions. Similarly, unemployment—and especially long-term

unemployment—is associated with difficulties in family relationships and losing touch with friends (Morin and Kochhar 2010). This illustrates how the circumstances outside someone's control, such as being the victim of corporate downsizing or layoffs, can work to create social poverty.

23. Seefeldt 2016.

24. Maestas et al. 2017.

25. See also Cacioppo and colleagues for a discussion of how loneliness is distinct from social support. Because the provision of support can come with judgment or be available only in certain circumstances, for example, it may meet some social needs without attenuating one's feelings of social isolation (Cacioppo et al. 2006).

26. See, for example, Lasgaard, Friis, and Shevlin 2016; M. Luhmann and Hawkley 2016.

27. Beveridge 1942.

28. For example, while those with low incomes are more likely to suffer from material hardships, most do not; among those under 200 percent of the poverty line, one in four report having been unable to pay housing or utility bills and just over one in ten report food insecurity (Boushey et al. 2001); this means that the vast majority of those with low incomes did not experience these problems recently.

29. Maslow 1943.

30. See, for example, Kenrick et al. 2010.

31. Maslow 1970, 21.

32. Kenrick et al. 2010, 307.

33. This association holds over and above a whole range of control variables, including health behaviors and socioeconomic status. See Holt-Lunstad et al. 2015; Kiecolt-Glaser and Newton 2001; Luo et al. 2012; Uchino, Cacioppo, and Kiecolt-Glaser 1996; Perissinotto, Cenzer, and Covinsky 2012. In addition, this association does not seem to be driven by personality characteristics like sociability (for a discussion, see S. Cohen 2004).

34. See, for example, Campos 2015; Kiecolt-Glaser and Newton 2001; Lakey and Orehek 2011; M. Newman and Roberts 2013; Repetti, Taylor, and Seeman 2002; Thoits 2011.

35. Holt-Lunstad et al. 2015.

36. Murthy n.d. See also Almendrala 2016.

37. Cacioppo, Cacioppo, and Boomsma 2014; Cacioppo and Hawkley 2009; Cacioppo, Chen, and Cacioppo 2017.

38. Twenge et al. 2001.

39. Those who are more disadvantaged economically are likely to also be more disadvantaged socially, being far more likely to experience loneliness, even after controlling for confounding factors (Bosma et al. 2015; Creed and Reynolds 2001; Hawkley et al. 2008; M. Luhmann and Hawkley 2016; Savikko et al. 2005).

40. Gallo and Matthews 2003.

41. Marcus et al. 2016.

42. Stack 1974, 27.

43. Brewster and Padavic 2002; Desmond 2012, 2015; Miller-Cribs and Farber 2008; Sarkisian and Gerstel 2004; S. S. Smith 2007. This builds on a strong historical basis, including Liebow's (1967) description of rampant distrust among the poor residents of Tally's Corner, Rainwater's (1970) points about poor people choosing isolation over social immersion to avoid the troubles such ties can bring, and Howell's (1973) reporting of poor people seeing themselves as "loners," without a strong social grounding.

44. Research on neighborhoods—especially their collective efficacy, social disorganization, and social cohesion—and their effects on residents might be seen as an exception (Anderson 1999; Chetty and Hendren 2018; Perkins and Sampson 2015; Quillian and Redd 2010; Sampson, Raudenbusch, and Earls 1997; Sharkey and Elwert 2011; Sharkey and Faber 2014). However, this focus on neighborhood- and community-level social deprivation does not attend to the residents' experience of micro-level social deprivation (for an exception, see, for example, Ross, Mirowsky, and Pribesh 2001).

45. Benin and Keith 1995; Dominguez and Watkins 2003; Eggebeen 1992; Hogan, Eggebeen, and Clogg 1993; McDonald and Armstrong 2001; Sarkisian and Gerstel 2004.

46. Dominguez and Watkins 2003.

47. Desmond 2012, 2015.

48. D'Angelo et al. 2016.

49. Holcomb et al. 2015.

50. D'Angelo et al. 2016.

51. Kaplan 1997, 11. See also Jacobs and Mollborn 2012.

52. Arlie Hochschild in Kaplan 1997, xiv.

53. Rates of loneliness and social isolation among young adults rival or surpass those among older adults. Hawthorne 2008; Lasgaard, Friis, and Shevlin 2016; Qualter et al. 2015.

54. M. Luhmann and Hawkley 2016.

55. W. A. Collins, Welsh, and Furman 2009.

56. Lee and Goldstein 2016; Segrin 2003.

57. Arnett 2004, 2006; Schwartz, Côté, and Arnett 2005. See also Hartmann and Swartz 2006; K. Newman and Aptekar 2007; C. Smith 2011.

58. Silva 2012, 2013; Waters et al. 2011.

59. Bureau of Labor Statistics 2014; Kendig, Mattingly, and Bianchi 2014.

60. Wang and Parker 2011.

61. Cherlin, Talbert, and Yasutake 2014.

62. Cherlin 2009.

63. Silva 2012, 2013.

64. Gallo and Matthews 2003.

65. Unplanned pregnancies constituted less than one-third of pregnancies among married women, nearly two-thirds among cohabiting women, and more than eight in ten among unmarried, noncohabiting women (Finer and Zolna 2014).

66. Edin et al. 2007; Mosher, Jones, and Abma 2012.
67. Edin et al. 2007.
68. Edin and Kefalas 2005; Edin and Nelson 2013.
69. Edin and Kefalas 2005, 34.
70. Edin and Kefalas 2005, 34, 211.
71. Edin and Kefalas 2005, 34. See also Kaplan 1997.
72. Edin and Kefalas 2005.
73. M. Luhmann and Hawkley 2016. In addition to a child being an ineffective personal solution to social poverty, it also places a heavy and inappropriate burden on children, who ought not be tasked with solving their parents' feelings of social isolation.
74. Doss et al. 2009, 601.
75. Doss et al. 2009.
76. Because all the participants in this study are opposite-sex couples, I focus on family behavior trends among opposite-sex couples here.
77. Cherlin 2011, 81.
78. Manning and Sykes 2015.
79. Some nine out of ten cohabiting unions end within five years; today, a majority of these unions end in breakup, with only a minority ending in marriage. Seeing a cohabiting union end in marriage is less likely for lower-income women; only one in three cohabiting unions among poor women end in marriage (Lichter, Qian, and Mellott 2006).
80. Edin and Kefalas 2005; Edin, Kefalas, and Reed 2004; Edin and Reed 2005; Gibson-Davis, Edin, and McLanahan 2005.
81. Cherlin 2004, 2009. See also Beck and Beck-Gernsheim 1995; Beck-Gernsheim 2002; Gerson 2009.
82. Edin and Reed 2005; Willoughby and James 2017.
83. Manlove et al. 2010.
84. Hamilton, Martin, and Ventura 2009; Upchurch, Lillard, and Panis 2002.
85. Manning 2004; Manning, Smock, and Majumdar 2004.
86. Lichter, Turner, and Sassler 2010.
87. For a discussion of the lack of norms in stepfamilies and cohabiting families, see Cherlin 1978; Marsiglio 2004; Nock 1995. For a discussion of the lack of norms for social fathers, see Cherlin 1978; Cherlin and Furstenberg 1994; Edin and Nelson 2013; Furstenberg and Cherlin 1991. For a discussion of the decline in father involvement following parents' repartnering, see Berger, Cancian, and Meyer 2012; Kamp Dush, Kotila, and Schoppe-Sullivan 2011; Tach, Mincy, and Edin 2010.
88. Edin and Kefalas 2005; Gerson 2009.
89. Karney, Garvan, and Thomas 2003; Waller 2001.
90. While trust is a quality of a dyadic relationship, social poverty assesses a person's broader social "portfolio." Just as holding a low-wage job is not equivalent to living in economic poverty (as the worker may have other sources of income), having a relationship that is not trusting does not mean one is experiencing social

poverty (as the person may have other sources of social connection and support). If trust is the currency of relationships, social poverty asks how much of this "wealth" a person has.

91. Burton et al. 2009.

92. It is useful to distinguish between a lack of trust in marriage as an institution versus in a specific partner, given that there is a good deal of public discourse over the retreat from marriage. The evidence for this retreat is found in demographic trends of rising rates of cohabitation and nonmarital births, and high rates of divorce. However, we ought not confuse people lacking confidence in marriage as an institution and their not trusting themselves or their partners to fulfill the demands of marriage. While policies and campaigns focused on marriage promotion efforts assume that people are shying away from marriage as an institution (not valuing or having confidence in it), relationship education programs assume that couples need help building trust and other relationship skills, as opposed to needing to be convinced of the value of marriage. The Family Expectations program profiled in this book is an example of the latter approach.

93. Beck and Beck-Gernsheim 1995, 7.

94. Portes and Sensenbrenner 1993.

95. N. Luhmann 1988.

96. Weber and Carter 2003.

97. Goffman 1963; Zucker 1986.

98. Weber and Carter 2003.

99. Luhmann 1979 in Elofson 2001.

100. Liebow 1967, 180.

101. Bandura 1997; Brehm and Rahn 1997; T. W. Smith 1997; Uslaner 2002; Yamagishi 2001.

102. Levine 2013.

103. The evidence from Glanville, Andersson, and Paxton (2013) indicates that this is causal, as opposed to an artifact of selection, as this result holds even in fixed effects analyses.

104. Welch, Sikkink, and Loveland 2007.

105. Rotenberg 1994.

106. Hardin 1993; King 2002; Rotenberg 1995; Weissman and LaRue 1998.

107. K. S. Cook, Hardin, and Levi 2005; T. W. Smith 1997.

108. See also Burton and Tucker 2009.

109. This is due in part to the fact that few have seen such relationships while growing up (a result, in part, of the deinstitutionalization of marriage playing out in their parents' generation). Researchers posit that there are three primary avenues through which parents' relationship practices can influence their children's relationship behaviors in adulthood: (1) inherited characteristics; (2) having the parents' relationship struggles spill over into the quality of their parenting, resulting in emotional dysregulation for the children and, thus, future challenges in intimate relationships; and (3) through social learning, with children develop-

ing attitudes and skills in line with those they saw practiced by the adults in their lives. Studies have established empirical support for these latter two mechanisms (Amato and Booth 2001; Cui and Fincham 2010; Herzog and Cooney 2002; Kim et al. 2009; Rhoades et al. 2012; Stocker and Richmond 2007).

110. Arnett 2000, 469.
111. See also Carr and Kefalas 2011; Silva 2012.
112. Cherlin 2004; Giddens 1991, 1992.
113. Gross 2005; Lauer and Yodanis 2010; Willoughby and James 2017.
114. Carlson, McLanahan, and England 2004; Edin and Kefalas 2005; Estacion and Cherlin 2010; Nomaguchi et al. 2017; Waller and McLanahan 2005.
115. Edin, England, and Linnenberg 2003.
116. Stanley 2003, 7.
117. Cherlin 2009.
118. Oliker 1989.
119. The influence of holding hands with one's spouse was compared with not holding hands with anyone or holding hands with a stranger (Coan, Schaefer, and Davidson 2006). The quality of the perceived social support also influenced how calming holding hands with a significant other was (Coan et al. 2017).

CHAPTER 2. BECOMING AN ADULT

1. The Department of Human Services is the agency in Oklahoma that administers the state's child support enforcement activities.
2. Kathryn Edin and Maria Kefalas (2005) detail how a pregnancy often brings about higher expectations of partners among mothers-to-be. In their study of unmarried fathers, Edin and Timothy Nelson (2013) describe how despite their deep desires to be fathers, these men often "rip and run" during and after their partners' pregnancies.
3. Hogan and Astone 1986; Shanahan 2000.
4. Arnett 1997, 1998; Greene, Wheatley, and Aldava 1992.
5. Arnett 1998, 2000, 2004, 2005.
6. Arnett 2005, 239.
7. Arnett 2000; Settersten, Furstenberg, and Rumbaut 2005.
8. Arnett 2005.
9. Halperin 1998.
10. Sum et al. 2011.
11. P. Cohen et al. 2003; Meier and Allen 2008.
12. Elliott and Simmons 2011.
13. Uecker and Stokes 2008.
14. Mathews and Hamilton 2016.
15. Kearney and Levine 2007.
16. Bowlby 1979; Furman and Buhrmester 1992; Hazan and Zeifman 1994; Markiewicz et al. 2006; Rosenthal and Kobak 2010.
17. For a comparison to a national sample, see table A.2. in the appendix.

18. This is not unique to this sample; see also Toguchi Swartz, Hartmann, and Mortimer 2011.
19. See also Toguchi Swartz, Hartmann, and Mortimer 2011.
20. Some 40 percent of American workers are not covered by the Family and Medical Leave Act, meaning that many who are employed during their pregnancies do not have a job that offers any type of leave, even without pay (Klerman, Daley, and Pozniak 2012).
21. I present couple income data here even though not all couples were living together or combining their incomes, and some couples were combining resources with other household members. Since they are parents, this couple-level income information tells us about the resources immediately at their disposal to care for their child. For 2009 HHS Poverty Guidelines, see www.aspe.hhs.gov.
22. Cheng and Chan 2008; T. W. Smith 1997.
23. Fehr 1996; Fine 1986; McGuire 2007; Sias and Cahill 1998.
24. Creed and Reynolds 2001.
25. Zach's experiences with an employer who turns out to be untrustworthy are not unique, as detailed by Judith Levine (2013).
26. Bureau of Labor Statistics 2016.
27. Bureau of Labor Statistics 2016. This is in contrast to two-thirds of jobs being held for more than six months among those with a college degree.
28. This age pattern is also borne out in national statistics. Bureau of Labor Statistics 2016.
29. I cannot disentangle the impact of age and education here in explaining these variations in employment trajectories, as Marvin and Ken are rare in the sample both in being older and in having college degrees.
30. Eccles 2009; Nurmi 2004.
31. Malanchuk, Messersmith, and Eccles 2010.
32. Chiu 1990; Malanchuk, Messersmith, and Eccles 2010.
33. C. Smith 2011.
34. Parker 2012.
35. For a discussion of the impact on parenting of sharing housing, see Harvey n.d.
36. Even if I wasn't able to conduct interviews with some couples, I was able to get information about whether or not they had moved (for example, by having the post office mark a letter to the couple "returned to sender—no forwarding address available").
37. Accepting in-kind and economic help from kin can weigh on these relationships and on the recipients of this support (Finch et al. 1997; Kissane and Clampet-Lundquist 2012; Trobst 2000). This underlines the distinction between the socioemotional support necessary to prevent social poverty and financial support delivered via social ties. In conflating these two types of support, we can miss out on the potential tensions or trade-offs between having adequate social and financial resources.
38. See, for example, Desmond 2012; Sarkisian and Gerstel 2004; S. S. Smith 2007.

39. Most millennials own a car, and most of those who don't already own one want to (Accel + Qualtrics n.d.).
40. Carasso and McKernan 2007.
41. Chetty and Hendren 2018.
42. This was not a topic about which I specifically asked, but it emerged spontaneously in interviews. Transportation issues, therefore, may be more widespread than is represented here.
43. Kimball 2012.
44. Kneebone 2009.
45. Tomer et al. 2011.
46. Conger and Elder 1994; Conger, Rueter, and Elder 1999; Gomel et al. 1998; Vinokur, Price, and Caplan 1996.
47. See also Edin and Kefalas 2005; Edin and Reed 2005.
48. WIC is the Supplemental Nutrition Assistance Program for Women, Infants, and Children, which provides vouchers for staple food items to low-income pregnant and nursing women and children under age five.
49. Low-income women with incarcerated partners spend approximately a quarter of their monthly incomes maintaining these relationships (Grinstead et al. 2001).
50. Arnett 1998, 295.

CHAPTER 3. COMMITTING TO A RELATIONSHIP

1. See also Edin and Nelson 2013.
2. Taleisha is clearly cash strapped, yet she's more than willing to spend her money to take care of Darrell. This contrasts with some other research, for example, Kathryn Edin's (2000) discussion of low-income women maintaining a "pay and stay rule," requiring men to contribute financially or get kicked out of the household. The present study shows how some are willing to spend money to care for and maintain their ties to significant others. Future research should examine under what circumstances women are willing to support men financially versus ending the relationship because of their partners' need for financial support.
3. Biddle 1986; Eggebeen, Knoester, and McDaniel 2013; Townsend 2002.
4. Biddle 1986.
5. Cherlin 1978, 2004.
6. See, for example, Cettina 2009; Farr n.d.; Jay and Kovarick 2007; Stock n.d.
7. See, for example, the *Huffington Post* (Work family balance n.d.); *Harvard Business Review* (Groysberg and Abrahams 2014); thinkprogress.org (Covert 2013); and *Cosmopolitan* (Corneal 2013).
8. Burr 1972; Cottrell 1942; Merton 1968.
9. Berger and Bzostek 2014; Fox and Bruce 2001.
10. Stets and Cast 2007.
11. Burke and Stets 1999; Cast and Burke 2002; Stets and Burke 2005a.
12. Berger and Bzostek 2014.
13. Cherlin 2004.

14. Gusfield and Michalowicz 1984; Stanley, Rhoades, and Whitton 2010.
15. Manning and Smock 2005; Sassler 2004; Stanley, Rhoades, and Markman 2006.
16. Marsiglio and Roy 2012: 180.
17. In twenty-two of the thirty-one couples (71 percent), at least one partner had cohabited in a previous relationship. In twenty couples (65 percent), at least one partner had previously been engaged or married to another partner. In ten couples (32 percent), at least one partner had a child from a previous relationship.
18. Cherlin 2009; Edin and Nelson 2013.
19. Berger, Cancian, and Meyer 2012; Edin, Tach, and Mincy 2009; Guzzo 2009; Marsiglio and Roy 2012; Meyer and Cancian 2012; Tach, Mincy, and Edin 2010; Townsend 2002.
20. Cross-Barnett, Cherlin, and Burton 2011; Nepomnyaschy and Teitler 2013; Roy, Buckmiller, and McDowell 2008.
21. Cherlin 2004, 2009.
22. Amato and Booth 2001; Hazan and Shaver 1987; Kim et al. 2009; Mikulincer 1998; Rhoades et al. 2012.
23. Burton and Tucker 2009; Carlson, McLanahan, and England 2004; Edin and Kefalas 2005; Hill 2007; Silva 2013, 17, 56.
24. Trail and Karney 2012.
25. Cherlin 2009.
26. Giddens 1992.
27. For a review, see Karney and Bradbury 2005. See also Gibson-Davis 2009; Lichter, Qian, and Mellott 2006; McLanahan and Beck 2010; Smock, Manning, and Porter 2005.
28. Beck and Beck-Gernsheim 1995; Cherlin 2004, 2009.
29. Gerson 2009; Silva 2013.
30. Edin and Kefalas 2005.
31. Beck and Beck-Gernsheim 1995; Cherlin 2004, 2009.
32. Nationally, nearly three-quarters of men and women say that being "able to support a family financially is very important for a man to be a good husband/partner"; in contrast, only a quarter of men and over a third of women say the same about women being good wives or partners (Parker and Stepler 2017). The millennial generation may have more traditional views of the gendered division of labor than previous generations (Cotter and Pepin 2017; Fate-Dixon 2017; but see also Beam 2017).
33. Edin and Kefalas 2005; Gibson-Davis, Edin, and McLanahan 2005.
34. Silva 2013, 59.

CHAPTER 4. BECOMING A PARENT

1. Edin and Kefalas 2005; Edin and Nelson 2013; Settersten et al. 2014.
2. For related discussion, see Settersten et al. 2014.
3. Edin and Nelson 2013.

4. Edin and Kefalas 2005; Marsiglio and Hutchinson 2002; Silva 2013; Silva and Pugh 2010; Toguchi Swartz, Hartmann, and Mortimer 2011.

5. Addo 2014; Edin and Kefalas 2005; Edin, Kefalas, and Reed 2004; Edin and Reed 2005; Gibson-Davis 2009; Gibson-Davis, Edin, and McLanahan 2005; Kuo and Raley 2016; Smock, Manning and Porter 2005.

6. Bronfenbrenner 1979; Silva and Pugh, 2010.

7. Burr 1972, 414.

8. Mothers with more personal resources, like higher educational attainment, experience less stress during transitions (S. L. Brown 2000; Cooper et al. 2009; Tach 2012).

9. C. P. Cowan and Cowan 2000.

10. Marsiglio and Roy 2012, 175. See also Settersten et al. 2014.

11. Marsiglio and Roy 2012; Schneider 2011; Silva 2013.

12. Astone et al. 2010; Eggebeen, Dew, and Knoester 2010; Settersten and Cancel-Tirado 2010.

13. Berger and Bzostek 2014, 100.

14. See also Marsiglio and Roy 2012, 16.

15. Edin and Nelson 2013.

16. Burke and Stets 1999; Cast and Burke 2002; Stets and Burke 2005a, 2005b.

17. Carlson and Turner 2010.

18. Center for Research on Child Wellbeing 2003, 2007. Tach, Mincy, and Edin 2010; Townsend 2005. Walsh et al. 2014.

19. Cottrell 1942, 619.

CHAPTER 5. FAMILY EXPECTATIONS

1. See promotional materials on the Family Expectations website (www.familyexpectations.com), accessed August 1, 2017.

2. Either or both partners can remain in the program if they break up during the course of their participation.

3. This was the case during the time when data were collected for this project.

4. Program information described here comes from program reports. Oklahoma City's overall population is 15 percent black, 63 percent white, and 17 percent Hispanic. Eighty-five percent of Oklahoma City residents have graduated from high school. The median annual household income is around $47,000 (www.census.gov n.d.).

5. These topics emerged spontaneously in interviews, not in response to specific questions.

6. Here I discuss only the *primary* reasons couples gave for participation in Family Expectations. These total to more than 100 percent because couples offered more than one reason for participation.

7. Men are less likely to find out about the programs in the first place due to how they are advertised, in places where pregnant women and newborns are likely to be.

8. Cordell was exceptional in this regard; this was not an issue raised by other parents.

9. Mothers averaged 82 percent of workshop sessions; fathers averaged 79 percent of workshop sessions.

10. Dion, Avellar, and Clary 2010; Moore et al. 2012.

11. This is also in line with attendance trends in 2016–2017.

12. Each cohort's workshops are taught by a team of three "marriage educators" (a term that I never heard any of the parents use). These teams include both men and women and educators of various races.

13. See also Quirk et al. 2013.

14. Among the couples in this study, mothers averaged 9.4 office visits and fathers 8.2; this does not include contacts with family support coordinators by phone and e-mail, which were common.

15. See chapter 3 for a discussion of identity verification.

16. Edin and Lein 1997; London et al. 2004; E. K. Scott et al. 2004.

17. See also Watkins-Hayes 2009.

18. Family support coordinators provide information in response to the types of programs or services in which couples express interest. There is not a stock list of phone numbers they hand out. Therefore, they must be aware of a wide array of assistance available in the community.

19. I met with ten family support coordinators as well as their supervisor to discuss how they viewed and approached their role in couples' experiences at Family Expectations.

20. Except in those instances where it is not possible—as in the case of a language barrier, for example.

21. See also Finch et al. 1997; Kissane and Clampet-Lundquist 2012; Trobst 2000.

CHAPTER 6. LEARNING SKILLS

1. See also Edin, Kefalas, and Reed 2004.

2. Often, the voices of the participants in the programs have been absent from this debate; for exceptions, see Manning et al. 2010; Randles 2017.

3. See, for example, Halford, Sanders, and Behrens 2001; Rogge et al. 2013; Stanley et al. 2010; Stanley et al. 2014.

4. Blanchard et al. 2009; Hawkins et al. 2008; Hawkins et al. 2012.

5. Hawkins and Fackrell 2010.

6. Amato 2014.

7. Bradford et al. 2014.

8. P. A. Cowan et al. 2009; Rienks et al. 2011.

9. Hawkins 2014; Hawkins, Amato, and Klinghorn 2013; Hawkins et al. 2013.

10. Johnson 2013.

11. Johnson 2012.

12. Gardner and Boellaard 2007; Gubits et al. 2014; Kerpelman et al. 2009.

13. Markman et al. 1993.

14. Heath 2012. Heath's fieldwork, conducted in 2004, was done before the Building Strong Families and Supporting Healthy Marriage initiatives were implemented and so did not include an examination of programs under these initiatives.

15. See Randles (2017, 58) for a discussion of how relationship education program staff recognize how participants entered the programs already embracing marriage as a family form.

16. Heath 2012, 198. This is not to say that a critical analysis is an incorrect methodological approach; rather, here I recognize the limitations of such an approach for understanding the impact of policy on targeted participants.

17. Randles 2017; see also Karney and Bradbury 2005.

18. Couples with stronger marriages prior to the Depression were less susceptible to declining marital quality in the face of financial stressors (Liker and Elder 1983). Couples with good relationship problem-solving skills do not see an increase in conflict when faced with economic stressors; those with poorer coping skills do see a marked increase in hostility (Masarik et al. 2016). A representative sample of low-income coresidential couples shows relatively high levels of and variation in relationship quality (Addo and Sassler 2010, table 1). Although finances are predictive of couple conflict, they are not predictive of all relationship quality characteristics, such as affection (Hardie and Lucas 2010). Therefore, while relationship quality and stability can be affected by financial circumstances, they are not simply a function of them.

19. Randles and Woodward 2018, 42.

20. Randles and Woodward 2018, 46.

21. Randles 2017, 175.

22. Anne Sparks (2008) evaluated a relationship education program for welfare recipients in Oklahoma and found that it largely aligned with the participants' views of their relationship needs.

23. Of the three couples who did not participate in the second round of interviews, all had moved, no forwarding information was available, and cell phones were no longer in service. I attempted contact by phone, mail, and e-mail (when available).

24. For information about parents' employment at the time of program enrollment, see chapter 2.

25. Relationship education workshops are more effective in improving couples' communication when they teach the speaker listener technique (Owen, Manthos, and Quirk 2013).

26. Curriculum developers expect some adaptation (Stanley, Bradbury, and Markman 2000).

27. This material comes from PREP and the Becoming Parents Program (Jordan, Stanley, and Markman 1999).

28. Some couples had not yet participated in enough of the workshops to report either changes or no changes.

29. For a similar point, see also Randles 2017.

30. I performed additional analyses to examine whether partners' reactions to the program are related to various characteristics, including initial relationship quality, whether or not they were engaged or cohabiting, women's ages, whether they had children with previous partners, and race/ethnicity. There are no strong trends differentiating course reactions along these lines. The small sample size precludes me from drawing strong conclusions.

CHAPTER 7. RELATIONSHIP AND PARENTING CHANGES

1. This possibility may be more likely among the Family Expectations population than among all parents or couples in general. Unmarried parents are more likely to describe traumatic childhood experiences (Davies, Avison, and McAlpine 1997; Lippman, MacMillan, and Boyle 2001). Childhood trauma may make it more likely that partners' conflicts escalate quickly and that they have more limited abilities to follow through on calling a needed time out to halt such escalations (Linder and Collins 2005; Styron and Janoff-Bulman 1997; van der Kolk and Fisler 1994). To address this, some approaches to relationship education focus on individuals' development of emotional self-regulation (Halford 2011), although Family Expectations does not.
2. See also Avishai, Gerber, and Randles 2013.
3. Halpern-Meekin et al. 2013; Halpern-Meekin and Turney 2016.
4. See also Avishai, Gerber, and Randles 2013.
5. See also Randles 2017.
6. Wood et al. 2010.
7. Carlson, McLanahan, and England 2004.
8. In Fragile Families data, approximately 16 percent of parents report churning (breaking up and reuniting) over the first five years of their children's lives (Halpern-Meekin and Turney 2016).
9. These patterns are in line with the broader employment trends in Oklahoma City during the Great Recession (Bureau of Labor Statistics n.d.).
10. There is now no mention of LCLC on the Gottman Institute's extensive website (www.gottman.com, accessed September 18, 2017).
11. Dion et al. 2008.
12. Treatment group couples in Baltimore were more likely to have broken up and to report physical violence in their relationships. But there were low program participation rates among couples in Baltimore—just less than half of treatment couples did one session, and of those who started the program, they received less than half of the curriculum, on average. Therefore, it is difficult to determine how the program itself may have such an effect, given the large proportion of the treatment group that received little or no intervention. This also emphasizes the issue of whether measuring relationship stability is an appropriate outcome. The couples in Baltimore had some of the lowest-quality relationships across sites initially. The dissolution of low-quality relationships may be a positive outcome, a possibility not captured by existing studies' measures.
13. See also Braithwaite and Fincham 2014.

CONCLUSION

1. Reeves, Rodrigue, and Kneebone 2016.
2. Fussell and Furstenberg 2005.
3. Fussell and Furstenberg 2005.
4. Lundberg, Pollak, and Stearns 2016.
5. Copen, Daniels, and Mosher 2013.
6. Amato and Patterson 2017.
7. Amato 2000; Conger, Conger, and Martin 2010; Hardie and Lucas 2010; Osborne, Manning, and Smock 2007; Williamson, Karney, and Bradbury 2013.
8. Raley and Bumpass 2003.
9. Edin and England 2007, 14.
10. Conger, Rueter, and Elder 1999; Masarik et al. 2016; Neff and Broady 2011.
11. Kearney and Wilson 2017.
12. Schneider 2015. However, consistent with Schneider's findings, the New Hope project showed that improvements in financial well-being were associated with a greater likelihood of marriage among mothers (Gassman-Pines and Yoshikawa 2006).
13. Conger, Rueter, and Elder 1999; Masarik et al. 2016; Neff and Broady 2011. See also Brock and Lawrence 2008; Cox et al. 1999; Schokker et al. 2010.
14. A. C. Huston 2011.
15. Holcomb et al. 2015.
16. Dominguez and Watkins (2003) and Small (2006) also describe low-income mothers turning to the staff of organizations such as child care centers to create social ties; the result can be "reliable, high quality resources and relationships that are less stressful and burdensome in terms of reciprocity" compared with those with family and friends (Dominguez and Watkins 2003, 129).
17. Similarly, Edin and Kefalas explain, "We must recognize that young people growing up in poor communities have few positive models of marriage. Poor young women and men need some sense of what constitutes a healthy couple relationship to learn what helps couples who want to stay together and even someday marry. So some form of relationship-skills training is needed, though it must impart far more than mere speaker-listener techniques" (2005, 218).
18. Burke et al. 2011.
19. Davies, Avison, and McAlpine 1997; Lippman, MacMillan, and Boyle 2001.
20. Cloitre et al. 2009; Cook et al. 2005.
21. Executive function n.d.
22. Toxic stress n.d.
23. Bandura 1997.
24. Dutra et al. 2009; van der Kolk, Perry, and Herman 1991.
25. Linder and Collins 2005; Styron and Janoff-Bulman 1997; van der Kolk and Fisler 1994.

26. Some other approaches to relationship education focus on individuals' development of emotional self-regulation (Curtis 2015; Halford 2011); that, however, was not the focus of the Family Expectations curriculum.
27. For more discussion of this issue, see Edin and Nelson 2013.
28. See also Heflin and Iceland 2009.
29. Angry silents, disengaged millennials 2011.
30. Riffkin 2014.
31. As marriage and parenthood drift apart 2007.
32. Cherlin 2009.
33. Copen et al. 2012; Isen and Stevenson 2010.
34. In Kaplan 1997, xiv.
35. Center for Promise 2015.
36. Drentea et al. 2006.
37. Span 2017.
38. In Britain, social isolation costs employers £2.5 billion per year, in part due to lost days of work among caregivers (Jeffrey, Abdallah, and Michaelson 2017).
39. Similar efforts are also under way in other countries. See Jansen 2015.
40. The way the centers serve as a response to social poverty is visible in Chen's descriptions of them as offering "the more and less tangible benefits of personal relationships, cooperation, and community" (2015, 62).
41. Small 2006.
42. Center for the Study of Social Policy n.d.
43. This is compared to nearly universal participation among college-educated men (The long-term decline in prime-age male labor force participation 2016).
44. Mishel et al. 2012.
45. Bureau of Labor Statistics 2016.
46. Livingston and Parker 2011.
47. A discussion of how to bolster men's economic standing is beyond the scope of this book; however, this could potentially include addressing men's educational attainment, increasing worker protections, and bolstering wages, either directly or via the Earned Income Tax Credit.
48. Marsiglio and Roy 2012.
49. The insights the book has to offer are limited in key ways. First, the sample size is too small to permit analyses by race and ethnicity. Second, it includes only a sample of couples in opposite-sex relationships. Third, the program is situated in the particular cultural climate of Oklahoma. Future research should examine whether and how the conclusions of the current study stand up to examination across racial and ethnic groups, among same-sex couples, and in other state contexts.
50. Research shows that low-income married couples rate relational problems and those external to the relationship (such as employment or child care issues) as equally severe (Jackson et al. 2016).
51. While social poverty is a subjective experience, this does not mean instruments cannot be developed to measure it (just as has been done for other subjective

experiences, such as feelings of self-efficacy or relationship satisfaction). These could include measures of time and frequency of contact with others, quality of relationships with others, trust in others, and feelings of social isolation and loneliness. For a review of existing and proposed measures, see OECD 2011; Stiglitz, Sen, and Fitoussi 2009; Zavaleta, Samuel, and Mills 2017.

52. This is under way with military couples, same-sex couples, and couples forming stepfamilies: Allen et al. 2011; Buzzella, Whitton, and Tompson 2012; Lucier-Greer and Adler-Baeder 2012.

53. Futris, Sutton, and Richardson 2013; Gardner and Boellaard 2007; Halpern-Meekin 2011; Kerpelman et al. 2009, 2010; Ma et al. 2014; Sparks, Lee, and Spjeldnes 2012.

54. Some relationship education curricula for youth, such as Relationship Smarts Plus, do address issues around sex.

APPENDIX

1. T. Brown 2016; Oklahoma Marriage Initiative n.d.

2. After several years of conducting research in the state and attending the research advisory group meetings as a guest, I was asked to formally join the group in 2010.

3. Becoming Parents Program n.d.

4. See, for example, Antle et al. 2011; Stanley et al. 2010.

5. PREP, Inc. n.d.

6. In the cases of two couples who were having relationship problems at the time, I conducted separate interviews with each partner. In two other instances, only one partner was available, so I interviewed only one partner from two couples at this round.

7. In one case, only one partner was able to meet, so I interviewed only one member of this couple. In two other cases, in which couples had broken up and there were potential issues with violence, I interviewed only the women and did not contact their exes. While this meant sacrificing data, the risks to the women's safety and my own did not seem worth what I lost in not hearing both sides of these stories. In two final cases, the men were in jail, and so I met only with their partners.

8. Charmaz 2006.

9. This is in line with the approach Kristin Seefeldt (2016) describes in analyzing her interviews with low-income women.

10. T. Brown 2016; Adcock 2013; Associated Press 2017; Clark 2016; Liou 2016.

11. Associated Press 2017; Cobb 2017; Wingerter 2017.

BIBLIOGRAPHY

Accel + Qualtrics. n.d. The Millennial Study. www.qualtrics.com. Accessed July 10, 2017.

Adcock, Clifton. 2013. Oklahoma watch: Effectiveness of Oklahoma marriage initiative questioned by some. *The Oklahoman, December 1.* www.newsok.com. Accessed September 6, 2017.

Addo, Fenaba. 2014. Debt, cohabitation, and marriage in young adulthood. *Demography* 51: 1677–1701.

Addo, Fenaba R., and Sassler, Sharon. 2010. Financial arrangements and relationship quality in low-income couples. *Family Relations* 59: 408–423.

Ainsworth, Mary S. 1989. Attachments beyond infancy. *American Psychologist* 44: 709–716.

Alkire, Sabina, and Foster, James. 2008. Counting and multidimensional poverty measurement. Oxford Poverty and Human Development Initiative Working Paper Series No. 7. Oxford, UK. www.ophi.org.uk.

Allard, Scott W., and Small, Mario L. 2013. Reconsidering the urban disadvantaged: The role of systems, institutions, and organizations. *ANNALS of the American Academy of Political and Social Sciences* 647: 6–20.

Allen, Elizabeth, Stanley, Scott M., Rhoades, Galena K., Markman, Howard J., and Loew, Benjamin A. 2011. Marriage education in the army: Results of a randomized clinical trial. *Journal of Couple and Relationship Therapy* 10: 309–326.

Almendrala, Anna. 2016. The U.S. surgeon general wants to bring you health via happiness. www.huffingtonpost.com, November 23. Accessed July 15, 2016.

Amato, Paul R. 2000. Consequences of divorce for adults and children. *Journal of Marriage and the Family* 62: 1269–1287.

Amato, Paul R. 2014. Does social and economic disadvantage moderate the effects of relationship education on unwed couples? An analysis of data from the 15-month Building Strong Families evaluation. *Family Relations* 63: 343–355.

Amato, Paul R., and Booth, Alan. 2001. The legacy of parents' marital discord: Consequences for children's marital quality. *Journal of Personality and Social Psychology* 81: 627–638.

Amato, Paul R., and Patterson, Sarah E. 2017. The intergenerational transmission of union instability in early adulthood. *Journal of Marriage and Family* 79: 723–738.

Anderson, Elijah. 1999. *Code of the street.* New York: Norton.

Angley, Meghan, Divney, Anna, Magriples, Urania, and Kershaw, Trace. 2015. Social support, family functioning and parenting competence in adolescent parents. *Maternal and Child Health Journal* 19: 67–73.

Angry silents, disengaged millennials: The generation gap and the 2012 election. 2011. Pew Research Center. www.people-press.org. Accessed June 11, 2015.

Antle, Becky, Karam, Eli, Christensen, Dana N., Barbee, Anita P., and Sar, Bibhuti K. 2011. An evaluation of healthy relationship education to reduce intimate partner violence. *Journal of Family Social Work* 14: 387–406.

Arnett, Jeffrey J. 1997. Young people's conceptions of the transition to adulthood. *Youth and Society* 29: 1–23.

Arnett, Jeffrey J. 1998. Learning to stand alone: The contemporary American transition to adulthood in cultural and historical context. *Human Development* 41: 295–315.

Arnett, Jeffrey J. 2000. Emerging adulthood: A theory of development from the late teens through the twenties. *American Psychologist* 55: 469–480.

Arnett, Jeffrey J. 2004. Adolescence in the twenty-first century: A worldwide survey. In *Childhood and adolescence: Cross-cultural perspectives and applications*, edited by Uwe P. Gielen and Jaipaul Roopnarine, 277–294. Westport, CT: Praeger.

Arnett, Jeffrey J. 2005. The developmental context of substance use in emerging adulthood. *Journal of Drug Issues* 35: 235–253.

Arnett, Jeffrey J. 2006. Emerging adulthood: Understanding the new way of coming of age. In *Emerging adults in America: Coming of age in the 21st century*, edited by Jeffrey J. Arnett and Jennifer L. Tanner, 3–19. Washington, DC: APA Books.

As marriage and parenthood drift apart, public is concerned about social impact. 2007. Pew Research Center. www.pewsocialtrends.org. Accessed June 11, 2015.

Associated Press. August 27, 2017. Charities try to help Oklahoma teachers survive pay collapse. www.wtop.com. Accessed September 6, 2017.

Astone, Nan M., Dariotis, Jacinda K., Sonenstein, Freya L., Pleck, Joseph H., and Hynes, Katheryn. 2010. Men's work efforts and the transition to fatherhood. *Journal of Family and Economic Issues* 31: 3–13.

Avishai, Orit, Gerber, Lynne, and Randles, Jennifer. 2013. The feminist ethnographer's dilemma: Reconciling progressive research agendas with fieldwork realities. *Journal of Contemporary Ethnography* 42: 394–426.

Bandura, Albert. 1997. *Self-efficacy: The exercise of control*. New York: W. H. Freeman.

Barrera, Manuel, Jr. 2000. Social support research in community psychology. In *Handbook of community psychology*, edited by Julian Rappaport and Edward Seidman, 215–245. Boston: Springer US.

Baumeister, Roy F., and Leary, Mark R. 1995. The need to belong: Desire for interpersonal attachments as a fundamental human motivation. *Psychological Bulletin* 117: 497–529.

Beam, Emily. 2017. Adventures in garbage millennial confirmation bias. www.scatter. wordpress.com. Accessed July 12, 2017.

Beck, Ulrich, and Beck-Gernsheim, Elisabeth. 1995. *The normal chaos of love*. Malden, MA: Blackwell.

Beck-Gernsheim, Elisabeth. 2002. *Reinventing the family: In search of new lifestyles*. Cambridge, UK: Wiley.

Becoming Parents Program. n.d. Program for couples. www.becomingparents.com. Accessed September 6, 2017.

Benin, Mary, and Keith, Verna M. 1995. The social support of employed African American and Anglo mothers. *Journal of Family Issues* 16: 275–297.

Berger, Lawrence M., and Bzostek, Sharon H. 2014. Young adults' roles as partners and parents in the context of family complexity. *Annals of the American Academy of Political and Social Science* 654: 87–109.

Berger, Lawrence M., Cancian, Maria, and Meyer, Daniel R. 2012. Maternal re-partnering and new-partner fertility: Associations with nonresident father investments in children. *Children and Youth Services Review* 34: 426–436.

Beveridge, William H. 1942. *Social insurance and allied services*. London: HMSO.

Biddle, Bruce J. 1986. Recent developments in role theory. *Annual Review of Sociology* 12: 67–92.

Blanchard, Victoria L., Hawkins, Alan J., Baldwin, Scott A., and Fawcett, Elizabeth B. 2009. Investigating the effects of marriage and relationship education on couples' communication skills: A meta-analytic study. *Journal of Family Psychology* 23: 203–214.

Blank, Rebecca M. 2008. Presidential address: How to improve poverty measurement in the United States. *Journal of Policy Analysis and Management* 27: 233–254.

Bono, Katherine E., Sy, Susan R., and Kopp, Claire B. 2016. School readiness among low-income black children: Family characteristics, parenting, and social support. *Early Child Development and Care* 186: 419–435.

Boo, Katherine. 2003. The marriage cure: Is wedlock really a way out of poverty? *New Yorker, August 18*. www.newyorker.com.

Bosma, Hans, Jansen, Maria, Schefman, Suzanne, Hajema, Klaas Jan, and Feron, Frans. 2015. Lonely at the bottom: A cross-sectional study on being ill, poor, and lonely. *Public Health* 129: 185–187.

Bourdieu, Pierre. 1986. The forms of capital. In *Handbook of theory and research for the sociology of education*, edited by John G. Richardson, 241–258. Westport, CT: Greenwood Press.

Boushey, Heather, Gundersen, Bethney, Brocht, Chauna, and Bernstein, Jared. 2001. *Measuring hardships*. Washington, DC: Economic Policy Institute.

Bowlby, John. 1979. *The making and breaking of affectional bonds*. London: Tavistock.

Bradford, Angela B., Adler-Baeder, Francesca, Ketring, Scott A., Bub, Kristen L., Pittman, Joe F., and Smith, Thomas A. 2014. Relationship quality and depressed affect among a diverse sample of relationally unstable relationship education participants. *Family Relations* 63: 219–231.

Braithwaite, Scott R., and Fincham, Frank D. 2014. Computer-based prevention of intimate partner violence in marriage. *Behavior Research and Therapy* 54: 12–21.

Brehm, John, and Rahn, Wendy. 1997. Individual-level evidence for the causes and consequences of social capital. *American Journal of Political Science* 41: 999–1023.

Brewster, Karen L., and Padavic, Irene. 2002. No more kin care? Change in black mothers' reliance on relatives for child care, 1977–94. *Gender and Society* 16: 546–563.

Briggs, Xavier de Souza. 1998. Brown kids in white suburbs: Housing mobility and the many faces of social capital. *Housing Policy Debate* 9: 177–221.

Brisson, Daniel S., and Usher, Charles L. 2005. Bonding social capital in low-income neighborhoods. *Family Relations* 54: 644–653.

Brock, Rebecca L., and Lawrence, Erika. 2008. A longitudinal investigation of stress spillover in marriage: Does spousal support adequacy buffer the effects? *Journal of Family Psychology* 22: 11–20.

Bronfenbrenner, Urie. 1979. *The ecology of human development: Experiments by nature and design*. Cambridge, MA: Harvard University Press.

Brown, Susan L. 2000. The effect of union type on psychological well-being: Depression among cohabitors versus marrieds. *Journal of Health and Social Behavior* 41: 241–255.

Brown, Trevor. 2016. State ends marriage initiative as part of budget cuts. Oklahoma Watch, August 3. www.oklahomawatch.org.

Bureau of Labor Statistics. 2014. America's young adults at 27: Labor market activity, education, and household composition: Results from a longitudinal survey. March 26. US Department of Labor USDL-14-0491.

Bureau of Labor Statistics. 2016. Labor market activity, education, and partner status among America's young adults at 29: Results from a longitudinal survey. DOL-16-0700.

Bureau of Labor Statistics. n.d. www.data.bls.gov. Accessed June 28, 2016.

Burke, Nadine J., Hellman, Julia L., Scott, Brandon G., Weems, Carl F., and Carrion, Victor G. 2011. The impact of adverse childhood experiences on an urban pediatric population. *Child Abuse and Neglect* 35: 408–413.

Burke, Peter J., and Stets, Jan E. 1999. Trust and commitment through self-verification. *Social Psychology Quarterly* 62: 347–366.

Burr, Wesley R. 1972. Role transitions: A reformulation of theory. *Journal of Marriage and Family* 34: 407–416.

Burton, Linda M., Cherlin, Andrew, Winn, Donna-Marie, Estacion, Angela, and Holder-Taylor, Clara. 2009. The role of trust in low-income mothers' intimate unions. *Journal of Marriage and Family* 71: 1107–1124.

Burton, Linda M., and Tucker, M. Belinda. 2009. Romantic unions in an era of uncertainty: A post-Moynihan perspective on African American women and marriage. *Annals of the American Academy of Political and Social Science* 621: 132–148.

Buzzella, Brian A., Whitton, Sarah A., and Tompson, Martha C. 2012. A preliminary evaluation of a relationship education program for male same-sex couples. *Couple and Family Psychology: Research and Practice* 1: 306–322.

Byrnes, Hilary F., and Miller, Brenda A. 2012. The relationship between neighborhood characteristics and effective parenting behaviors: The role of social support. *Journal of Family Issues* 33: 1658–1687.

Cacioppo, John T., and Cacioppo, Stephanie. 2014. Social relationships and health: The toxic effects of perceived social isolation. *Social and Personality Psychology Compass* 8: 58–72.

Cacioppo, John T., Cacioppo, Stephanie, and Boomsma, Dorret. 2014. Evolutionary mechanisms for loneliness. *Cognition and Emotion*: 28: 3–21.

Cacioppo, John T., Chen, Hsi Yuan, and Cacioppo, Stephanie 2017. Reciprocal influences between loneliness and self-centeredness: A cross-lagged panel analysis in a population-based sample of African American, Hispanic, and Caucasian adults. *Personality and Social Psychology Bulletin* 43: 1125–1135.

Cacioppo, John T., and Hawkley, Louise C. 2009. Perceived social isolation and cognition. *Trends in Cognitive Sciences* 13: 447–454.

Cacioppo, John T., Hughes, Mary Elizabeth, Waite, Linda J., Hawkley, Louise C., and Thisted, Ronald A. 2006. Loneliness as a specific risk factor for depressive symptoms: Cross-sectional and longitudinal analyses. *Psychology and Aging* 21: 140–151.

Cacioppo, John T., and Patrick, William. 2008. *Loneliness: Human nature and the need for social connection.* New York: W. W. Norton.

Campos, Belinda. 2015. What is the role of culture in the association of relationships with health? *Social and Personality Psychology Compass* 9: 661–677.

Carasso, Adam L., and McKernan, Signe-Mary. 2007. The balance sheets of low-income households: What we know about their assets and liabilities. www.papers.ssrn.com.

Carlson, Marcia, McLanahan, Sara, and England, Paula. 2004. Union formation in fragile families. *Demography* 41: 237–261.

Carlson, Marcia J., and Turner, Kimberly. 2010. Fathers' involvement and fathers' wellbeing over children's first five years. Working paper. University of Wisconsin–Madison, Institute for Research on Poverty.

Carr, Patrick J., and Kefalas, Maria J. 2011. Straight from the heartland: Coming of age in Ellis, Iowa. In *Coming of age in America: The transition to adulthood in the twenty-first century*, edited by Mary C. Waters, Patrick J. Carr, and Maria J. Kefalas, 28–58. Berkeley: University of California Press.

Cast, Alicia D., and Burke, Peter J. 2002. A theory of self-esteem. *Social Forces* 80: 1041–1068.

Catlett, Beth S., and Artis, Julie E. 2004. Critiquing the case for marriage promotion. *Violence against Women*, 10: 1226–1244.

Center for Promise. 2015. *Don't quit on me: What young people who left school say about the power of relationships.* Washington, DC: America's Promise Alliance.

Center for Research on Child Wellbeing. 2003. Union formation and dissolution in fragile families. Fragile Families Research Brief No. 14, Princeton University.

Center for Research on Child Wellbeing. 2007. Parents' relationship status five years after a non-marital birth. Fragile Families Research Brief No. 39, Princeton University.

Center for the Study of Social Policy. n.d. Intensive permanence services: Any Family Services. www.cssp.org.

Cettina, Teri. 2009. How to save your marriage from your kids. CNN. July 29. www.cnn.com. Accessed October 4, 2014.

Charmaz, K. 2006. *Constructing grounded theory.* Thousand Oaks, CA: Sage.

Chen, Victor T. 2015. *Cut loose: Jobless and hopeless in an unfair economy.* Berkeley: University of California Press.

Cheng, Grand H. L., and Chan, Darius K. S. 2008. Who suffers more from job insecurity? A meta-analytic review. *Applied Psychology* 57: 272–303.

Chetty, Raj, and Hendren, Nathaniel. 2018. The impacts of neighborhoods on intergenerational mobility I: Childhood exposure effects. *Quarterly Journal of Economics* 133: 1107–1162.

Cherlin Andrew. 1978. Remarriage as an incomplete institution. *American Journal of Sociology* 84: 634–650.

Cherlin, Andrew J. 2004. The deinstitutionalization of American marriage. *Journal of Marriage and Family* 66: 848–861.

Cherlin, Andrew J. 2009. *The marriage-go-round: The state of marriage and the family in America today.* New York: Random House.

Cherlin, Andrew J. 2011. Between poor and prosperous: Do the family patterns of moderately educated Americans deserve a closer look? In *Social class and changing families in an unequal America,* edited by Marcia J. Carlson and Paula England, 68–84. Stanford, CA: Stanford University Press.

Cherlin Andrew J., and Furstenberg, Frank F., Jr. 1994. Stepfamilies in the United States: A reconsideration. *Annual Review of Sociology* 20: 359–381.

Cherlin, Andrew J., Talbert, Elizabeth, and Yasutake, Suzumi. 2014. Changing fertility regimes and the transition to adulthood: Evidence from a recent cohort. Paper presented at the annual meeting of the Population Association of America, Boston, May 3.

Chiu, Lian-Hwang. 1990. The relationship of career goal and self-esteem among adolescents. *Adolescence* 25: 593–597.

Clark, Krissy. 2016. "Oh my God—We're on welfare?!" www.slate.com, June 2. Accessed September 6, 2017.

Clark, Krissy, Esch, Caitlin, and Delvac, Gina. 2016. What's love (styles) got to do with it? *The Uncertain Hour,* Marketplace S01-3. May 26. www.marketplace.org.

Cloitre, Marylene, Stolbach, Bradley C., Herman, Judith L., van der Kolk, Bessel, Pynoos, Robert, Wang, Jing, and Petkova, Eva. 2009. A developmental approach to complex PTSD: Childhood and adult cumulative trauma as predictors of symptom complexity. *Journal of Traumatic Stress* 22: 399–408.

Coan, James A., Beckes, Lane, Gonzalez, Marlen Z., Maresh, Erin L., Brown, Casey L., and Hasselmo, Karen. 2017. Relationship status and perceived support in the social regulation of neural responses to threat. *Social Cognitive and Affective Neuroscience* 12: 1574–1583.

Coan James A., Schaefer, Hillary S., and Davidson Richard J. 2006. Lending a hand: Social regulation of the neural response to threat. *Psychological Science* 17: 1032–1039.

Cobb, Russell. 2017. Oklahoma isn't working. Can anyone fix this failing American state? *The Guardian,* August 29. www.theguardian.com. Accessed September 6, 2017.

Cohen, Patricia, Kasen, Stephanie, Chen, Henian, Hartmark, Claudia, and Gordon, Kathy. 2003. Variations in patterns of developmental transmissions in the emerging adulthood period. *Developmental Psychology* 39: 657–669.

Cohen, Sheldon. 2004. Social relationships and health. *American Psychologist* 59: 676–684.

Cohen, Sheldon, Mermelstein, Robin, Kamarck, Tom, and Hoberman, Harry M. 1985. Measuring the functional components of social support. In *Social support: Theory, research and applications*, edited by Irwin G. Sarason and Barbara R. Sarason, 73–94. Dordrecht: Springer Netherlands.

Cohen, Sheldon, and Wills, Thomas A. 1985. Stress, social support, and the buffering hypothesis. *Psychological Bulletin* 98: 310–357.

Coleman, James S. 1988. Social capital in the creation of human capital. *American Journal of Sociology* 9: S95–S121.

Coleman, James S. 1990. *Foundations of social theory.* Cambridge, MA: Harvard University Press.

Collins, Nancy L., Dunkel-Schetter, Christine, Lobel, Marci, and Scrimshaw, Susan C. 1993. Social support in pregnancy: Psychosocial correlates of birth outcomes and postpartum depression. *Journal of Personality and Social Psychology* 65: 1243–1258.

Collins, W. Andrew, Welsh, Deborah P., and Furman, Wyndol. 2009. Adolescent romantic relationships. *Annual Review of Psychology* 60: 631–652.

Conger, Rand D., Conger, Katherine J., and Martin, Monica J. 2010. Socioeconomic status, family processes, and individual development. *Journal of Marriage and Family* 72: 685–704.

Conger, Rand D., and Elder, Glen H. 1994. *Families in troubled times: Adapting to change in rural America.* New York: Aldine de Gruyter.

Conger, Rand D., Rueter, Martha A., and Elder, Glen H. 1999. Couple resilience to economic pressure. *Journal of Personality and Social Psychology* 76: 54–71.

Cook, Alexandra, Spinazzola, Joseph, Ford, Julian, Lanktree, Cheryl, Blaustein, Margaret, Cloitre, Marylene, DeRosa, Ruth, Hubbard, Rebecca, Kagan, Richard, Liautaud, Joan, Mallah, Karen, Olafson, Erna, and van der Kolk, Bessel. 2005. Complex trauma in children and adolescents. *Psychiatric Annals* 35: 390–398.

Cook, Karen S., Hardin, Russell, and Levi, Margaret. 2005. *Cooperation without trust?* New York: Russell Sage Foundation.

Cooper, Carey E., McLanahan, Sara S., Meadows, Sarah O., and Brooks-Gunn, Jeanne. 2009. Family structure transitions and maternal parenting stress. *Journal of Marriage and Family* 71: 558–574.

Copen, Casey E., Daniels, Kimberly, and Mosher, William D. 2013. First premarital cohabitation in the United States: 2006–2010 National Survey of Family Growth. National Health Statistics Reports, 64. www.cdc.gov.

Copen, Casey E., Daniels, Kimberly, Vespa, Jonathan, and Mosher, William D. 2012. First marriages in the United States: Data from the 2006–2010 National Survey of Family Growth. National Health Statistics Reports, 49. www.cdc.gov.

Corneal, Devon. 2013. The question we should all be asking about success. *Cosmopolitan*, December 27. www.cosmopolitan.com. Accessed October 4, 2014.

Cotter, David, and Pepin, Joanna. 2017. Trending toward traditionalism? Changes in youths' gender ideology. www.contemporaryfamilies.org. Accessed July 12, 2017.

Cottrell, Leonard S., Jr. 1942. The adjustment of the individual to his age and sex roles. *American Sociological Review* 7: 617–620.

Covert, Bryce. 2013. Work-family balance is important to both genders, but it comes harder to women. www.thinkprogress.org. Accessed October 4, 2014.

Cowan, Carolyn P., and Cowan, Philip A. 2000. *When partners become parents: The big life change for couples.* Mahwah, NJ: Lawrence Erlbaum.

Cowan, Philip A., Cowan, Carolyn P., Pruett, Marsha Kline, Pruett, Kyle, and Wong, Jessie J. 2009. Promoting fathers' engagement with children: Preventive interventions for low-income families. *Journal of Marriage and Family* 71: 663–679.

Cox, Martha J., Paley, Blair, Burchinal, Margaret, and Payne, C. Chris. 1999. Marital perceptions and interactions across the transition to parenthood. *Journal of Marriage and the Family* 61: 611–625.

Creed, Peter A., and Reynolds, Judith. 2001. Economic deprivation, experiential deprivation and social loneliness in unemployed and employed youth. *Journal of Community and Applied Social Psychology* 11: 167–178.

Cross-Barnett, Caitlin, Cherlin, Andrew, and Burton, Linda. 2011. Bound by children: Intermittent cohabitation and living together apart. *Family Relations* 60: 633–647.

Cui, Ming, and Fincham, Frank D. 2010. The differential effects of parental divorce and marital conflict on young adult romantic relationships. *Personal Relationships* 17: 331–343.

Curtin, Melanie. 2017. This 75-year Harvard study found the 1 secret to leading a fulfilling life. www.inc.com. Accessed March 12, 2017.

Curtis, Carolyn R. 2015. Introduction to a trauma informed approach in relationship education. The Dibble Institute. www.youtube.com/watch?v=_s-WiAknj-c. Accessed August 30, 2017.

Cutrona, Carolyn E. 1982. Transition to college: Loneliness and the process of social adjustment. *Loneliness: A Sourcebook of Current Theory, Research, and Therapy* 36: 291–309.

Cutrona, Carolyn E., and Russell, Daniel W. 1990. Type of social support and specific stress: Toward a theory of optimal matching. In *Social support: An interactional view*, edited by B. R. Sarason, I. G. Sarason, and G. R. Pierce, 319–366. Oxford: John Wiley.

D'Angelo, Angela V., Knas, Emily, Holcomb, Pamela, and Edin, Kathryn. 2016. The role of social networks among low-income fathers: Findings from the PACT evaluation. OPRE Report 2016-60. www.acf.hhs.gov.

Davies, Lorraine, Avison, William R., and McAlpine, Donna D. 1997. Significant life experiences and depression among single and married mothers. *Journal of Marriage and Family* 59: 294–308.

Desmond, Matthew. 2012. Disposable ties and the urban poor. *American Journal of Sociology* 117: 1295–1335.

Desmond, Matthew. 2015. Severe deprivation in America: An introduction. *RSF: The Russell Sage Foundation Journal of the Social Sciences* 1: 1–11.

Dion, M. Robin, Avellar, Sarah, and Clary, Elizabeth. 2010. *The Building Strong Families Project: Implementation of eight programs to strengthen unmarried parent families.* Office of Planning, Research, and Evaluation, Administration for Children and Families, US Department of Health and Human Services.

Dion, M. Robin, Hershey, Alan M., Zaveri, Heather H., Avellar, Sarah A., Strong, Debra A., Silman, Timothy, and Moore, Ravaris. 2008. Implementation of the Building Strong Families Program. Mathematica Policy Research. www.acf.hhs.gov.

Dominguez, Silvia. 2010. *Getting ahead: Social mobility, public housing, and immigrant networks.* New York: NYU Press.

Dominguez, Silvia, and Watkins, Celeste. 2003. Creating networks for survival and mobility: Social capital among African-American and Latin-American low-income mothers. *Social Problems* 50: 111–135.

Doss, Brian D., Rhoades, Galena K., Stanley, Scott M., and Markman, Howard J. 2009. The effect of the transition to parenthood on relationship quality: An eight-year prospective study. *Journal of Personality and Social Psychology* 96: 601–619.

Drentea, Patricia, Clay, Olivio J., Roth, David L., and Milttelman, Mary S. 2006. Predictors of improvement in social support: Five-year effects of a structured intervention for caregivers of spouses with Alzheimer's disease. *Social Science and Medicine* 63: 957–967.

Dutra, Lissa, Bureau, Jean-François, Holmes, Bjarne, Lyubchik, Amy, and Lyons-Ruth, Karlen. 2009. Quality of early care and childhood trauma: A prospective study of developmental pathways to dissociation. *Journal of Nervous and Mental Disease* 197: 383–390.

Eccles, Jacquelynne S. 2009. Who am I and what am I going to do with my life? Personal and collective identities as motivators of action. *Educational Psychologist* 44: 78–89.

Edin, Kathryn. 2000. What do low-income single mothers say about marriage? *Social Problems* 47: 112–133.

Edin, Kathryn, and England, Paula. 2007. Unmarried couples with children: Hoping for love and the white picket fence. In *Unmarried couples with children*, edited by Kathryn Edin and Paul England, 3–22. New York: Russell Sage Foundation.

Edin, Kathryn, England, Paula, and Linnenberg, Kathryn. 2003. Love and distrust among unmarried parents. Paper presented at the annual research conference of the National Poverty Center. Washington, DC, September 4–5.

Edin, Kathryn, England, Paula, Shafer, Emily F., and Reed, Joanna. 2007. Forming fragile families: Was the baby planned, unplanned, or in between? In *Unmarried couples with children*, edited by Kathryn Edin and Paula England, 25–54. New York: Russell Sage Foundation.

Edin, Kathryn, and Kefalas, Maria. 2005. *Promises I can keep: Why poor women put motherhood before marriage.* Berkeley: University of California Press.

Edin, Kathryn, Kefalas, Maria, and Reed, Joanna. 2004. A peek inside the black box: What marriage means for poor unmarried parents. *Journal of Marriage and Family* 66: 1007–1014.

Edin, Kathryn, and Lein, Laura. 1997. *Making ends meet: How single mothers survive welfare and low-wage work.* New York: Russell Sage Foundation.

Edin, Kathryn, and Nelson, Timothy. 2013. *Doing the best I can: Fathering in the inner city.* Berkeley: University of California Press.

Edin, Kathryn, and Reed, Joanna. 2005. Why don't they just get married: Barriers to marriage among the disadvantaged. *Future of Children* 15: 117–137.

Edin, Kathryn, Tach, Laura, and Mincy, Ron. 2009. Claiming fatherhood: Race and the dynamics of paternal involvement among unmarried men. *Annals of the American Academy of Political and Social Science* 621: 149–177.

Eggebeen, David. 1992. Family structure and intergenerational exchanges. *Research on Aging* 14: 427–447.

Eggebeen, David J., Dew, Jeffrey, and Knoester, Chris. 2010. Fatherhood and men's lives at middle age. *Journal of Family Issues* 31: 113–130.

Eggebeen, David J., Knoester, Chris, and McDaniel, Brandon. 2013. The implications of fatherhood for men. In *Handbook of father involvement: Multidisciplinary perspectives,* edited by Natasha J. Cabrera and Catherine S. Tamis-LeMonda, 338–357. New York: Routledge.

Elliott, Diana B., and Simmons, Tavia. 2011. Marital events of Americans: 2009. American Community Survey Reports. www.census.gov.

Elofson, Greg. 2001. Developing trust with intelligent agents: An exploratory study. In *Trust and deception in virtual societies,* edited by Cristiano Castelfranchi and Yao-Hua Tan, 125–138. Dordrecht: Springer.

Estacion, Angela, and Cherlin, Andrew. 2010. Gender distrust and intimate unions among low-income Hispanic and African American women. *Journal of Family Issues* 31: 475–498.

Executive function. n.d. Center on the Developing Child, Harvard University. www.developingchild.harvard.edu. Accessed August 30, 2017.

Farr, Robin. n.d. Losing yourself to motherhood. www.scarymommy.com. Accessed November 14, 2017.

Fate-Dixon, Nika. 2017. Are some millennials rethinking the gender revolution? Long-range trends in views of non-traditional roles for women. www.contemporaryfamilies.org. Accessed July 12, 2017.

Fehr, Beverley. 1996. *Friendship processes.* Thousand Oaks, CA: Sage.

Ferlander, Sara. 2004. E-learning, marginalised communities and social capital: A mixed methods approach. In *Researching widening access to lifelong learning: Issues and approaches in international research,* edited by Michael Osborne, Jim Gallacher, and Beth Crossan, 180–194. London: Routledge/Falmer.

Finch, John F., Barrera, Manuel, Jr., Okun, Morris A., Bryant, William H. M., Pool, Gregory J., and Snow-Turek, A. Lynn. 1997. The factor structure of received social support: Dimensionality and the prediction of depression and life satisfaction. *Journal of Social and Clinical Psychology* 16: 323–342.

Fine, Gary A. 1986. Friendships in the workplace. In *Friendship and social interaction*, edited by Valerian J. Derlega and Barbara A. Winstead, 185–206. New York: Springer-Verlag.

Finer, Lawrence B., and Zolna, Mia R. 2014. Shifts in intended and unintended pregnancies in the United States, 2001–2008. *American Journal of Public Health* 104 (S1): S44–S48.

Fox, Greer L., and Bruce, Carol. 2001. Conditional fatherhood: Identity theory and parental investment theory as alternative sources of explanation of fathering. *Journal of Marriage and Family* 63: 394–403.

Fragile Families Research Brief. 2002. Is marriage a viable objective for fragile families? July. www.fragilefamilies.princeton.edu.

Furman, Wyndol, and Buhrmester, Duane. 1992. Age and sex differences in perceptions of networks of personal relationships. *Child Development* 63: 103–115.

Furstenberg, Frank F. 2007. Should government promote marriage? *Journal of Policy Analysis and Management* 26: 956–961.

Furstenberg, Frank F. 2008. The intersections of social class and the transition to adulthood. *New Directions for Child and Adolescent Development* 119: 1–10.

Furstenberg, Frank F., Jr., and Cherlin, Andrew. 1991. *Divided families: What happens to children when parents part*. Cambridge, MA: Harvard University Press.

Fussell, Elizabeth, and Furstenberg, Frank F., Jr. 2005. The transition to adulthood during the twentieth century. In *On the frontier of adulthood: Theory, research, and public policy*, edited by Richard A. Settersten Jr., Frank F. Furstenberg Jr., and Rubén G. Rumbaut, 29–75. Chicago: University of Chicago Press.

Futris, Ted G., Sutton, Tara E., and Richardson, Evin W. 2013. An evaluation of the Relationship Smarts Plus program on adolescents in Georgia. *Journal of Human Sciences and Extension* 1: 1–15.

Gallo, Linda C., and Matthews, Karen A. 2003. Understanding the association between socioeconomic status and physical health: Do negative emotions play a role? *Psychological Bulletin* 129: 10–51.

Gardner, Scott P., and Boellaard, Rila. 2007. Does youth relationship education continue to work after a high school class? A longitudinal study. *Family Relations* 56: 490–500.

Gassman-Pines, Anna, and Yoshikawa, Hirokazu. 2006. Five-year effects of an antipoverty program on marriage among never-married mothers. *Journal of Policy Analysis and Management* 25: 11–30.

Gerson, Kathleen. 2009. *The unfinished revolution: Coming of age in a new era of gender, work, and family*. New York: Oxford University Press.

Gibson-Davis, Christina M. 2009. Money, marriage, and children: Testing the financial expectations and family formation theory. *Journal of Marriage and Family* 71: 146–160.

Gibson-Davis, Christina, Edin, Kathryn, and McLanahan, Sara. 2005. High hopes, but even higher expectations: The retreat from marriage among low-income couples. *Journal of Marriage and Family* 67: 1301–1312.

Giddens, Anthony. 1991. *Modernity and self-identity: Self and society in the late modern age*. Stanford, CA: Stanford University Press.

Giddens, Anthony. 1992. *The transformation of intimacy: Sexuality, love, and eroticism in modern societies*. Stanford, CA: Stanford University Press.

Glanville, Jennifer L., Andersson, Matthew A., and Paxton, Pamela. 2013. Do social connections create trust? An examination using new longitudinal data. *Social Forces* 92: 545–562.

Goffman, Erving. 1963. *Stigma: Notes on the management of spoiled identity*. Englewood Cliffs, NJ: Prentice Hall.

Gomel, Jessica N., Tinsley, Barbara J., Parke, Ross D., and Clark, Kathleen M. 1998. The effects of economic hardship on family relationships among African American, Latino, and Euro-American families. *Journal of Family Issues* 19: 436–467.

Granovetter, Mark. 1973. The strength of weak ties. *American Journal of Sociology* 78: 1360–1380.

Greene, A. L., Wheatley, Susan M., and Aldava, John F., IV. 1992. Stages on life's way: Adolescents' implicit theories of the life course. *Journal of Adolescent Research* 7: 364–381.

Grinstead, Olga, Faigeles, Bonnie, Bancroft, Carrie, and Zack, Barry. 2001. The financial cost of maintaining relationships with incarcerated African American men: A survey of women prison visitors. *Journal of African American Men* 6: 59–69.

Gross, Neil. 2005. The detraditionalization of intimacy reconsidered. *Sociological Theory* 23: 286–311.

Groysberg, Boris, and Abrahams, Robin. 2014. Manage your work, manage your life. *Harvard Business Review*. March. www.hbr.org. Accessed October 4, 2014.

Gubits, Daniel, Lowenstein, Amy, Harris, Jorgen, and Hsueh, JoAnn. 2014. Do the effects of a relationship education program vary for different types of couples? Exploratory subgroup analysis in the Supporting Healthy Marriage evaluation. MDRC. www.mdrc.org.

Gusfield, Joseph R., and Michalowicz, Jerzy. 1984. Secular symbolism: Studies of ritual, ceremony, and the symbolic order of modern life. *Annual Review of Sociology* 10: 417–435.

Guzzo, Karen B. 2009. Maternal relationships and nonresident father visitation of children born outside of marriage. *Journal of Marriage and Family* 71: 632–649.

Halford, W. Kim. 2011. *Marriage and relationship education: What works and how to provide it*. New York: Guilford Press.

Halford, W. Kim, Sanders, Matthew R., and Behrens, Brett C. 2001. Can skills training prevent relationship problems in at-risk couples? Four-year effects of a behavioral relationship education program. *Journal of Family Psychology* 15: 750–768.

Halperin, Samuel. 1998. *The forgotten half revisited: American youth and young families, 1988–2008*. Washington, DC: American Youth Policy Forum.

Halpern-Meekin, Sarah. 2011. High school relationship and marriage education: A comparison of mandated and self-selected treatment. *Journal of Family Issues* 32: 394–419.

Halpern-Meekin, Sarah, Manning, Wendy D., Giordano, Peggy C., and Longmore, Monica A. 2013. Relationship churning in emerging adulthood: On/off relationships and sex with an ex. *Journal of Adolescent Research* 26: 166–188.

Halpern-Meekin, Sarah, and Turney, Kristin. 2016. Relationship churning and parenting stress among mothers and fathers. *Journal of Marriage and Family* 78: 715–729.

Hamilton, Brady E., Martin, Joyce A., and Ventura, Stephanie J. 2009. Births: Preliminary data for 2007. *National Vital Statistics Reports* 57 (12): 1–23.

Hardin, Russell. 1993. The street-level epistemology of trust. *Politics and Society* 21: 505–529.

Hardie, Jessica H., and Lucas, Amy. 2010. Economic factors and relationship quality among young couples: Comparing cohabitation and marriage. *Journal of Marriage and Family* 72: 1141–1154.

Harknett, Kristen. 2006. The relationship between private safety nets and economic outcomes among single mothers. *Journal of Marriage and Family* 68: 172–191.

Harvey, Hope. n.d. When mothers can't pay the cost to be the boss: Doubled-up mothers' desires for residential independence. Unpublished manuscript.

Hartigan, John. 1999 *Racial situations: Class predicaments of whiteness in Detroit*. Princeton, NJ: Princeton University Press.

Hartmann, Douglas, and Swartz, Teresa T. 2006. The new adulthood? The transition to adulthood from the perspective of transitioning young adults. *Advances in Life Course Research* 11: 253–286.

Hawe, Penelope, and Shiell, Alan. 2000. Social capital and health promotion: A review. *Social Science and Medicine* 51: 871–885.

Hawkins, Alan J. 2014. Continuing the important debate on government-supported Healthy Marriages and Relationships Initiatives: A brief response to Johnson's (2014) comment. *Family Relations* 63: 305–308.

Hawkins, Alan J., Amato, Paul R., and Klinghorn, Andrea. 2013. Are government-supported Healthy Marriage Initiatives affecting family demographics? A state-level analysis. *Family Relations* 62: 501–513.

Hawkins, Alan J., Blanchard, Victoria L., Baldwin, Scott A., and Fawcett, Elizabeth B. 2008. Does marriage and relationship education work? A meta-analytic study. *Journal of Consulting and Clinical Psychology* 76: 723–734.

Hawkins, Alan J., and Fackrell, Tamara A. 2010. Does relationship and marriage education for lower-income couples work? A meta-analytic study of emerging research. *Journal of Couple and Relationship Therapy* 9: 181–191.

Hawkins, Alan J., Stanley, Scott M., Blanchard, Victoria L., and Albright, Michael. 2012. Exploring programmatic moderators of the effectiveness of marriage and relationship education programs: A meta-analytic study. *Behavior Therapy* 43: 77–87.

Hawkins, Alan J., Stanley, Scott M., Cowan, Philip A., Fincham, Frank D., Beach, Steven R. H., Cowan, Carolyn P., Rhoades, Galena K., Markman, Howard J., and

Daire, Andrew P. 2013. A more optimistic perspective on government-supported marriage and relationship education programs for lower income couples. *American Psychologist* 68: 110–111.

Hawkley, Louise C., Hughes, Mary E., Waite, Linda J., Masi, Christopher M., Thisted, Ronald A., and Cacioppo, John T. 2008. From social structural factors to perceptions of relationship quality and loneliness: The Chicago Health, Aging, and Social Relations Study. *Journals of Gerontology Series B: Psychological Sciences and Social Sciences* 63: S375–S384.

Hawthorne, Graeme. 2008. Perceived social isolation in a community sample: Its prevalence and correlates with aspects of people's lives. *Social Psychiatry and Psychiatric Epidemiology* 43: 140–150.

Hazan, Cindy, and Shaver, Philip. 1987. Romantic love conceptualized as an attachment process. *Journal of Personality and Social Psychology* 52: 511–524.

Hazan, Cindy, and Zeifman, Debra. 1994. Sex and the psychological tether. In *Advances in personal relationships*. Vol. 5, *Attachment processes in adulthood*, edited by Kim Bartholomew and Daniel Perlman, 151–177. London: Jessica Kingsley.

Heath, Melanie. 2012. *One marriage under God: The campaign to promote marriage in America*. New York: NYU Press.

Heflin, Colleen M., and Iceland, John. 2009. Poverty, material hardship, and depression. *Social Science Quarterly* 90: 1051–1071.

Herzog, Melissa J., and Cooney, Teresa M. 2002. Parental divorce and perceptions of past interparental conflict: Influences on the communication of young adults. *Journal of Divorce and Remarriage* 36: 89–109.

Hill, Heather. 2007. Steppin' out: Infidelity and sexual jealousy among unmarried parents. In *Unmarried couples with children*, edited by Kathryn Edin and Paula England, 104–123. New York: Russell Sage Foundation.

Hogan, Dennis P., and Astone, Nan M. 1986. The transition to adulthood. *Annual Review of Sociology* 12: 109–130.

Hogan, Dennis, Eggebeen, David, and Clogg, Clifford. 1993. The structure of intergenerational exchanges in American families. *American Journal of Sociology* 98: 1428–1458.

Holcomb, Pamela, Edin, Kathryn, Max, Jeffrey, Young, Alford, Jr., D'Angelo, Angela V., Friend, Daniel, Clary, Elizabeth, and Johnson, Waldo E., Jr. 2015. In their own voices: The hopes and struggles of responsible fatherhood program participants in the Parents and Children Together Evaluation. OPRE Report 2015-67. www.acf.hhs.gov.

Holt-Lunstad, Julianne, Smith, Timothy B., Baker, Mark, Harris, Tyler, and Stephenson, David. 2015. Loneliness and social isolation as risk factors for mortality: A meta-analytic review. *Perspectives on Psychological Science* 10: 227–237.

House, James S., Kahn, Robert L., McLeod, Jane D., and Williams, David. 1985. Measures and concepts of social support. In *Social support and health*, edited by S. Cohen and S. L. Syme, 83–108. San Diego: Academic Press.

Howell, Joseph. 1973. *Hard living on Clay Street: Portraits of blue collar families*. Garden City, NY: Anchor.

Huston, Aletha C. 2011. Children in poverty: Can public policy alleviate the consequences? *Family Matters* 87: 13–26.

Huston, Ted L., and Melz, Heidi. 2004. The case for (promoting) marriage: The devil is in the details. *Journal of Marriage and Family* 66: 943–958.

Hutchinson, Judy. 2004. Social capital and community building in the inner city. *Journal of the American Planning Association* 70: 168–175.

Interactive: A portrait of five generations. 2010. Pew Research Center. www.pewsocialtrends.org. Accessed July 14, 2013.

Isen, Adam, and Stevenson, Betsey. 2010. Women's education and fertility behavior: Trends in marriage, divorce, and fertility. NBER Working Paper No. 15725. www.nber.org.

Jackson, Grace L., Trail, Thomas E., Kennedy, David P., Williamson, Hannah C., Bradbury, Thomas N., and Karney, Benjamin R. 2016. The salience and severity of relationship problems among low-income couples. *Journal of Family Psychology* 30: 2–11.

Jacobs, Janet, and Mollborn, Stefanie. 2012. Early motherhood and the disruption in significant attachments: Autonomy and reconnection as a response to separation and loss among African American and Latina mothers. *Gender and Society* 26: 922–944.

Jansen, Tiffany R. 2015. The nursing home that's also a dorm. October 2. www.citylab.com. Accessed August 30, 2017.

Jay, Joelle, and Kovarick, Amy. 2007. *Baby on board: Becoming a mother without losing yourself: A guide for moms-to-be*. New York: AMACOM.

Jeffrey, Karen, Abdallah, Saamah, and Michaelson, Juliet. 2017. The cost of loneliness to UK employers. New Economics Foundation and Co-op. www.campaigntoendloneliness.org.

Johnson, Matthew D. 2012. Healthy marriage initiatives: On the need for empiricism in policy implementation. *American Psychologist* 67: 296–308.

Johnson, Matthew D. 2013. Optimistic or quixotic? More data on marriage and relationship education programs for lower income couples. *American Psychologist* 68: 111–112.

Jordan, Pamela, Stanley, Scott, and Markman, Howard. 1999. *Becoming parents: How to strengthen your marriage as your family grows*. San Francisco: Jossey-Bass.

Kalil, Ariel, and Ryan, Rebecca M. 2010. Mothers' economic conditions and sources of support in fragile families. *Future of Children* 20: 39–61.

Kamp Dush, Claire M., Kotila, Letitia E., and Schoppe-Sullivan, Sarah J. 2011. Predictors of supportive coparenting after relationship dissolution among at-risk parents. *Journal of Family Psychology* 25: 356–365.

Kaplan, Elaine B. 1997. *Not our kind of girl: Unraveling the myths of black teenage motherhood*. Berkeley: University of California Press.

Karney, Benjamin R., and Bradbury, Thomas N. 2005. Contextual influences on marriage: Implications for policy and intervention. *Current Directions in Psychological Science* 14: 171–174.

Karney, Benjamin R., Garvan, Cynthia W., and Thomas, Michael S. 2003. *Family formation in Florida: 2003 baseline survey of attitudes, beliefs, and demographics relating to marriage and family formation.* University of Florida.

Kearney, Melissa S., and Levine, Phillip B. 2007. Socioeconomic disadvantage and early childbearing. In *The problems of disadvantaged youth: An economic perspective,* edited by Jonathan Gruber, 181–209. Chicago: University of Chicago Press.

Kearney, Melissa S., and Wilson, Riley. 2017. Male earnings, marriageable men, and nonmarital fertility: Evidence from the fracking boom. NBER Working Paper No. 23408. www.nber.org. Accessed September 21, 2017.

Kendig, Sarah M., Mattingly, Marybeth J., and Bianchi, Suzanne M. 2014. Childhood poverty and the transition to adulthood. *Family Relations* 63: 271–286.

Kenrick, Douglas T., Griskevicius, Vladas, Neuberg, Steven L., and Schaller, Mark. 2010. Renovating the pyramid of needs: Contemporary extensions built upon ancient foundations. *Perspectives on Psychological Science* 5: 292–314.

Kerpelman, Jennifer L., Pittman, Joe F., Adler-Baeder, Francesca, Eryigit, Suna, and Paulk, Amber. 2009. Evaluation of a statewide youth-focused relationships education curriculum. *Journal of Adolescence* 32: 1359–1370.

Kerpelman, Jennifer L., Pittman, Joe F., Adler-Baeder, Francesca, Stringer, Kate J., Eryigit, Suna, Cadely, Hans S., and Harrell-Levy, Marinda K. 2010. What adolescents bring to and learn from relationship education classes: Does social address matter? *Journal of Couple and Relationship Therapy: Innovations in Clinical and Educational Interventions* 9: 95–112.

Kiecolt-Glaser, Janice K., and Newton, Tamara L. 2001. Marriage and health: His and hers. *Psychological Bulletin* 127: 472–503.

Kieselbach, Thomas. 2003. Long-term unemployment among young people: The risk of social exclusion. *Community Psychology* 32 (1–2): 69–76.

Kim, Hyoun K., Pears, Katherine C., Capaldi, Deborah M., and Owen, Lee D. 2009. Emotion dysregulation in the intergenerational transmission of romantic relationship conflict. *Journal of Family Psychology* 23: 585–595.

Kimball, Michael. 2012. Oklahoma City Council studies transit options for Sundays. July 7. www.newsok.com.

King, Valarie. 2002. Parental divorce and interpersonal trust in adult offspring. *Journal of Marriage and Family* 64: 642–656.

Kissane, Rebecca J., and Clampet-Lundquist, Susan. 2012. Social ties, social support, and collective efficacy among families from public housing in Chicago and Baltimore. *Journal of Sociology and Social Welfare* 39: 157–181.

Klerman, Jacob, Daley, Kelly, and Pozniak, Alyssa. 2012. Family and Medical Leave in 2012: Executive summary. Cambridge, MA: Abt Associates.

Kneebone, Elizabeth. 2009. Job sprawl revisited: The changing geography of metropolitan employment. Metro Economy Series for the Metropolitan Policy Program at Brookings.

Kuo, Janet C., and Raley, R. Kelly. 2016. It is all about the money? Work characteristics and women's and men's marriage formation in early adulthood. *Journal of Family Issues* 37: 1046–1073.

Lakey, Brian, and Orehek, Edward. 2011. Relational regulation theory: A new approach to explain the link between perceived social support and mental health. *Psychological Review* 118: 482–495.

Lasgaard, Mathias, Friis, Karina, and Shevlin, Mark. 2016. "Where are all the lonely people?": A population-based study of high-risk groups across the life span. *Social Psychiatry and Psychiatric Epidemiology* 51: 1373–1384.

Lauer, Sean, and Yodanis, Carrie. 2010. The deinstitutionalization of marriage revisited: A new institutional approach to marriage. *Journal of Family Theory and Review* 2: 58–72.

Laursen, Brett, and Hartl, Amy C. 2013. Understanding loneliness during adolescence: Developmental changes that increase the risk of social isolation. *Journal of Adolescence* 36: 1261–1268.

Lee, Chi-Yuan S., and Goldstein, Sara E. 2016. Loneliness, stress, and social support in young adulthood: Does the source of support matter? *Journal of Youth and Adolescence* 45: 568–580.

Levine, Judith. 2013. *Ain't no trust: How bosses, boyfriends, and bureaucrats fail low-income mothers and why it matters.* Berkeley: University of California Press.

Lewandowski, Joseph D. 2008. On social poverty: Human development and the distribution of social capital. *Journal of Poverty* 12: 27–48.

Lichter, Daniel T., Qian, Zhenchao, and Mellott, Leanna M. 2006. Marriage or dissolution? Union transitions among poor cohabiting women. *Demography* 43: 223–240.

Lichter, Daniel T., Turner, Richard N., and Sassler, Sharon. 2010. National estimates of the rise in serial cohabitation. *Social Science Research* 39: 754–765.

Liebow, Elliott. 1967. *Talley's corner.* Boston: Little, Brown.

Light, Ivan. 2004. Social capital's unique accessibility. *Journal of the American Planning Association* 70: 145–151.

Liker, Jeffrey K., and Elder, Glen H. 1983. Economic hardship and marital relations in the 1930s. *American Sociological Review* 48: 343–359.

Lillbacka, Ralf. 2006. Measuring social capital: Assessing construct stability of various operationalizations of social capital in a Finnish sample. *Acta Sociologica* 49: 201–220.

Lin, Nan. 2001. Building a network theory of social capital. In *Social capital: Theory and research*, edited by Nan Lin, Karen Cook, and Ronald S. Burt, 3–30. New Brunswick, NJ: Transaction.

Linder, Jennifer R., and Collins, W. Andrew. 2005. Parent and peer predictors of physical violence and conflict management in romantic relationships in early adulthood. *Journal of Family Psychology* 19: 252–262.

Liou, Tiffany. 2016. OK marriage initiative among programs cut due to DHS budget shortfall. News 9. www.news9.com. Accessed September 6, 2017.

Lippman, Ellen L., MacMillan, Harriet L., and Boyle, Michael H. 2001. Childhood abuse and psychiatric disorders among single and married mothers. *American Journal of Psychiatry* 158: 73–77.

Livingston, Gretchen, and Parker, Kim. 2011. A tale of two fathers: More are active, but more are absent. Pew Research Center.

Lochner, Kimberly, Kawachi, Ichiro, and Kennedy, Bruce P. 1999. Social capital: A guide to its measurement. *Health and Place* 5: 259–270.

London, Andrew S., Scott, Ellen K., Edin, Kathryn, and Hunter, Vicki. 2004. Welfare reform, work-family tradeoffs, and child well-being. *Family Relations* 53: 148–158.

The long-term decline in prime-age male labor force participation. 2016. Office of the President of the United States.

Lucier-Greer, Mallory, and Adler-Baeder, Francesca. 2012. Does couple and relationship education work for individuals in step-families? A meta-analytic study. *Family Relations* 61: 756–769.

Luecken, Linda J., Lin, Betty, Coburn, Shayna S., MacKinnon, David P. Gonzales, Nancy A., and Crnic, Keith A. 2013. Prenatal stress, partner support, and infant cortisol reactivity in low-income Mexican American families. *Psychoneuroendocrinology* 38: 3092–3101.

Luhmann, Maike, and Hawkley, Louise C. 2016. Age differences in loneliness from late adolescence to oldest old age. *Developmental Psychology* 52: 943–959.

Luhmann, Niklas. 1988. Familiarity, confidence, trust: Problems and alternatives. In *Trust: Making and breaking cooperative relations*, edited by Diego Gambetta, 94–107. Oxford: Blackwell.

Lundberg, Shelly, Pollak, Robert, A., and Stearns, Jenna. 2016. Family inequality: Diverging patterns in marriage, cohabitation, and childbearing. *Journal of Economic Perspectives* 30: 79–102.

Lundquist, Erika, Hsueh, JoAnn, Lowenstein, Amy E., Faucette, Kristen, Gubits, Daniel, Michalopoulos, Charles, and Knox, Virginia. 2014. A family-strengthening program for low-income families: Final impacts from the Supporting Healthy Marriage evaluation. MDRC. www.mdrc.org.

Luo, Ye, Hawkley, Louise C., Waite, Linda J., and Cacioppo, John T. 2012. Loneliness, health, and mortality in old age: A national longitudinal study. *Social Science and Medicine* 74: 907–914.

Ma, Yanling, Pittman, Joe F., Kerpelman, Jennifer L., and Adler-Baeder, Francesca. 2014. Relationship education and classroom climate impact on adolescents' standards for partners/relationships. *Family Relations* 63: 453–468.

Maestas, Nicole, Mullen, Kathleen J., Powell, David, von Wachter, Till, and Wenger, Jeffrey B. 2017. Working conditions in the United States: Results of the 2015 American Working Conditions Survey. Santa Monica, CA: RAND Corporation. www.rand. org. Accessed September 20, 2017.

Malanchuk, Oksana, Messersmith, Emily E., and Eccles, Jacquelynne S. 2010. The ontogeny of career identities in adolescence. *New Directions for Child and Adolescent Development* 130: 97–110.

Malveaux, Julianne. 2002. More jobs, not more marriages, lift poor. *USA Today*, February 22.

Manlove, Jennifer, Ryan, Suzanne, Wildsmith, Elizabeth, and Franzetta, Kerry. 2010. The relationship context of nonmarital childbearing in the US. *Demographic Research* 23: 615–653.

Manning, Wendy D. 2004. Children and the stability of cohabiting couples. *Journal of Marriage and Family* 66: 674–689.

Manning, Wendy D., and Smock, Pamela J. 2005. Measuring and modeling cohabitation: New perspectives from qualitative data. *Journal of Marriage and Family,* 67: 989–1002.

Manning, Wendy D., Smock, Pamela J., and Majumdar, Debarun. 2004. The relative stability of cohabiting and marital unions for children. *Population Research and Policy Review* 23: 135–159.

Manning, Wendy D., and Sykes, Bart. 2015. Twenty-five years of change in cohabitation in the U.S., 1987–2013. Research Family Profile FP-15-01. National Center for Marriage and Family Research, Bowling Green State University.

Manning, Wendy D., Trella, Deanna, Lyons, Heidi, and Du Toit, Nola C. 2010. Marriageable women: A focus on participants in a community healthy marriage program. *Family Relations* 59: 87–102.

Marcus, Andrea F., Echeverria, Sandra E., Holland, Bart K., Abraido-Lanza, Ana F., and Passannante, Marian R. 2016. The joint contribution of neighborhood poverty and social integration to mortality risk in the United States. *Annals of Epidemiology* 26: 261–266.

Markiewicz, Dorothy, Lawford, Heather, Doyle, Anna Beth, and Haggart, Natalie. 2006. Developmental differences in adolescents' and young adults' use of mothers, fathers, best friends, and romantic partners to fulfill attachment needs. *Journal of Youth and Adolescence* 35: 127–140.

Markman, Howard J., Renick, Mari Jo, Floyd, Frank J., Stanley, Scott M., and Clements, Mari. 1993. Preventing marital distress through communication and conflict management training: A 4- and 5-year follow-up. *Journal of Consulting and Clinical Psychology* 61: 70–77.

Marsiglio, William. 2004. *Stepdads: Stories of Love, Hope, and Repair.* Lanham, MD: Rowman and Littlefield.

Marsiglio, William, and Hutchinson, Sally. 2002. *Sex, men, and babies: Stories of awareness and responsibility.* New York: NYU Press.

Marsiglio, William, and Roy, Kevin. 2012. *Nurturing dads: Fatherhood initiatives beyond the wallet.* New York: Russell Sage Foundation.

Masarik, April S., Martin, Monica J., Ferrer, Emilio, Lorenz, Frederick O., Conger, Katherine J., and Conger, Rand D. 2016. Couple resilience to economic pressure over time and across generations. *Journal of Marriage and Family* 78: 326–345.

Maslow, Abraham H. 1943. A theory of human motivation. *Psychological Review* 50: 370–396.

Maslow, Abraham H. 1970. *Motivation and personality.* 3rd ed. New York: Longman.

Mathews, T. J., and Hamilton, Brady E. 2016. Mean age of mothers is on the rise: United States, 2000–2014. NCHS Data Brief No. 232. Centers for Disease Control and Prevention. www.cdc.gov.

Mazelis, Joan M. 2017. *Surviving poverty: Creating sustainable ties among the poor.* New York: NYU Press.

McDonald, Katrina B., and Armstrong, Elizabeth M. 2001. De-romanticizing black intergenerational support: The questionable expectations of welfare reform. *Journal of Marriage and Family* 63: 213–223.

McGuire, Gail M. 2007. Intimate work: A typology of the social support that workers provide to their network members. *Work and Occupations* 34: 125–147.

McLanahan, Sara, and Beck, Audrey N. 2010. Parental relationships in fragile families. *Future of Children* 20: 17–37.

Meier, Ann, and Allen, Gina. 2008. Intimate relationship development during the transition to adulthood: Differences by social class. *New Directions for Child and Adolescent Development* 119: 25–39.

Merton, Robert K. 1968. *Social theory and social structure*. New York: Simon and Schuster.

Meyer, Daniel R., and Cancian, Maria. 2012. "I'm not supporting his kids": Nonresident fathers' contributions given mothers' new fertility. *Journal of Marriage and Family* 74: 132–151.

Mikulincer, Mario. 1998. Attachment working models and the sense of trust: An exploration of interaction goals and affect regulation. *Journal of Personality and Social Psychology* 74: 1209–1224.

Miller-Cribbs, Julie, and Farber, Naomi. 2008. Kin networks and poverty among African Americans: Past and present. *Social Work* 53: 43–51.

Mishel, Lawrence, Bivens, Josh, Gould, Elise, and Shierholz, Heidi. 2012. *The state of working America*. 12th ed. Ithaca, NY: ILR Press.

Misra, Sophie, and Brucker, Debra L. 2017. Income poverty and multiple deprivations in a high-income country: The case of the United States. *Social Science Quarterly* 98: 37–56.

Moore, Quinn, Wood, Robert G., Clarkwest, Andrew, Killewald, Alexandra, and Monahan, Shannon. 2012. The Building Strong Families project: The long-term effects of Building Strong Families: A relationship skills education program for unmarried parents, technical supplement. Mathematica Policy Research. www.acf.hhs.gov.

Morin, Rich, and Kochhar, Rakesh. 2010. Lost income, lost friends—and loss of self-respect. Pew Research Center. www.assets.pewresearch.org.

Mosher, William D., Jones, Jo, and Abma, Joyce C. 2012. Intended and unintended births in the United States: 1982–2010. National Health Statistics Reports, No. 55. www.cdc.gov.

Murthy, Vivek. n.d. www.surgeongeneral.gov. Accessed July 15, 2016.

Neff, Lisa A., and Broady, Elizabeth F. 2011. Stress resilience in early marriage: Can practice make perfect? *Journal of Personality and Social Psychology* 101: 1050–1067.

Nepomnyaschy, Lenna, and Teitler, Julien. 2013. Cyclical cohabitation among unmarried parents in fragile families. *Journal of Marriage and Family* 75: 1248–1265.

Newman, Katherine. 1999. *No shame in my game: The working poor in the inner city*. New York: Russell Sage Foundation.

Newman, Katherine, and Aptekar, Sofya. 2007. Sticking around: Delayed departure from the parental nest in Western Europe. In *The price of independence: The economics of early adulthood*, edited by Sheldon Danziger and Cecilia E. Rouse, 207–230. New York: Russell Sage Foundation.

Newman, Matthew L., and Roberts, Nicole A. 2013. *Health and social relationships: The good, the bad, and the complicated.* Washington, DC: American Psychological Association.

Nock, Steven L. 1995. A comparison of marriages and cohabiting relationships. *Journal of Family Issues* 16: 53–76.

Nomaguchi, Kei M., Giordano, Peggy C., Manning, Wendy D., and Longmore, Monica M. 2017. Adolescents' gender mistrust: Variations and implications for the quality of romantic relationships. *Journal of Marriage and Family* 73: 1032–1047.

Nurmi, Jari-Erik. 2004. Socialization and self-development. *Handbook of Adolescent Psychology* 2: 85–124.

Nylen, Kimberly J., O'Hara, Michael W., and Engeldinger, Jane. 2013. Perceived social support interacts with prenatal depression to predict birth outcomes. *Journal of Behavioral Medicine* 36: 427–440.

OECD. 2011. *How's life? Measuring well-being.* Paris: OECD.

Oklahoma Marriage Initiative. n.d. www.publicstrategies.com. Accessed December 7, 2017.

Oliker, Stacey J. 1989. *Best friends and marriage: Exchange among women.* Berkeley: University of California Press.

Osborne, Cynthia, Manning, Wendy, and Smock, Pamela. 2007. Married and cohabiting parents' relationship stability: A focus on race and ethnicity. *Journal of Marriage and Family* 69: 1345–1366.

Owen, Jesse, Manthos, Megan, and Quirk, Kelley. 2013. Dismantling study of Prevention and Relationship Education Program: The effects of a structured communication intervention. *Journal of Family Psychology* 27: 336–341.

Parker, Kim. 2012. The boomerang generation: Feeling OK about living with Mom and Dad. Pew Social and Demographic Trends. www.pewsocialtrends.org.

Parker, Kim, and Stepler, Renee. 2017. Americans see men as the financial providers, even as women's contributions grow. Pew Research Center. www.pewresearch.org. Accessed October 16, 2017.

Perissinotto, Carla M., Cenzer, Irena S., and Covinsky, Kenneth E. 2012. Loneliness in older persons: A predictor of functional decline and death. *Archives of Internal Medicine* 172: 1078–1084.

Perkins, Kristin L., and Sampson, Robert J. 2015. Compounded deprivation in the transition to adulthood: The intersection of racial and economic inequality among Chicagoans, 1995–2013. *RSF: The Russell Sage Foundation Journal of the Social Sciences* 1: 35–54.

Pilkauskas, Natasha V., Campbell, Colin, and Wimer, Christopher. 2017. Giving unto others: Private financial transfers and hardship among families with children. *Journal of Marriage and Family* 79: 705–722.

Portes, Alejandro, and Sensenbrenner, Julia. 1993. Embeddedness and immigration: Notes on the social determinants of economic action. *American Journal of Sociology* 98: 1320–1350.

Putnam, Robert, Light, Ivan, Briggs, Xavier de Souza, Rohe, William M., Vidal, Avis C., Hutchinson, Judy, Gress, Jennifer, and Woolcock, Michael. 2004. Using social capital to help integrate planning theory, research, and practice. *Journal of the American Planning Association* 70: 142–192.

PREP, Inc. n.d. About PREP, Inc. www.prepinc.com. Accessed September 6, 2017.

Qualter, Pamela, Brown, Stephen L., Rotenberg, Ken J., Vanhalst, Janne, Harris, Rebecca A., Goossens, Luc, Bangee, M., and Munn, P. 2013. Trajectories of loneliness during childhood and adolescence: Predictors and health outcomes. *Journal of Adolescence* 36: 1283–1293.

Qualter, Pamela, Vanhalst, Janne, Harris, Rebecca, Van Roekel, Eeske, Lodder, Gerine, Bangee, Munirah, Maes, Marlies, and Verhagen, Maaike. 2015. Loneliness across the lifespan. *Perspectives on Psychological Science* 10: 250–264.

Quillian, Lincoln, and Redd, Rozlyn. 2010. Can social capital explain persistent racial poverty gaps? In *The colors of poverty: Why racial and ethnic disparities persist*, edited by Ann Chih Lin and David R. Harris, 170–197. New York: Russell Sage Foundation.

Quirk, Kelley, Owen, Jesse, Inch, Leslie J., France, Tiffany, and Bergen, Carrie. 2013. The alliance in relationship education programs. *Journal of Marital and Family Therapy* 40: 178–192.

Rainwater, Lee. 1970. *Behind ghetto walls: Black family life in a federal slum*. Chicago: Aldine.

Raley, R. Kelly, and Bumpass, Larry. 2003. The topography of the divorce plateau: Levels and trends in union instability in the United States after 1980. *Demographic Research* 8: 245–260.

Randles, Jennifer. 2017. *Proposing prosperity? Marriage education policy and inequality in America*. New York: Columbia University Press.

Randles, Jennifer, and Woodward, Kerry. 2018. Learning to labor, love, and live: Shaping the good neoliberal citizen in state work and marriage programs. *Sociological Perspectives* 61: 31–56.

Reeves, Richard, Rodrigue, Edward, and Kneebone, Elizabeth. 2016. Five evils: Multidimensional poverty and race in America. Metropolitan Policy Program and Center on Children and Families. Brookings Institution. www.brookings.edu. Accessed May 31, 2016.

Repetti, Rena L., Taylor, Shelley E., and Seeman, Teresa E. 2002. Risky families: Family social environments and the mental and physical health of offspring. *Psychological Bulletin* 128: 330–366.

Rhoades, Galena K., Stanley, Scott M., Markman, Howard J., and Ragan, Erica P. 2012. Parents' marital status, conflict, and role modeling: Links with adult romantic relationship quality. *Journal of Divorce and Remarriage* 53: 348–367.

Rienks, Shauna L., Wadsworth, Martha E., Markman, Howard J., Einhorn, Lindsey, and Etter, Erica M. 2011. Father involvement in urban low-income fathers: Baseline associations and changes resulting from preventive interventions. *Family Relations* 60: 191–204.

Riffkin, R. 2014. New record highs in moral acceptability. Gallup. www.gallup.com. Accessed June 11, 2015.

Rogge, Ronald D., Cobb, Rebecca J., Lawrence, Erika, Johnson, Matthew D., and Bradbury, Thomas N. 2013. Is skills training necessary for the primary prevention of marital distress and dissolution? A 3-year experimental study of three interventions. *Journal of Consulting and Clinical Psychology* 81: 949–961.

Rohe, William M. 2004. Building social capital through community development. *Journal of the American Planning Association* 70: 158–164.

Rosen, Rebecca J. 2016. Marriage will not fix poverty. *Atlantic, March.* www.theatlantic.com. Accessed August 8, 2016.

Rosenthal, Natalie L., and Kobak, Roger. 2010. Assessing adolescents' attachment hierarchies: Differences across developmental periods and associations with individual adaptation. *Journal of Research on Adolescence* 20: 678–706.

Ross, Catherine E., Mirowsky, John, and Pribesh, Shana. 2001. Powerlessness and the amplification of threat: Neighborhood disadvantage, disorder, and mistrust. *American Sociological Review* 66: 568–591.

Rotenberg, Ken J. 1994. Loneliness and interpersonal trust. *Journal of Social and Clinical Psychology* 13: 152–173.

Rotenberg, Ken J. 1995. The socialisation of trust: Parents' and children's interpersonal trust. *International Journal of Behavioral Development* 18: 713–726.

Rotenberg, Ken J., Addis, Nick, Betts, Lucy R., Corrigan, Amanda, Fox, Claire, Hobson, Zoe, Rennison, Sarah, Trueman, Mark, and Boulton, Michael J. 2010. The relation between trust beliefs and loneliness during early childhood, middle childhood, and adulthood. *Personality and Social Psychology Bulletin* 36: 1086–1100.

Roy, Kevin M., Buckmiller, Nicolle, and McDowell, April. 2008. Together but not "together": Trajectories of relationship suspension for low-income unmarried parents. *Family Relations* 57: 198–210.

Sampson, Robert J., Raudenbusch, Stephen W., and Earls, Felton. 1997. Neighborhoods and violent crime: A multilevel study of collective efficacy. *Science* 277 (5328): 918–924.

Samuel, Kim, Alkire, Sabina, Zavaleta, Diego, Mills, China, and Hammock, John. 2017. Social isolation and its relationship to multidimensional poverty. *Oxford Development Studies* 46: 83–97.

Sarason, Barbara R., Sarason, Irwin G., and Pierce, Gregory R. 1990. *Social support: An interactional view*. Oxford: John Wiley.

Sarkisian, Natalia, and Gerstel, Naomi. 2004. Kin support among blacks and whites: Race and family organization. *American Sociological Review* 69: 812–837.

Sassler, Sharon. 2004. The process of entering a cohabiting unions. *Journal of Marriage and Family* 66: 491–505.

Savikko, Niina, Routasalo, Pirkko, Tilvis, Reijo S., Strandberg, Timo E., and Pitkälä, Kaisu H. 2005. Predictors and subjective causes of loneliness in an aged population. *Archives of Gerontology and Geriatrics* 41: 223–233.

Schinka, Katherine C, van Dulmen, Manfred H. M., Mata, Andrea D., Bossarte, Robert, and Swahn, Monica. 2013. Psychosocial predictors and outcomes of loneliness trajectories from childhood to early adolescence. *Journal of Adolescence* 36: 1251–1260.

Schneider, Daniel. 2011. Wealth and the marital divide. *American Journal of Sociology* 117: 627–667.

Schneider, Daniel. 2015. Lessons learned from non-marriage experiments. *Future of Children* 25: 155–178.

Schokker, Marike C., Stuive, Ilse, Bouma, Jelte, Keers, Joost C., Links, Thera P., Wolffenbuttel, Bruce H. R., Sanderman, Robbert, and Hagedoorn, Mariët. 2010. Support behavior and relationship satisfaction in couples dealing with diabetes: Main and moderating effects. *Journal of Family Psychology* 24: 578–586.

Schwartz, Seth J., Côté, James E., and Arnett, Jeffrey J. 2005. Identity and agency in emerging adulthood: Two developmental routes in the individualization process. *Youth and Society* 37: 201–229.

Scott, Ellen K., Edin, Kathryn, London, Andrew S., and Kissane, Rebecca Joyce. 2004. Unstable work, unstable income: Implications for family well-being in the era of time-limited welfare. *Journal of Poverty* 8: 61–88.

Scott, Shelby B., and Rhoades, Galena K. 2014. Relationship education for lesbian couples: Perceived barriers and content considerations. *Journal of Couple and Relationship Therapy* 4: 339–364.

Seefeldt, Kristin. 2016. *Abandoned families: Social isolation in the twenty-first century.* New York: Russell Sage Foundation.

Segrin, Chris. 2003. Age moderates the relationship between social support and psychosocial problems. *Human Communication Research* 29: 317–342.

Settersten, Richard A., Jr., and Cancel-Tirado, Doris. 2010. Fatherhood as a hidden variable in men's development and life courses. *Research in Human Development* 7: 83–102.

Settersten, Richard A., Jr., Day, Jack K., Cancel-Tirado, Doris, and Driscoll, Debra M. 2014. Fathers' accounts of struggle and growth in early adulthood: An exploratory study of disadvantaged men. *New Directions in Child and Adolescent Development* 143: 73–89.

Settersten, Richard A., Jr., Furstenberg, Frank F., and Rumbaut, Ruben G., eds. 2005. *On the frontier of adulthood: Theory, research, and public policy.* Chicago: University of Chicago Press.

Shanahan, Michael J. 2000. Pathways to adulthood in changing societies: Variability and mechanisms in life course perspective. *Annual Review of Sociology* 26: 667–692.

Sharkey, Patrick, and Elwert, Felix. 2011. The legacy of disadvantage: Multigenerational neighborhood effects on cognitive ability. *American Journal of Sociology* 116: 1934–1981.

Sharkey, Patrick, and Faber, Jacob W. 2014. Where, when, why, and for whom do residential contexts matter? Moving away from the dichotomous understanding of neighborhood effects. *Annual Review of Sociology* 40: 559–579.

Shaver, Philip, Furman, Wyndol, and Buhrmester, Duane. 1985. Transition to college: Network changes, social skills, and loneliness. In *Understanding personal relation-*

ships: An interdisciplinary approach, edited by S. Duck and D. Perlman, 193–219. Thousand Oaks, CA: Sage.

Sias, Patricia M., and Cahill, Daniel J. 1998. From coworkers to friends: The development of peer friendships in the workplace. *Western Journal of Communication* 62: 273–299.

Silva, Jennifer M. 2012. Constructing adulthood in an age of uncertainty. *American Sociological Review* 77: 505–522.

Silva, Jennifer M. 2013. *Coming up short: Working-class adulthood in an age of uncertainty*. New York: Oxford University Press.

Silva, Jennifer M., and Pugh, Allison J. 2010. Beyond the depleting model of parenting: Narratives of childrearing and change. *Sociological Inquiry* 80: 605–627.

Simmel, Georg. 1950. *The Sociology of Georg Simmel*. Translated and edited by Kurt H. Wolff. New York: Free Press.

Small, Mario L. 2006. Neighborhood institutions as resource brokers: Childcare centers, interorganizational ties, and resource access among the poor. *Social Problems* 53: 274–292.

Small, Mario L. 2009. *Unanticipated gains: Origins of network inequality in everyday life*. New York: Oxford University Press.

Small, Mario L. 2013. The ties that bind: How childcare centers build social capital. *Huffington Post*, November 7.

Smith, Christian. 2011. *Lost in transition: The dark side of emerging adulthood*. New York: Oxford University Press.

Smith, Sandra Susan. 2005. "Don't put my name on it": Social capital activation and job-finding assistance among the black urban poor. *American Journal of Sociology* 111: 1–57.

Smith, Sandra Susan. 2007. *Lone pursuit: Distrust and defensive individualism among the black poor*. New York: Russell Sage Foundation.

Smith, Tom W. 1997. Factors relating to misanthropy in contemporary American society. *Social Science Research* 26: 170–196.

Smock, Pamela J., Manning, Wendy D., and Porter, Meredith. 2005. "Everything's there except money": How money shapes decisions to marry among cohabitors. *Journal of Marriage and Family* 67: 680–696.

Span, Paula. 2017. Caregiving is hard enough. Isolation can make it unbearable. *New York Times*, August 4. www.nytimes.com. Accessed August 31, 2017.

Sparks, Anne. 2008. Implementation of "Within My Reach": Providing a relationship awareness and communications skills program to TANF recipients in Oklahoma. Working paper of the National Poverty Center. Ann Arbor, Michigan. www.npc.umich.edu.

Sparks, Anne, Lee, Mingun, and Spjeldnes, Solveig. 2012. Evaluation of the high school relationship curriculum *Connections: Dating and Emotions. Child and Adolescent Social Work Journal* 29: 21–40.

Stack, Carol. 1974. *All our kin: Strategies for survival in a black community*. New York: Harper and Row.

Stanley, Scott M. 2003. Comments on Cherlin, Burton, Hurt, and Purvin; Edin, England, and Linnenberg; and Ahituv and Lerman. Paper presented at the annual research conference of the National Poverty Center, Washington, DC, September 4–5.

Stanley, Scott M., Allen, Elizabeth S., Markman, Howard J., Rhoades, Galena K., and Prentice, Donnella L. 2010. Decreasing divorce in U.S. Army couples: Results from a randomized controlled trial using PREP for Strong Bonds. *Journal of Couple and Relationship Therapy* 9: 149–160.

Stanley, Scott M., Bradbury, Thomas N., and Markman, Howard J. 2000. Structural flaws in the bridge from basic research on marriage to interventions for couples. *Journal of Marriage and Family* 62: 256–264.

Stanley, Scott M., Rhoades, Galena K., Loew, Benjamin A., Allen, Elizabeth S., Carter, Sarah, Osborne, Laura J., Prentice, Donnella, and Markman, Howard J. 2014. A randomized controlled trial of relationship education in the U.S. Army: 2-year outcomes. *Family Relations* 63: 482–495.

Stanley, Scott M., Rhoades, Galena K., and Markman, Howard J. 2006. Sliding versus deciding: Inertia and the premarital cohabitation effect. *Family Relations* 55: 499–509.

Stanley, Scott M., Rhoades, Galena K., and Whitton, Sarah W. 2010. Commitment: Functions, formation, and the securing of romantic attachment. *Journal of Family Theory and Review* 2: 243–257.

Stapleton, Lynlee R. T., Schetter, Christine D., Westling, Erika, Rini, Christine, Glynn, Laura M., Hobel, Calvin J., and Sandman, Curt A. 2012. Perceived partner support in pregnancy predicts lower maternal and infant distress. *Journal of Family Psychology* 26: 453–463.

Starr, Alexandra. 2001. Shotgun wedding by Uncle Sam? *Business Week*, June 4.

Steptoe, Andrew, Owen, Natalie, Kunz-Ebrecht, Sabine, and Brydon, Lena. 2004. Loneliness and neuroendocrine, cardiovascular, and inflammatory stress responses in middle-aged men and women. *Psychoneuroendocrinology* 29: 593–611.

Stets, Jan E., and Burke, Peter J. 2005a. Identity verification, control, and aggression in marriage. *Social Psychology Quarterly* 68: 160–178.

Stets, Jan E., and Burke, Peter J. 2005b. New directions in identity control theory. In *Social identification in groups*, edited by Shane R. Thye and Edward J. Lawler, 43–64. Bingley: Emerald Group Publishing.

Stets, Jan E., and Cast, Alicia D. 2007. Resources and identity verification from an identity theory perspective. *Sociological Perspectives* 50: 517–543.

Stiglitz, Joseph E., Sen, Amartya, and Fitoussi, Jean-Paul. 2009. Report by the Commission on the Measurement of Economic Performance and Social Progress. Paris: Commission on the Measurement of Economic Performance and Social Progress.

Stock, Pamela. n.d. Marriage after baby: Problems and solutions. www.parents.com. Accessed October 4, 2014.

Stocker, Clare M., and Richmond, Melissa K. 2007. Longitudinal associations between hostility in adolescents' family relationships and friendships and hostility in their romantic relationships. *Journal of Family Psychology* 21: 490–497.

Stone, Wendy. 2001. Measuring social capital: Towards a theoretically informed measurement framework for researching social capital in family and community life. Research paper 24. Australian Institute for Family Studies.

Styron, Thomas, and Janoff-Bulman, Ronnie. 1997. Childhood attachment and abuse: Long-term effects on adult attachment, depression, and conflict management. *Child Abuse and Neglect* 21: 1015–1023.

Sum, Andrew, Khatiwada, Ishwar, McLaughlin, Joseph, and Palma, Sheila 2011. No country for young men: Deteriorating labor market prospects for low-skilled men in the United States. *Annals of the American Academy of Political and Social Science* 635: 24–55.

Tach, Laura. 2012. Family complexity, childbearing, and parenting stress: A comparison of mothers' and fathers' experiences. National Center for Family and Marriage Research, Working Paper Series WP-12-09.

Tach, Laura, Mincy, Ronald, and Edin, Kathryn. 2010. Parenting as a "package deal": Relationships, fertility, and nonresident father involvement among unmarried parents. *Demography* 47: 181–204.

Teen attitudes about marriage and family. 2010. www.stateofourunions.org.

Thoits, Peggy A. 2011. Mechanisms linking social ties and support to physical and mental health. *Journal of Health and Social Behavior* 52: 145–161.

Thurston, Rebecca C., and Kubzansky, Laura D. 2009. Women, loneliness, and incident coronary heart disease. *Psychosomatic Medicine* 71: 836–842.

Tigges, Leann M., Browne, Irene, and Green, Gary P. 1998. Social isolation of the urban poor: Race, class, and neighborhood effects on social resources. *Sociological Quarterly* 39: 53–77.

Toguchi Swartz, Teresa, Hartmann, Douglas, and Mortimer, Jeylan T. 2011. Transitions to adulthood in the land of Lake Wobegon. In *Coming of age in America: The transition to adulthood in the twenty-first century*, edited by Mary C. Waters, Patrick J. Carr, Maria J. Kefalas, and Jennifer Holdaway, 59–105. Berkeley: University of California Press.

Tomer, Adie, Elizabeth Kneebone, Robert Puentes, and Alan Berube. 2011. Missed opportunity: Transit and jobs in metropolitan America. Metropolitan Infrastructure Initiative Series and Metropolitan Opportunity Series. Metropolitan Policy Program at Brookings.

Townsend, Nicholas. 2002. *Package deal: Marriage, work and fatherhood in men's lives.* Philadelphia: Temple University Press.

Townsend, Nicholas. 2005. Fatherhood and the mediating role of women. In *Gender in cross-cultural perspective*, edited by Caroline Brettell and Carolyn Sargent, 105–119. Upper Saddle River, NJ: Pearson Prentice Hall.

Toxic stress. n.d. Center on the Developing Child. Harvard University. www.developingchild.harvard.edu. Accessed August 30, 2017.

Trail, Thomas E., and Karney, Benjamin R. 2012. What's (not) wrong with low-income marriages. *Journal of Marriage and Family* 74: 413–427.

Trobst, Krista K. 2000. An interpersonal conceptualization and quantification of social support transactions. *Personality and Social Psychology Bulletin* 26: 971–986.

Twenge, Jean M., Baumeister, Roy F., Tice, Dianne M., and Stucke, Tanja S. 2001. If you can't join them, beat them: Effects of social exclusion on aggressive behavior. *Journal of Personality and Social Psychology* 81: 1058–1069.

Uchino, Bert N. 2004. *Social support and physical health: Understanding the health consequences of relationships.* New Haven, CT: Yale University Press.

Uchino, Bert N., Cacioppo, John T., and Kiecolt-Glaser, Janice K. 1996. The relationship between social support and physiological processes: A review with emphasis on underlying mechanisms and implications for health. *Psychological Bulletin* 119: 488–531.

Uecker, Jeremy E., and Stokes, Charles E. 2008. Early marriage in the United States. *Journal of Marriage and Family* 70: 835–846.

Upchurch, Dawn M., Lillard, Lee A., and Panis, Constantijn W. 2002. Nonmarital childbearing: Influences of education, marriage, and fertility. *Demography* 39: 311–329.

Uslaner, Eric M. 2002. *The moral foundations of trust.* Cambridge: Cambridge University Press.

van der Kolk, Bessel A., and Fisler, Rita E. 1994. Childhood abuse and neglect and loss of self-regulation. *Bulletin of the Menninger Clinic* 58: 145–168.

van der Kolk, Bessel A., Perry, J. Christopher, and Herman, Judith L. 1991. Childhood origins of self-destructive behavior. *American Journal of Psychiatry* 148: 1665–1671.

Veenstra, Gerry. 2002. Social capital and health. *Social Science and Medicine* 54: 849–868.

Vinokur, Amiram D., Price, Richard H., and Caplan, Robert D. 1996. Hard times and hurtful partners: How financial strain affects depression and relationship satisfaction of unemployed persons and their spouses. *Journal of Personality and Social Psychology* 71: 166–179.

Wadsworth, Martha E. 2012. Working with low-income families: Lessons learned from basic and applied research on coping with poverty-related stress. *Journal of Contemporary Psychotherapy* 42: 17–25.

Wadsworth, Martha E., and Markman, Howard J. 2012. Where's the action? Understanding what works and why in relationship education. *Behavior Therapy* 43: 99–112.

Wagle, Udaya R. 2008a. Multidimensional poverty: An alternative measurement approach for the United States. *Social Science Research* 37: 559–580.

Wagle, Udaya R. 2008b. *Multidimensional poverty measurement: Concepts and applications.* New York: Springer.

Wagle, Udaya R. 2014. The counting-based measurement of multidimensional poverty: The focus on economic resources, inner capabilities, and relational resources in the United States. *Social Indicators Research* 115: 223–240.

Wagmiller, Robert L. 2010. How representative are the Fragile Families Study families? A comparison of the Early Childhood Longitudinal Study-Birth Cohort and Fragile Families samples. Fragile Families Working Paper 2010-01-FF. www.crcw.princeton. edu. Accessed July 14, 2013.

Waller, Maureen R. 2001. High hopes: Unwed parents' expectations about marriage. *Children and Youth Services Review* 23: 457–484.

Waller, Maureen R., and McLanahan, Sara S. 2005. "His" and "her" marriage expectations: Determinants and consequences. *Journal of Marriage and Family* 67: 53–67.

Walsh, Tova, Tolman, Richard M., Davis, R. Neal, Palladino, Christie L., Romero, Vivian C., and Singh, Vijay. 2014. Moving up the "magic moment": Fathers' experience of prenatal ultrasound. *Fathering* 12: 18–37.

Wang, Wendy, and Parker, Paul. 2011. For millennials, parenthood trumps marriage. Pew Research Center. www.pewsocialtrends.org.

Waters, Mary C., Carr, Patrick J., Kefalas, Maria J., and Holdaway, Jennifer A., eds. 2011. *Coming of age in America: The transition to adulthood in the twenty-first century.* Berkeley: University of California Press.

Watkins-Hayes, Celeste. 2009. *The new welfare bureaucrats: Entanglements of race, class, and policy reform.* Chicago: University of Chicago Press.

Weber, Linda R., and Carter, Allison I. 2003. *The social construction of trust.* New York: Kluwer Academic/Plenum.

Weiss, Robert S. 1974. The provisions of social relations. In *Doing unto others,* edited by Z. Rubin, 17–26. Englewood Cliffs, NJ: Prentice Hall.

Weissman, Marsha, and LaRue, Candace M. 1998. Earning trust from youths with none to spare. *Child Welfare* 77: 579–594.

Welch, Michael R., Sikkink, David, and Loveland, Matthew T. 2007. The radius of trust: Religion, social embeddedness and trust in strangers. *Social Forces* 86: 23–46.

Whitton, Sarah W., and Buzzella, Brian A. 2012. Using relationship education programs with same-sex couples: A preliminary evaluation of program utility and needed modifications. *Marriage and Family Review* 48: 667–688.

Williamson, Hannah C., Karney, Benjamin R., and Bradbury, Thomas N. 2013. Financial strain and stressful events predict newlyweds' negative communication independent of relationship satisfaction. *Journal of Family Psychology* 27: 65–75.

Willoughby, Brian J., and James, Spencer L. 2017. *The marriage paradox: Why emerging adults love marriage yet push it aside.* New York: Oxford University Press.

Wingerter, Meg. 2017. Oklahoma cuts case management for people with mental illnesses. *The Oklahoman,* August 25. www.newsok.com. Accessed September 6, 2017.

Wood, Robert G., McConnell, Sheena, Moore, Quinn, Clarkwest, Andrew, and Hsueh, JoAnn. 2010. *Strengthening unmarried parents' relationships: The early impacts of Building Strong Families.* Princeton, NJ: Mathematica Policy Research. www.mathematica-mpr.com.

Wood, Robert G., Moore, Quinn, Clarkwest, Andrew, Killewald, Alexandra, and Monahan, Shannon. 2012. The long-term effects of Building Strong Families: A relationship skills education program for unmarried parents. OPRE Report 2012-28B. www.acf.hhs.gov.

Woolcock, Michael. 2004. Why and how planners should take social capital seriously. *Journal of the American Planning Association* 70: 183–189.

Work family balance. n.d. www.huffingtonpost.com. Accessed October 4, 2014.

www.census.gov. n.d. Quick facts: Oklahoma City, Oklahoma. Accessed June 28, 2016.

Yamagishi, Toshio. 2001. Trust as a form of social intelligence. In *Russell Sage Foundation series on trust. Vol. 2, Trust in society*, edited by K. S. Cook, 121–147. New York: Russell Sage Foundation.

Zavaleta, Diego, Samuel, Kim, and Mills, China T. 2017. Measures of social isolation. *Social Indicators Research* 131: 367–391.

Zucker, Lynne G. 1986. Production of trust: Institutional sources of economic structure, 1840–1920. *Research in Organizational Behavior* 8: 53–111.

INDEX

Anu Family Services, 221

Arnett, Jeffrey, 30, 47

Becoming Parents Program (BPP), 11, 197, 228–29

Beveridge, William, 23

Boo, Katherine, 2–3, 4, 5–6

"Boomerang Generation," 61

Bringing Baby Home, 197

Building Strong Families (BSF), 3–4, 11, 157, 195, 197–99; comparison to current study, 11n28, 142–43, 195, 198; Family Expectations as program site, 11, 142–43 197–99; findings from, 157, 195, 197–99

Burr, Wesley, 120

Bush, George W. *See* George W. Bush Administration

Bush, Jeb, 227

Cacioppo, John, 25

careers: goals of participants, 51, 58–60; occupational identity and, 31, 60. *See also* employment

cars, 64–69, 70, 71, 154, 205; symbolic importance of, 65–66, 69. *See also* transportation

Cherlin, Andrew, 33, 94, 219

child care, 54, 74, 84, 112, 217, 228; as provided by Family Expectations, 12, 129, 132, 184, 200; relationship to social resources, 20, 209, 221

childhood trauma, 175, 191n1, 212–14

child support, 45, 72, 123, 191, 214, 222

churning (relationships). *See* romantic relationships: and instability

cohabitation, 15, 18, 33, 34, 89n17, 140; differences by socioeconomic status, 207. *See also* marriage; romantic relationships

communication skills, 162–67, 181–82, 184; speaker listener technique, 162–63, 178; time out technique, 63, 163–65

complex families, 34–35, 88–89, 219

Crib Cash. *See under* Family Expectations

custody (children), 52, 66, 108, 145, 191

Desmond, Matthew, 26–27

disadvantaged fathers, 27–28, 214–16, 221–22; complex needs of, 214–16. *See also* fatherhood

divorce, 15, 33, 140, 207. *See also* marriage; romantic relationships

domestic violence, 130, 223

Edin, Kathryn, 31–32, 124, 207

education, 39, 40, 47, 77, 97, 114, 206; and transition to adulthood, 50–54

emerging adulthood, 30, 41, 47, 105, 114–15, 120–21. *See also* role malintegration; transition to adulthood

employment, 14, 47–48, 54–57; instability during transition to adulthood, 54–57; participant trajectories of, 54–57, 161–62, 196; and social poverty, 54, 57; and transition to adulthood, 30, 47–48, 54–57, 114

expressive individualism. *See* individualism

ABOUT THE AUTHOR

Sarah Halpern-Meekin is Associate Professor of Human Development and Family Studies at the University of Wisconsin–Madison and co-author of *It's Not Like I'm Poor: How Working Families Make Ends Meet in a Post-Welfare World.* She received her PhD in Sociology and Social Policy from Harvard University. Her research and teaching focus on poverty and social policy.